D1557195

The Twisted Tale of Glam Rock

THE TWISTED TALE OF GLAM ROCK

Stuart Lenig

 PRAEGER

AN IMPRINT OF ABC-CLIO, LLC
Santa Barbara, California • Denver, Colorado • Oxford, England

Library of Congress Cataloging-in-Publication Data

Lenig, Stuart.
    The twisted tale of glam rock / Stuart Lenig.
        p. cm.
    Includes bibliographical references and index.
    ISBN 978–0–313–37986–4 (hard copy : alk. paper) — ISBN 978–0–313–37987–1 (ebook)
1. Glam rock music—History and criticism. 2. Glam rock musicians.   I. Title.
ML3534.L452   2010
781.66—dc22   2010004677

ISBN: 978–0–313–37986–4
EISBN: 978–0–313–37987–1

14 13 12 11 10   1 2 3 4 5

This book is also available on the World Wide Web as an eBook.
Visit www.abc-clio.com for details.

Praeger
An Imprint of ABC-CLIO, LLC

ABC-CLIO, LLC
130 Cremona Drive, P.O. Box 1911
Santa Barbara, California 93116-1911

This book is printed on acid-free paper ∞

Manufactured in the United States of America

This work is dedicated to my mother and father, Robert John Bopp and Frances Naomi Lenig, who always believed in everything I did. Thanks, Father and Mother, for giving me the confidence to believe in my own ideas.

To my wife, Joni Lenig, for having endless patience with me while I wrote, and rewrote, and rewrote . . .

To my good friend and reference librarian Lyn Bayless, for kindly and diligently obtaining varied and rare books, magazines, and articles that were not available in Nashville or in most libraries anywhere. Most librarians would not have bothered with me.

Thanks to ABC-CLIO editor Dan Harmon for patiently guiding me through the writing process.

Lastly, thanks to the countless musicians who labored in the field of glam and often felt rejected, ridiculed, and ignored for a vibrant musical form that has endured beyond its critics.

CONTENTS

Chapter 1

THE COMING OF GLAM

I am a deeply superficial person.

—Andy Warhol (1994)

Glam music has been around for over 30 years, and during that time it has lived a closeted life as rock and roll with lipstick or simply rock in costume. Glam was born out of the turbulent musical era of the early seventies, and it was called various things: theatre rock, glitter rock, shock rock, and gay rock. Most of these terms were derisive, but the form was durable and influential, and it inspired MTV and popular artists such as Madonna, the Cure, and My Chemical Romance. Its blend of theatricality, postmodernism, and identity politics make it a contemporary style that seems more at home with Madonna's Confessions tour, rogue music labels selling groups through YouTube videos, Imax concert presentations, and American Idol–wannabe performers than at any time during its disturbing birth. It continues to captivate new fans through its mix of theatre, camp, and endless variety. For years it was ignored by the legitimate rock press and was routinely marginalized in the United States. However, after Dick Hebdige's breakthrough *Subculture, the Meaning of Style*, in 1979, and Hebdige's passing mention of glam as a prelude to the visual codes of punk rock, there has been a growing, fitful, and sometimes *confused* new interest in glam.

Scholarly and semi-scholarly descriptions of the music did not help it to be understood. Larry Starr and Christopher Waterman's *American Popular Music* lauded David Bowie's *Ziggy Stardust* album but derided the music, saying, "the coherence of the album derives more from the imaginative and magnetic

Though the Rolling Stones distilled their act to only rock and roll by the seventies, they were once experimental performers, flaunting theatricality, costuming, and identities as pop bad boys. (Courtesy of Photofest.)

persona of the singer and his character than from the music itself" (Starr and Waterman 2008, 185). David Szatmary's *Rockin' in Time* describes Alice Cooper's act as "an elaborate, degenerate show that included throwing live chickens into the crowd, axing off the heads of dolls, staging mock executions in fake electric chairs, Alice draping himself with a live boa constrictor, and beating fans over the head with six-feet-long inflated phalluses" (Szatmary 2006, 240). Loyd Grossman's *A Social History of Rock Music* accused glams of being "sexually ambiguous rockers and razzle-dazzle glitter stars who sought attention through an image of unmitigated chrome-plated maladjust-ment" (Grossman 1976, 135). Frankly, I'm not even sure I know what that means, but it doesn't sound good. Throughout its history, glam had to over-come an overemphasis on visuals and to demand a critical hearing on music and aesthetics. Now, due to 35 years of scholarship, we may be able to see glam's project more accurately. The perspective of distance may also help us to know why glam was so difficult for audiences and critics to understand, what the artists themselves were doing, and what codes and subtexts were embedded in the music.

This chapter sets the stage for understanding glam and placing it in a few contexts. First, glam is a form influenced by the pop art styles of the seventies—the fiction, art, theatre, music, and emerging media ideas of the times. Glam also arrived with the beginnings of postmodernism, a time when everything seemed to be collapsing, and confused genres and historical periods took center stage. What you will quickly discover is that glam history is inelegant. Nothing is simple and direct. Unlike San Francisco rock or Mersey Beat, glam is not comfortably situated in one place or form. It arrived in fits and starts as artists struggled desperately for fame. It limped and stuttered along, often forgotten, overlooked, and marginalized. But what one will hopefully also discover is that glam was extremely diverse, filled with artists who had spectacular visual and sonic imaginations. Despite critical abandonment, they have and continue to exert a strong influence on pop performance. Finally, we'll see how critics saw and simultaneously obscured glam.

We have to look at glam's turbulent history in the seventies and beyond and define musical and performance elements that either caught or eluded the public eye. A critical question was, "Who are the glams?" This is harder to answer for glam than other pop genres. A band such as Black Sabbath or Metallica would fall into the category of metal, but glam is more diverse. First, glams were distinguished by their general sense of theatricality. David Bowie, Marc Bolan, Bryan Ferry, Alice Cooper, and Queen all showed a continuing interest in performing theatrical rock. They are core acts of glam and have remained theatrical while changing to accommodate the times. However, other cases are more complex. Later, Alice Cooper trended towards metal, a less ambiguous style. Kate Bush was a hybrid with art rock, and *Mojo Magazine* classified her as an "English eccentric." Arriving after glam's heyday, Bush always expressed an interest in theatre, dance, character, and performance. Bush's friend and sometime coworker Peter Gabriel was also an early proponent of glam, dressing in elaborate costumes and telling art rock mythic stories while acting out characters on stage in "The Musical Box" and *The Lamb Lies Down on Broadway*. But recently, Gabriel's work has championed world music. Though still eclectic and deeply involved in sets, special effects, stage configurations, and choreography, he personally does not perform in character, preferring to sing as himself. Later artists like the Pet Shop Boys have invoked the costuming, the role playing, and the perverse subject matter of glam rock; but they arrived in the eighties New Romantic/MTV era, and they are often categorized as such. Many goth groups (the Cure/Siouxsie and the Banshees) possessed glam elements (narrative songs, character portrayals, costumes, makeup, elaborate sets, and videos), but they are usually classified as goths. So to simplify the definition, we will view artists that participate in the theatrical impulse and share tendencies towards pop culture, media, and fantasy themes as participants in the glam sensibility.

POPULAR CULTURE INFLUENCES GLAM

I can hide behind a role on stage and really enjoy performing.
—Kate Bush (quoted in Sutcliffe 2003, 77)

America and the world changed by the end of the sixties, and so had the music. Between the relaxation of soft rock, the triumph of hard mainstream rock, and the excesses of progressive music, glam arrived. At the time, glam was widely criticized for its narcissism. People saw characters like David Bowie, Gary Glitter, and Marc Bolan as completely self-absorbed. Few of these artists espoused the sort of obvious leftist politics that permeated the liberal hippie credos of the sixties, and in fact, it was assumed that glams were largely apolitical. In truth, the liberal consensus of the sixties had fallen apart as individual groups (such as gays, women, and minorities) became progressively factionalized. America in particular had grown tired of 10 years of war and civil strife and desired a time of reflective, self-centered hedonism. Wayne Robins wrote in *A Brief History of Rock* that "exhausted by protest, by death, by the relentless war, young people and the pop-music culture began to turn inward" (Robins 2008, 154).

It took some time before people understood that a new politics had emerged, based on a new set of issues. An emerging, pop, visual culture was inspired by diverse visionaries. Artists such as Andy Warhol, Bertolt Brecht, Marshall McLuhan, and Philip K. Dick showed different ways of seeing the world. The magnified power of the media, the political theatre of Watergate, and the rise of exotic and expensive blockbuster film spectacles captivated public attention. Glam maintained a politics, but it was built on those seventies values, not the issues of the sixties, and often it was overlooked.

First, there was a notion of media fame and spectacle that was borrowed from Andy Warhol. Warhol, during the sixties, provided the notion that anyone could be a star if they looked like one, courted the right image and attitudes, and nurtured a certain visual style. Warhol himself was such a self-generated persona, rejecting his immigrant, shy, stuttering self to recreate a persona as a hip, wigged, vacant, bizarre organizer of art and happenings. He inspired artists such as David Bowie and Bryan Ferry. Warhol told audiences that one day everyone would be famous for 15 minutes. Even he didn't envision today's society, in which someone on YouTube would be famous for 15 people. Glams learned from Warhol that they could become anything, and the characters they played were the types of strange personas that Warhol himself had manufactured.

Glams wanted to theatricalize their performance, and for that they needed more than Warhol's visions; they needed a stage director. Just playing rock music wasn't enough. What kinds of characters and stories could the glams invent? They took their theatrical cues from an odd source. Bertolt Brecht was a socialist playwright who had died during the fifties at the height of his powers as a director and writer. His techniques of a deeply committed social theatre had spread across Europe and America during the sixties. His style of drama encouraged deeply political plays such as *Inherit the Wind*, a play about the Scopes Monkey trail of the twenties, and *The Night Thoreau Spent in Jail*, chronicling Thoreau's acts of civil disobedience. During the sixties, Brecht became one of the most produced playwrights in American colleges, and yet none of his plays had achieved commercial success on Broadway. He appealed to the sixties youth movement, who saw theatre as a means to protest the conventional, the conservative, and the establishment values that youth opposed. Brecht's ideas inspired young playwrights such as Stephen Sondheim, who merged musical comedy with sophisticated identity in *Company*, *Sweeney Todd*, and other plays. In plays by Sondheim, characters are often searching to find who they really are and to express the real self they discover. As in *Sweeney Todd*, sometimes these discoveries produce a dark and gruesome spectacle. The glams of the seventies, like Sondheim, saw Brecht as a way to protest social conditions and to present the psychology of the characters they played through visual displays: costume, makeup, effects, and sets. Despite the centrality of his politics, Brecht was a deeply visual playwright, employing a wide range of techniques to draw attention to the spectacle. He used fragments of sets, cheap tawdry subjects, music theatre, borrowed plots, and an arch, exaggerated/nonrealistic acting style to call attention to the politics of his plays. Where Brecht used theatre to interest audiences in his political views, often it was the clever spectacle itself that drew and held their attention. Glams learned from him that they could use spectacle to make visual messages to arouse an audience. When Tim Curry exploded on to the stage singing, "I'm just a sweet transvestite from Transsexual, Transylvania," he bridged the gap between Brecht's drama of liberation and the gay liberation movement. Brecht, as a socialist, practiced a form of politics situated against the greed and corruption of capitalism. The glams had little interest in the socialist messages of the previous generation's cold war, and most glams wanted capitalist success. Their theatre was inspired by science fiction B movies, old horror films, and extravagant musical showpieces. Performers such as Alice Cooper knew youths were far more inspired by monsters they had witnessed at a drive-in grindhouse movie than by politics. Cooper played a guy like them—rocking out, rebelling, and being a misunderstood monster himself. Bowie's theatre featured mime, Asian costumes, and gay themes. Bowie presented another kind of monster to society—the unconventional. If glam's theatre was political, it was about the politics of individual identity, gay rights, and freedom from convention.

Glams innovated in another way. One of the new topics that glams saw as important was the media itself. It played a big role in their lyrics and subject matter. Bowie writes about a *starman* on the radio, Alice Cooper imitates TV announcers, in "Elected," Queen complains of "Radio Ga-Ga," and Sparks writes songs about "Photoshop." Later, glam-inspired artists Duran Duran would write about "Girls on Film," Soft Cell rhapsodized about "Memorabilia,"and Kate Bush wrote "A Deeper Understanding," a love song about her computer.

Canadian media theorist Marshall McLuhan, one of the first popularizers of media studies, had said that the medium was the message, meaning that the medium itself was more important than the messages it contained. By the seventies, the media was dominating public attention. It became society's way to see the world. But McLuhan saw dangers, including the fear that our sense of historicism would be collapsed by the immediacy of the new media. McLuhan argued if we no longer read type in a straight line, we would start to hop and skip over the text like channel-surfers flipping a remote control. He predicted hypertext jumping through time and space. The glams turned McLuhan's observation into a strategy, mixing genres and eras with abandon. Bowie would move from the turn-of-the-century music hall, through Weimar cabaret song, to seventies metal in a single album side. Kate Bush would mix Celtic melodies, classical art song, and Broadway balladry in a single album.

A media determinist, McLuhan envisioned an acceleration of knowledge, a breakdown in old ways of learning (print), and a recognition that media would increase the speed of change and often become the content of communication. McLuhan saw everything as potential media, including art. In *Understanding Media*, he described cubism by saying, "in other words, cubism, by giving the inside and the outside, the top, bottom, back, and front and the rest in two dimensions, drops the illusion of perspective in favor of instant sensory awareness of the whole" (McLuhan 1964, 28). The glams put these ideas into practice. In songs by Brian Eno, Sparks, David Bowie, Roxy Music, and others, the future is repeatedly seen as a glowing spectacular age of new technologies. Bowie writes in "TVC 15," "he's quadraphonic, he's a, he's got more channels, So hologramic, oh my TVC one five." Bowie sees all the benefits of the future—quadraphonic sound, holographic imaging, more cable channels, all in a single device. McLuhan viewed this future mostly as positive, hoping the future would bring a "global village" of greater understanding, but often glam rockers saw it creating a dystopian era of alienation and confusion. As in everything, their vision of the future was more dramatic.

While glams were both fascinated by the media and weary of its power, they chose to write about their anxiety and problematize the coming media era in their songs. Alice Cooper sings of the next generation in "Generation Landslide," saying, "the over-indulgent machines were their children,

There wasn't a way down on Earth here to cool them." For Cooper, the super-powered machines of the future are likely to wrest control from the populace. For the glams, the future could be dangerous, and they took their fears from writers in the science fiction and fantasy fields. Often, their stories were hybrids wedding the future, technology, and fantasy together. For example, Bowie's "Man Who Sold the World" may have been inspired by Robert A. Heinlein's future history novella *Man Who Sold the Moon*, about Delos D. Harriman, future robber baron industrialist who engineers a buyout of the moon, but never gets to go there himself. Their fascination with alternative worlds was a response to a disappointing physical one. Unlike today, when fantasy literature is widely produced in the media, in the early seventies, fantasy could often be found only in novels or comic books. Glams provided a platform for visual fantasy in an era when youth had a growing appetite for surreal fantasy literature—J. R. R. Tolkien, H. P. Lovecraft, and mostly the paranoid visions of Philip K. Dick. The seventies ghettoized the genre to a dingy subculture, but glam gave it a brighter visual voice.

Slowly, these book ideas were arriving in film, and Hollywood would soon realize that this was the prime subject matter of youth culture. The difficulty that glams experienced in trying to sing about fantasy was equaled by filmmakers who wanted to produce fantasy films. When George Lucas tried to describe his *Star Wars* project, he found it difficult to express this new film form of sci-fi. David Rensin describes his struggle in *Very Seventies*: "it's a real crazy movie, like *Flash Gordon*, *Wizard of Oz* or *Gulliver's Travels*—a whole different kind of sci-fi film" (Rensin 1995, 235). But unlike Lucas's friendly space opera *Star Wars*, the writers whom the glams read were more negative. Philip K. Dick depicted paranoid societies filled with treacherous futures and diabolical plots. In Dick's story "Exhibit Piece," the protagonist, Miller, is a historian in charge of an exhibit of twentieth-century culture. He is criticized by his boss, who berates him with "idolize the past if you want, but remember—it's gone and buried. Times change. Society progresses" (Dick 2001, 156). Though he is criticized, Miller clings to his beloved displays. He finds a wormhole from his museum exhibit back to the past, and eventually he escapes the tyranny of the future, only to find a previous world on the brink of nuclear war. Many of the glams gained inspirations from such ironic and dark fantasy. The glams were registering the discontent of youth culture; many young people felt they had been sold out to merchandisers and dull, lifeless musicians. Frustrated by their inability to remake a recalcitrant, resistant real world, glams opted for a fictitious one they could control.

But glams weren't inspired just by images of science fiction. They were deeply impressed by the technologies that seemed just around the corner, and in many glam songs, there is praise of future technology and of ways of using that technology. The name of one of Marc Bolan's later albums,

Zinc Alloy and the Hidden Riders of Tomorrow, evokes all sorts of retro future images. Lou Reed entitled his breakthrough work *Transformer*, and Queen discussed the post-radio age in "Radio Ga-Ga." Everyone in glam was equally fascinated and fearful of the coming technological epoch.

Thus by 1970, youth culture was no longer dominated by the Beatles, Kennedy, and Communist philosophies, but by an emerging pop culture theorized by Warhol's notion of fame and glamour, Brecht's theory of political theatre, McLuhan's emphasis on media technology, and Dick's dark future worlds. But glam's new politics of a more visual music was often too glib, too campy, too remote from the national agenda, and simply too intellectual to reach a rock world that had embraced James Taylor, Bruce Springsteen, and the Carpenters as their leading voices. The *All Music Guide to Rock* describes Bowie's 1972 album, *Hunky Dory*, as "a kaleidoscopic array of pop styles, tied together only by Bowie's sense of vision, a sweeping cinematic mélange of high and low art, ambiguous sexuality, kitsch and class" (Erlewine 1989, 133). Glams like Bowie were doing so much that critics had trouble putting a finger on exactly what the albums were about. Still, despite public confusion, glams persisted in wedding startling images with theatrical music.

Often theatricalizing rock distracted critics and obscured musical ideas. Bowie wove messages about gay culture into songs like "Queen Bitch," and he dressed like a woman to complicate matters. Bryan Ferry appeared like a film matinee idol of the silver screen but sang in a strange parody of crooners. Kate Bush worked with a choreographer, toured with dancers, produced narrative stories, and used headsets years before Madonna. She told England's *MOJO Magazine*, "I saw our show as a complete experience like a play" (Sutcliffe 2003, 77). Sparks played with date song mechanics in the video "Cool Places." With singer Jane Wiedlin of the Go-Gos, Russell Mael bopped through sinister or mockingly trivial hot spots, making fun of yuppie notions of the privileged life. Lady Gaga assaulted our notion of upscale living with "Beautiful, Dirty Rich," in which a squad of dancers march through a Park Avenue brownstone, burning $100 bills, sexually assaulting statuary, and lounging on a baby grand. Peter Gabriel uses images of individuals in hermetically sealed water droplets as technologists build cities, drive toy cars, and eviscerate the natural environment. Glams used Brechtian devices disguising political, environmental, social, and identity issues in smart media packages that society would spend decades cryptographically decoding.

POSTMODERN GLAM

Another problem with understanding glam was its concurrent rise with postmodern culture. Both arrived in the seventies, and both dealt with a confused view of images in the era following modernism. Modernists were interested in experimenting with form through cubism, surrealism, and popism, styles retooled in the postmodern era. Modernist novels collaged the past and present and borrowed liberally from other cultures and codes. Glam and postmodernism extended these tendencies and accelerated them. Sadly, the term has been misused so much that scholar Umberto Eco said, "it is applied today to anything the user of the term happens to like" (Eco, "Postmodernism" 226). There are some meaningful definitions that interact with the way glam used postmodern strategies. M. Keith Booker, in his *Postmodern Hollywood*, described a range of defining elements, including, "a radical suspicion of totalizing narratives," "a dizzying and accelerating rate of change," "the vapid nature of messages," "pluralism in modern thought," "multiple genres and styles within a single work," "instability of personal identity," "loss of any sense of historical continuity," and "a general mode of playfulness and satire" (Booker 2007, xiv–xvi). Eco added to the definition *fantasy* as the new art, writing that "Disneyland makes it clear that within the magic enclosure it is fantasy that is absolutely reproduced" (Eco 1993, 202).

With glam, postmodern means a limited number of things:

1. Artists that collage and breakdown historical periods.
2. Artists that conflate and confuse identity.
3. Artists that ironically use media to comment on themselves and the media itself.
4. Artists that use pop strategies to theatricalize the everyday.

Most of the glam artists did or still do experiment using some or all of the strategies. For example, Bowie used music hall successfully in the *Hunky Dory* album, composing jaunty tunes such as "Fill Your Heart," "Kooks," and "Changes" that used midcentury pop styles to make commentary about contemporary problems of identity. Grace Jones, playing with her female identity, strutted onto the disco stage in a crewcut and topless, singing "I Need a Man" to mostly gay audiences of the seventies. Brittany Spears appeared as a slut bride on a birthday cake singing "Like a Virgin" for the 2003 MTV Music Awards show, and Madonna arose as a bridegroom singing "Hollywood." The unlikely couple was joined by Christina Aguilera and a rapper for a romping dance, and then Madonna tongue-kissed the bride. The Pet Shop Boys videoed "Pandemonium" as a tale of a robot head, popping out of a metal box to view a prettier static robot head on TV. The robot uses a television to watch a robot version of herself. Loaded with traditional PSB irony, the plain robot does a makeover of her appearance to match the TV screen image, stretches too far, fractures her metallic spine, and lays half-remake/half-ruin on the ground. The Bird and the Bee theatricalize the common in "Love Letter to Japan," becoming video avatars for a young Japanese gamer in an arcade. Overall, glams never avoided postmodern irony, identity issues, media references, or historical paradoxes, but embraced the new cultural paradigm with a passion.

GLAM'S RECURSIVE HISTORY

> The organizing topic was a big-top circus, complete with dancers, contortionists, stilt-walking, a deep voiced MC promising, "an amazing spectacle of sight and sound."
> —Mikael Wood, describing a Panic! At the Disco show (2007, 96)

Glam shined from 1972 to 1975, but glam ideas existed before the music was a movement, and long after glam was considered passé. The quote from *Spin* magazine shows that while people don't credit glam with a legitimate pop history, the theatrical qualities of glam are still being exploited by performers as diverse as Madonna, My Chemical Romance, Panic! At the Disco, The Bravery, Berlin's Cinema Bizarre, The Darkness, and Japan's Visual Kei movement. But it sometimes feels like glam is rock's illegitimate child. It is as if its tawdry adventures embarrass critics who once embraced it. Looking back at an issue of *CREEM* magazine from 1975, the cover illustrates stories on Alice Cooper, Sparks, Queen, Bowie, and other glam acts. The magazine was like a compendium of glam culture. But when *CREEM* editors Robert Matheu and Brian J. Bowe released a retrospective book on the magazine, *CREEM: America's Only Rock 'N' Roll Magazine*, in 2007, glam acts received only 8–10 articles out of a total of 60 articles on pop music. Glam may be rock's "Love Child," "afraid, ashamed, misunderstood" (Supremes, "Love Child").

Where did glam, with all its strange theatrics, come from? In the fifties, rock performers were wild men on stage, and youth such as John Lennon and Paul McCartney were captivated by Jerry Lee Lewis, Little Richard, and Elvis. Many British youth were also influenced by the American Beat writers, like Jack Kerouac and his book *On the Road*. Katherine Charlton writes in *Rock Music Styles* that youth like David Bowie (a.k.a. David Jones) were "impressed by the book's characters who were able to express their feelings of alienation from the conformist middle-class society that surrounded them" (Charlton 1994, 175). Teens like Bowie, the Beatles, the Who, and others enrolled in art schools and dreamed of a career in which they could merge their dual desires to be visual artists with their love of pop music stars. There were few other options for working-class youth in the high-unemployment and low-economic-opportunity environment afforded by postwar British culture. Many of these art school students emerged as members of pop bands that exploded on to the world stage as the British Invasion bands. They were the embodiment of the pop aesthetics of Warhol in America and Richard Hamilton in England. Their credo was superficial, pleasant, decorative music that was based on Muddy Waters blues (the Rolling Stones), Chuck Berry rave-ups (the Beatles), and British music hall (the Kinks). The British bands changed the form of pop rock by increasing the amplification using Vox and Marshall amplifiers, wearing their hair longer, and imbuing their compositions with more elements of the European classical music and art song tradition. Charlton described the scene by saying, "London was the hub for groups whose music and image were identified with youth cultures such as the mods and the rockers" (Charlton 1994, 109).

These groups polarized music fan groups. The rockers were a rough crowd who wore their hair like Elvis and clung to the fifties rock traditions. But most of the Invasion bands followed the social and visual codes of the mods. The mods were very stylish, and they had a format for everything from slang to transportation. Like the rockers, the mods were an aggressive social youth movement prone to gangish behavior and a wild social life. The story of the mods was perhaps most effectively portrayed in Pete Townshend and the Who's album and film, *Quadrophenia*. The mods' dress code included thin-lapeled jackets, button-down-collar shirts, thin ties, and longish, styled hair. Their ride was the Vespa scooter, and their drug of choice was prescription uppers that kept them hopping to an energized, rebellious beat music typified by bands like the Who. However as the movement progressed, mod pop became more eclectic and diverse. Bands began to seek wider and farther afield for inspiration. Asian sounds, nostalgia musical motifs from the twenties and thirties, jazz, and avant-garde sounds found their way into the music of the British pop bands. They in turn were influenced by the introspective and political lyrics of Dylan and the burgeoning psychedelic music from the San Francisco groups. Drug use was definitely part of the culture, but marijuana, and heroin had been common in the musical community for generations. LSD fueled the search for an otherworldly exotic sound palette, and prompted psychedelic pop towards excesses of colorfully orchestrated, international, longer, anarchic sounds. Rampant drug use deadened the music (notably even affecting the Beatles in *Let It Be*) and took from us many of the most prominent musicians in their prime. By the late sixties, many of the pop bands had either dissipated (as with the Beatles) or morphed into hard-rock, blues-based outfits (as with Hendrix, the Stones, the Who, and Cream). The British style moved to long, instrumental songs, with performance taking a back seat to compositional and improvisational skill. The apotheosis of the style was Cream, burdened with the title "supergroup," limited by ponderous 15-minute compositions, and enervated by lengthy guitar, bass, and unpleasant drum solos. The elements of performance were either minimized or sorely depleted. By 1969, the ponderous side of progressive rock had literally killed the performance instinct.

Glams illustrated the dream of common people promoted to stars. Bowie, Bolan, and Ferry emulated sixties idols and, through dress, style, and rigorous self-promotion, achieved musical and visual notoriety. But by 1975, the model of glam's self-made stardom was accelerated by discos. Instead of "real" stardom, discos democratized the notion of celebrity in which anyone could be an exhibitionist or a self-proclaimed celebrity. In contrast, punk's do-it-yourself aesthetic argued for a return to rock basics, primitive musicianship, teen angst, and sheer outrage. Bolan sought refuge in his own television show, Bowie retreated to soul for a time, and Roxy disbanded. Glam was dead.

But glam wasn't about to go out quietly. Bowie, Ferry, and Elton retained their popularity and adjusted to their smaller niche market. Each artist found a way to expand the performance vocabulary of glam. Elton John embraced pop. Bowie decamped to Berlin and engaged in aggressive sonic experiments with Brian Eno. Ferry and Roxy streamlined their sound to a slick Euro dance style that satisfied the club scene. By 1980, the glam impulse resurfaced in the form of MTV and a new generation of performing bands, now rechristened by the press as "new romantics." They were given the platform of television to reach audiences. The technologically oriented glams quickly embraced the new medium. Katherine Charlton commented that "the music of most glitter acts, particularly that of David Bowie, Roxy Music and Queen, reached beyond the standard rock styles, incorporating other forms of art music that became popular as art (or progressive) rock" (Charlton 1994, 181). Performers like David Bowie, who had already incorporated narrative into their works, used the video medium to craft extended narratives. Bands such as Duran Duran, Pet Shop Boys, Sparks, and the Cure applied makeup, mixed genders, and costumes in theatrical shows that challenged the glam works of the last decade.

GLAM MUSIC CHARACTERISTICS

A big question for critics was how to describe glam music. As glam changed, critics presumed the form had died. Glam qualities were ill-defined in the American press, and it was assumed the style had succumbed. Glam was a complex music that borrowed its identity from multiple musical traditions. Modern practitioners such as Souxsie Sioux, My Chemical Romance, and Suede still follow many of the formulas invented in the seventies. But glam's hybrid nature confounded critics. Glam was played and performed, but notably, American critics were blinded by an antiquarian literary tradition that reduced Dylan to a set of lyrics. American critics had no aptitude for assessing a music one must see as well as hear. They had no visual apparatus. Glam's eclecticism troubled critics. The glams dabbled in so many mixed forms that critics became lost trying to figure out glam's core style. Yet there was a complex codex underlying glam's rampant sampling. Like chaos theory, glam's melding of divergent strategies was so woven that it was possible to mistake its complexity for mere randomness. Glam had routinely returned to certain musical forms, including psychedelic music, English music hall, hard rock, ballad, and electronic music. The glams borrowed from these types because they were popular at the time or in the past. As time progressed, glams borrowed from an even wider palette.

Historicism helps us understand glam. It grew out of the sixties British Invasion, and much of its energy lies there. When Bowie released his *Pin-Ups* tribute album to the sixties in 1973, most of the songs were drawn from 1965 to 1967 and included works by the Who, the Kinks, the Pretty Things, the Yardbirds, and Pink Floyd. The *psychedelic* spirit that inspired the late-sixties music haunted glam as well. Psychedelic music had been inspired by drugs, mainly LSD, and Timothy Leary argued that, "God doesn't think in words . . . he thinks in visual images" (Warhol and Hackett 1989, 184). Leary argued that constructive drug use freed conscious, and that "everything we accept as reality is just social fabrication" (DeRogatis 2003, 17). While popsters put that into song, glams took it a step farther and rearranged their images, identities, and personas. The first psychedelic musicians, Syd Barrett and Pink Floyd, the Grateful Dead, and the Beatles showed drug influences through surreal whimsical songs with ornate tone color. In "See Emily Play," there are wild flourishes of piano notes, echoed basses, and freaky guitar solos to describe a simple childhood romp. The glams, seeing themselves as psychedelia's heirs, continued using synthesizers, production techniques, and obscure instruments to create exaggerated tonal colors. If the goal of psychedelic music was to take audiences along on a trip to see fantastic images, the glams more ambitiously wanted to *stage* that world. Bowie took us to space with Major Tom in "Ashes to Ashes," My Chemical Romance drove us to the dark fascistic world of "The Black Parade," Lou Reed escorted us inside Warhol's Factory of transsexual superstars in "Walk on the Wild Side," and Bryan Ferry and Roxy Music removed us to postwar Europe and disaster in a "Song For Europe."

Glam shared psychedelia's interest in science fiction, fantasy worlds, future and past eras, nostalgia movie images, and strange gender hybrids. Bowie evoked a burned-out future landscape in the wild guitar passage of "Moonage Daydream." Bowie's "Daydream" became our trip, a journey into an outer space world. Marc Bolan used a powerful sonic assault of fuzzed guitars to create an otherworldly effect in "20th Century Boy." Sparks used the technical sheen of disco beats to craft a euphoric tone for their single, "The Number One Song in Heaven" (1979), creating the image of shimmering angelic notes, with Russell Mael's high-pitched falsetto leading the charge. Most of the glam artists were working-class British youth who had grown up with the distinctly British tradition of *music hall* theatre, a common style that was popular with all segments of society. A music hall had rowdy, seedy, comical, lewd performers, often dressed in drag and behaving in an outrageous manner. Music hall entertainment played a primary role in British social history. The music hall allowed protest, expressed sexuality in Victorian Britain, and provided a field for transgressive performances such as drag, queer, and perverse behaviors.

Another complexity that made glam hard to follow was the fact that the form could mix hard and soft, aggressive rock riffs with subtle balladry. Many glams took their cue from pop music, lush romantic ballads, and popular singers of earlier eras. Notably, Bryan Ferry seemed to make sport of feverish torch singers in Roxy Music, but when he performed as a soloist, the distance between his performance and nostalgia-drenched renditions of classic songs melted. Probably confusing critics even more was glam's flirtation with metal rock. If glams appeared effeminate and swishy, mannish hard rock would seem an unlikely style, but groups like Roxy and Queen were vigorous rockers. Even in their last album, as lead singer Freddie Mercury was suffering from the ravages of AIDS, Queen delivered two of their best rocking songs, "Hit Man" and "Headlong." Yet even the extremes of ballads and metal failed to encompass the excesses of glam. Glam groups, despite ahistoric origins, had a keen relationship with past styles of music and inserted either references or direct interpolations of other eras into their music.

Adding to interpretive complexity was abundant interest in progressive electronic technology. Given the glams' interest in fantasy dystopias, it was inevitable that they would embrace the future sounds. Bowie and producer Tony Visconti forged nightmarish atmospheres in *Diamond Dogs*; and later, with Brian Eno, Bowie provided a series of ethereal instrumental landscapes. The dark, moody Berlin trilogy of albums features frequent instrumental tracks that Bowie still occasionally revisits. Ferry and Roxy Music entered the eighties further engaged in smoother exotic textures, and songs like Roxy's "India" and Ferry's "Don't Stop the Dance" reflect a great interest in trance club music styles.

Critics could reasonably argue that glam was eclectic to a fault. Artists of glam were often accused of having no musical style because they were facile at melding multiple styles. But glam artists thought of themselves as bigger than any one style, and they championed eclecticism in their albums. It was not uncommon to see all glam musical qualities in a single album. A case in point is Bowie's 1974 *Diamond Dogs* album. Critic Robert Christgau jokingly referred to it as an album "in which a man who has always turned his genuine if unendearing talent for image manipulation to the service of his dubious literary and theatrical gifts evolves from harmless kitsch to pernicious sensationalism" (Christgau 1981, 56).

GLAM VISUAL ELEMENTS

I don't know where I'm going from here, but I promise it won't be boring.
—David Bowie (quoted in Rose 1998)

If glam's musical proclivities towards exotic experimentalism weren't enough, glam artists' visual vocabulary was just as broad and confusing. Bowie's quote raised the aesthetic problem of a performance based on shock values. If glam's visuals were shocking, then they would have to change often to stay shocking. This left some glam artists in the continual bind of having to constantly increase the visual element of the show. Bowie gave up this demanding expense after the complex set for the 1974 Diamond Dogs tour simply weighed the performance down, and he found himself to be more effective under pure white light for the 1976 "Thin White Duke" tour. Also, glam was a cottage industry catering to eccentric acts that crafted their own distinctive shows. There was little uniformity. This created a marketing problem, since every show was different. The musical qualities of heavy metal: fuzzed guitar, throbbing bass, brutal drumming, lead guitar solos were well established, but what exactly constituted the perfect glam performance was far less clear. Glam remained hard to classify due to its schizophrenic personality, divided between music and performance. Glam routinely borrowed from both a visual vocabulary and a musical one. Just as grand opera had massive orchestras, big orchestra pits, extreme and colorful wardrobe, and vast cosmic sets (as in Wagner), so glam used both musical and extra-musical aspects to reach its adherents. Another problem was classifying the wide range of glam performances. Glam artists had as many genres as film. Alice Cooper was punkish and loud, like the kids he wrote about in "School's Out." Grace Jones wedded model/runway staging with exotic, trance continental beat music. Roxy Music and Bryan Ferry played screen-inspired Romeos and kinky B-movie space pirates. David Bowie played queer space creatures, beautiful hermaphrodites, and Nazi royalty.

But, despite their endless variety, glam artists shared four stylistic qualities. While glam artists focused on visuals more than previous rock performance, they mostly focused on low pop culture themes to balance the archness of their theatricality. They traded on gothic and eerie images, borrowing from the expressionist vocabulary of film. They presented a languid and exhausted façade to reinforce their sense of a collapsing culture, what Schaffner referred to as "harbinger's of civilization's decline and fall" (Schaffner 1983, 188). Finally, they luxuriated in the queer subculture of transsexuals, drag queens, homosexuality, and a carefully articulated use of aberrant sexuality.

Low Culture

Glams loved visual images, and each glam performer had a vivid theatrical imagination. Queen made mini operas, Bowie told sci-fi novellas, Roxy Music sold languid, broken love affairs, and Alice Cooper took his audience to late-night horror shows. Each was obsessed with visual codes and images. Stephen Valdez writes that "the primary aspect of these performers was the live show and the ability to shock their audiences" (Valdez 2006, 404).

Gothic

Creepy images and sounds haunt most of the glam artists. In Sparks' "The Rhythm Thief," the brothers Mael (Russell and Ron) slyly wink at the rise of new Euro-disco with a haunting composition dominated by a European classical string session. The only drums and rhythm on the track are the sounds of big orchestral kettle drums and Russell Mael's staccato delivery of the lyrics, saying, "I am the rhythm thief, Say goodbye to the beat." For all its dark Wagnerian intensity, the subject is pretty trivial, a lampooning of the Euro-disco sound. Throughout, goth music has been a coda to glam. It is costumed, theatrical, and intensely produced and orchestrated. Usually, it shares with glam an interest in expressionistic characters, either psychologically unbalanced or horror/sci-fi grotesques. There is plenty of lyric violence in these gothic glam odes, including Queen's "Death on Two Legs" with its doom-laden, hard rock style. Freddie Mercury sings, "you suck my blood like a leech, you break the law and you preach" (Queen, "Death on Two Legs").

Exhaustion

Glam began partially because contemporary forms of rock (at least to the glams) were exhausted and unoriginal. Nicholas Schaffner commented that by the seventies, pop was fairly repetitive. Glam sought to remedy that. He wrote that "rock and roll seemed to have become compulsively incestuous and self-referential, an elaborate 'in joke'" (Schaffner 1983, 190). Glams decided to energize rock while playing out characters, reflecting the form's implosion. Roxy played lounge lizards, while Grace Jones showed us a vamp model pose.

Queer

Queer elements were another strategy of glam music, with many glams embracing gay culture and adopting queer cultures and identities, or at least feeling liberated enough to discuss this taboo subculture. Gay issues were often censored from official historical accounts, and the American Psychological Association had listed homosexuality as a mental disease until 1974. Glam dealt with serious societal prejudices against gay politics. Lou Reed's "Walk on the Wild Side" reinserted that history back into his story of sixties New York. Reed described the lives of several of Warhol's transsexual superstars from the sixties. He began with a deadpan description of Holly Woodlawn (Haroldo Danhaki), "Shaved her legs, and then he was a she." Woodlawn was an actor in Warhol's *Trash* (1970) and *Women in Revolt* (1972).

When glam did gain critical attention, critics often misunderstood it. The mix of rock and theatre was written off as peripheral to real rock. The rock press moved on to embrace punk and some reactionary myths about rock. Presuming that glam was an outgrowth of rock's decadence, there was a violent reaction against it. Post glam, critics asserted that rock was basic, rhythm-and-blues-based, heterosexual, sexist, and unadorned. Paralleling the decline of liberalism and the rise of Thatcher/Reagan neoconservatism, Bowie was out, and Springsteen was in. Many critics saw performance and sophistication as the enemies of rock. But punk took many of its ideas from glam. The safety pin in the nose, the spiked hair, and tattered costumes of punk were simply another form of theatre, a theatre of rage. Most contemporary critics failed to notice what later critics like Philip Auslander and Dick Hebdige explained as the visual codes of rock. Hebdige and later Auslander realized that the dress, style, and norms that produced the subcultural worlds of various rock demi-cultures were vitally important to the form. Instead, seventies journalists had written off glam as an obscure boutique form enjoyed by a few fans and quickly absorbed by more enduring forms of pop. Even the astute Hebdige, who explored the subculture of punk, didn't see much critical value in Bowie and the glams at the end of the seventies. Hebdige wrote that, "not only was Bowie patently uninterested either in contemporary political and social issues or in working class life in general, but his entire aesthetic was predicated upon a deliberate avoidance of the real world and the prosaic language in which that world was habitually described, experienced, and reproduced" (Hebdige 1979, 61). Hebdige was ruled by a neo-Marxist ideology that rock must reflect social and proletarian struggles, he only tangentially perceived that visual codes could have intrinsic meaning in and of themselves.

Altogether, glam was misunderstood as a musical form. Perhaps importantly, glam ultimately can be separated from rock. It is not necessarily "glam rock"; it is "glam" *and* "rock." It was rock influenced by pop aesthetics, musical theatre, genre literature, and society's fascination with the media. It had a complicated turbulent history, with enormous difficulty finding and sustaining an audience. It was principally an English movement that discussed taboo topics of perversion, dystopia, and aberrant sexuality. It was a prelude and forefather of the punk, new romantic, alternative, and goth styles of pop, but received little credit for legitimizing a theatre of rock. It was a transitional form that transmitted rock to a post-rock era, and because of that, it may outlive the form that spurned it.

Chapter 2

PRE-GLAM

> Just look at the surface of my paintings and films and me, and there I am. There's nothing behind it.
>
> —Andy Warhol (quoted in Ratcliff 1983, 9)

In June 1968, a minor assistant and actress in Andy Warhol's films, Valerie Solanas, appeared at the entrance to The Factory, Warhol's studio, when Warhol and several associates were arriving for the day's work. Warhol and his colleagues were discussing recent business. Solanas, a radical feminist, had formed the group SCUM, the Society for Cutting Up Men, of which she was the sole member. Weeks earlier, she had accused Warhol of stealing a script she had written. Truthfully, Warhol had probably mislaid it or thrown it away, but to placate her, he cast her in a film and paid her $25.

It seemed to work, but on that June day, Solanas reached in her purse, retrieved a .32 caliber pistol, and began firing on the men. She hit Warhol twice, with one bullet passing through his chest, clipping internal organs, and exiting through his back. Solanas shot at other people in the room, wounding one of the other men. After 4:00 p.m. that afternoon, the doctors declared Warhol dead, but after several minutes, he was revived. He continued painting for almost another 20 years. As Warhol said, "I guess it was just being in the wrong place at the right time." Solanas later gave her rationale for shooting Warhol as "he had too much control over me." Maybe that's why glam music came to be. It was a group of musicians at the wrong place at the right time.

Warhol is often described as an epicenter of sixties media, and the story of his almost-assassination by Valerie Solanas shows the strange nexus of talent,

Warhol personally set the stage for glam aesthetics with his blend of glamour, publicity seeking, personal costuming, decorated musical landscapes, and the building of an artificial environment facade for art. (Courtesy of Photofest.)

notoriety, and fame that spurred the glam artists to their work. But there are many probable and conflicting explanations of how the music of glam arrived. The sixties provided many chaotic messages from a wide variety of subcultural groups that are still difficult to decode. There were divergent rumblings and urges towards a style of performance music.

First, media-centric people like Warhol, who were early adaptors of all sorts of technology, were immersed in ways to make more art and to follow the impetus of progress through mechanization. They believed that media held ways to extend their art, music, and contribution to larger audiences with greater efficiency. Philosophers such as Marshall McLuhan and Guy Debord explored how the media affected us. McLuhan looked at the media in the abstract as being more important than messages, and Debord thought of it as an enveloping concept that controlled how we interacted with the world. In either case, both McLuhan and Debord were media determinists who argued that media could have a powerful influence on us. Popular musicians like the Beatles and the Monkees used the media to reach a larger audience and to project a certain calculated persona. Both groups parlayed their natural talents for humor and an irreverent, acerbic wit into projecting the image of likable, everyday, boy-next-door characters who also happened to be musicians. Their use of the media made them seem remarkable because of the music they produced, but also accessible because of the image they portrayed.

Critics have arrived at different theories for the genesis of the genre, and some of the principal texts provide varying ways of seeing glam's origins. Van Cagle's *Restructuring Pop/Subculture* argues that Warhol's factory, circa 1965 to 1969, "provided glitter performers with the primary themes of flamboyance, style, and image construction, polymorphous sexuality, and multimedia montage as performance art" (Cagle 1995, 96). Cagle gives credit to Warhol suggesting that he imbued performers with the idea, the style, and a grammar of glam performance. Dave Thompson suggests that glam was born of a reaction to rock's new pretentiousness and self-importance. He wrote that "it represented nothing more than a return to the frivolous basics for which rock and roll had been condemned," adding that "musically, culturally, sexually, and anatomically, glam rock was to be the biggest, brightest, shiniest beast the music industry had ever known" (Thompson 2000, 5). Thompson, rather than make an argument for glam's intrinsic value and substance, goes the other direction by accepting that at its heart, glam was a very superficial form not to be taken seriously. Phillip Auslander's *Performing Glam Rock* takes a performance-studies approach to the field and argues that the genesis of the style must be viewed as a performance convention. Auslander explains that "it is never enough for rock performers to play a certain kind of music in order to claim membership in a particular rock subgenre; they must also present the right kind of image on stage, on screen and in print, even when part of the ideology is to deny the importance of the visual" (Auslander 2006, 39).

For Auslander, the total act of performance persona creates a pop genre, not just the form of music played. Further, Auslander argues that glam can be seen as a reaction to psychedelic music. In Auslander's thinking, psychedelic music was "anti-spectacular," virtuoso, serious, countercultural/noncommercial, and collectivist; while glam relished spectacle, disdained instrumental artistry, courted the marketplace, and spoke to the individual. Thus for Auslander, glam cannot be subtracted from its performance, nor can it be seen as a purely musical form. Similarly, in *Glam!* Barney Hoskyns called the music "a reaction . . . both to the pompous 'progressive' rock to which those older siblings were now in thrall and to the banal bubblegum with which teenagers had had to make do in the era of flared denims and free festivals" (Hoskyns 1998, 5). Hoskyns sees glam as all about stardom and the genre, "called into question received notions of truth and authenticity . . . it blurred the divide between straights and queens . . . and it flirted openly with a decadence pitched somewhere between *Cabaret* and *A Clockwork Orange*" (Hoskyns 1998, 6). Hoskyns sees glam as a style enamored of media images of stardom and rock fame in which not only performance, but the lifestyle of the performers was emblazoned in the minds of the listeners.

As wide-ranging as these descriptions are, there may be more to glam rock's origins and attributes. Artists like Warhol, television and an explosion of media, pop rockers with performance inclinations, psychedelic music's spectacular elements, and even Broadway musicals may have contributed to the inclinations and desires for a more visual form of pop rock.

Warhol's story is a good prelude to the dawn of the glam era. Glams were obsessed with image, media, and newness; so was Warhol. Besides his art, Warhol was intensively involved in the new emerging visual media. In the fifties, he had been a prominent New York art director, arriving with charming drawing skills from Carnegie Mellon in Pittsburgh. By the sixties, he was already wealthy, owned a townhouse in Manhattan, had won three art director awards, and was established as a stylish illustrator for I. Miller shoes. He was constantly in demand for his naive drawing style.

Warhol epitomized the media ferment of the era. He worked with local theatre groups, he attended film workshops, and developed a working relationship with independent New York film guru Jonathan Mekas. Warhol was deeply technological. He bought a Polaroid and used the instant camera to create exotic custom portraiture. He carried a cassette tape recorder everywhere and obsessively taped conversations, referring to the recorder as "his wife." He constructed films by letting the camera photo-document individuals and objects for hours at a time. Often when filming, he left the room to do something else. He said, "raw and crude was the way I liked our movies to look" (Warhol and Hackett 1989, 166). He was deeply obsessed with the idea of museumology, and he scrupulously archived himself, dumping the contents of his desk and workshop into a box, marking the date, and dubbing the projects "time capsules." Hundreds still exist, unopened.

Warhol was an aficionado of the fashion scene and refashioned himself, having his nose sanded, his dull, balding pate covered by a horrific blonde/white wig, and his wardrobe transformed to butch/punk, black leather jackets, turtleneck shirts, and blue jeans. He envisioned himself a talent scout/manager, and worked with singers and groups including the Velvet Underground, Nico, Mick Jagger, and later, David Bowie. Determined to stay current, he went to parties to find commissions and to keep up with new gossip. He founded his own film fan magazine, *Interview*, to feature events in Gotham and the world. After becoming dangerously mainstream in the seventies, he moved to reestablish his "street cred" in the eighties, working with Jean-Michel Basquiat, filming videos for the eighties pop band Curiosity Killed the Cat ("Misfit"), starting his own MTV show, *Andy Warhol's 15 Minutes*, and appearing on ABC's popular *Love Boat*. Finally, he was a gay man in a straight world, always labeled a freak, a neurotic, and an outsider. He forever played a double game with American society, who wrote him off from the start as a kook and a weirdo but failed to notice that he was an original voice and a media revolutionary.

Probably more than any other figure, Warhol—the legend and the reality— inspired the glam artists. He created a prototype for the glam world. He relished outrageous dress, believed in the power of costume, lived for the media, and liked exotic music (raw and hard, but also sensitive and moody styles). He desired the art event to be a happening, a confluence of media, spectacle, performer, and audience collaged in a surreal matrix from which the audience could graduate to the status of performer.

A SOCIETY OF SPECTACLE

Warhol's career was indicative of the rapid social changes of the sixties. It was a time when the media began to dominate public consciousness. McLuhan prophesied that the medium is the message, and he was right. McLuhan argued that no matter what the message, the format or media containing the message usually controlled the message's reception. Thus, a newspaper as a medium conveyed news in a far different manner from that of television. He predicted what he called the end of the Gutenberg galaxy, the time of print and literacy as the principal way to convey information. He argued that the new and completely absorbing media would engulf the entire world in a large network he called the global village. He was dubbed a media determinist, someone who believed that media determined our actions in much the same way monolithic socialists argued that economics governed our existence. Finally, he explained that when media were overextended or used too much or inappropriately, they could invert or have opposing effects. For instance, television was a potential great provider of news, but if overextended—if used as a social reference for knowledge—it could invert itself and provide less understanding and less knowledge. We see this lately when multiple 24-hour news stations actually provide less direct information than the traditional network newscasts and pad their programming with hours of opinion and editorial. But the key to understanding McLuhan was the notion that the media itself mattered much more than its content. People like Warhol glommed on to the media because they sensed its innate power.

One could extend the notion of a media society to a society completely dominated by spectacle, by big flashy media that compelled our attention. On the other hand, one could see society driven by small, less obtrusive, but insidious media that momentarily occupied us. For these situations, McLuhan theorized the idea of hot and cool media. He argued that spectacle did not have to be large and overwhelming; it could be small and unobtrusive, like the little 12-inch television set in the corner. He called this always-on but unnoticed and droning background cool media. It had a long range but subtle effect. Hot media, like film or loud music, was much easier to detect and recognize. On the other hand, cool media was noninvasive but insidious. Always on, and always being watched, television was the ultimate intruder into family life. It was a form of spectacle that was intimate and immediately compelling.

This idea of "spectacle" came to fruition in the philosophical writings of the French thinker Guy Debord. Debord argued that spectacle ran society. The marketers wanted us to be distracted by constant spectacle; whether it was big or small spectacle made no difference. Through commodities like media idols, the marketers dominated our attention and substituted these items for the real. Today, a simple item like the cell phone becomes this sort of spectacular appliance, constantly occupying us and commanding our attention. Who called? When? What did they say? Did they leave a video or text message? How can they be reached? Will they call again? Debord wrote that "the fetishism of the commodity, the domination of society by 'intangible as well as tangible things attains its ultimate fulfillment in the spectacle, where the real world is replaced by a selection of images which are projected above it, yet which at the same time succeed in making themselves regarded as the epitome of reality" (Debord 1983, 17).

In Warhol, McLuhan, and Debord, we have a philosophical groundwork for glam. Warhol cherished the media and saw it as a way to market art and as a subject for art. McLuhan saw the media as a dominant force in how we interact with the world, and alternately, that the media could impact us in extreme ways or in a slow subtle fashion. Debord saw the media as replacing real things with carefully crafted images. His ideas follow the tradition of scholarship on the media that include Walter Benjamin, Theodor Adorno, and Jean Baudrillard.

TELEVISION SELLS THE COUNTERCULTURE: THE BIRTHPLACE OF GLAM

The sixties was a time of vibrant new media exploding on the scene, and many of the artists who would later create glam music were listening. The audience was young and quick to adopt new products. Critic Archie Loss explained that the culture shifted towards youth and that, "by 1964 there were more people who were 17 years old than any other age group in the country. By 1965, 41 percent of the population would be under 20 years of age" (Loss 1999, 6). These new technologies promoted the emerging popular culture and courted a generation hungry to devour many new forms of entertainment. Music listening and consumption proliferated through records, cassettes, radio, magazines, film, and television.

But in 1964, a new force erupted in the Mersey Beat British Invasion bands, a series of rough, loud pop bands that borrowed from American blues,

European art song, and art school politics. Even if some musicians of glam weren't on the scene in the sixties, most of them had the chance to watch that scene and fantasize about the glamorous world of rock music because of television. Warhol made the media a background and subject of his art. McLuhan argued that youth would utilize television over books. Debord said that we would develop a society of spectacle. All of these things happened seemingly overnight. Many of the artists of glam grew up watching their favorite bands not in a live setting, but through the magic of television. Television's reifying and cleansing presentation of pop artists abstracted them and made them larger-than-life icons. While residents of the American coasts or London could easily see the Doors, the Stones, or other groups of the sixties era, many people in either nation's interior were only exposed to the culture of performance rock through the media.

The British Invasion itself was largely a media invasion, conducted through television, radio, and the press. Television produced the lure of exotic foreigners—those sexy Brits with their charming accents, playing an obscure blend of British and American pop with a smattering of more international influences. When the Beatles took the stage on the *Ed Sullivan Show* in February 1964, it was television that sold them to the American people. Television's demographic marketing produced a potent cocktail to youth.

Television marketed pop music, especially attractive and vibrant young performers like The Beatles. By the sixties, nearly every American family had a television set, and the medium quickly realized its power to sway the public as a more powerful cousin to radio. Television was on continually, pumping a steady stream of images, sounds, and commercial messages to an audience. Derived from radio, television took its early programming, commercial positioning, and worldview from the creators of radio. Major radio networks such as NBC and CBS became prominent television networks.

Further, television recognized its power as an agenda-setting device. Television started at first by broadcasting the daily HUAC hearings and inflaming the McCarthy red scare. It later chronicled school desegregation in Arkansas, tracked the rise of the civil rights movement, and promoted the anti–Vietnam War movement. Television welcomed cold war controversies and broadcast politically inflaming programming such as *I Led Three Lives*, recording the exploits of an FBI undercover man who infiltrated Communist Party cells working underground to destroy the United States. By focusing on a topic and keeping the public directed towards an issue, television could sell an idea or undermine it. Largely, the makers of television saw the sixties youth culture as an opportunity to capitalize on an emerging group with a distinct culture, a demographic, and, most importantly, flexible and disposable income. The proliferation of hair-coloring commercials, acne creams, and various soft drink products attested to the notice advertising gave to young people.

But to bring people to the market to buy their goods, the advertisers needed programming to attract youth to youth-culture products.

A flurry of youth-oriented shows emerged to court that market. Dick Clark's *American Bandstand* was an early success. Two evening youth shows, *Shindig* and *Hullabaloo*, featured musical acts in the mid-sixties. Both were party/dance programs that featured teens dancing to live performances by the hottest new bands. Ed Sullivan's variety show on Sunday nights featured a wide range of performers and was a staple of the CBS schedule. The Beatles began releasing their video performances to that venue after they stopped touring, to great marketing success. The Monkees television show debuted in 1966, with NBC hoping to capitalize on the success of the Beatles' films. The project auditioned four mop-top performers, and they were cast as a pop group trying to make it in the tough Los Angeles market. Weekly, the band would meet girls, become involved in harebrained plots, usually help someone, and find love. Of course, the Monkees' songs and the band's charming performances were the keys to the program's success.

TELEVISION ENABLES GLAM

> All of our songs are about love, death, and travel.
>
> —Jim Morrison

Not only did television play an important role for the marketers, but it also worked to the advantage of the bands. As Jim Morrison pointed out, rock songs had an obsession with travel the way country songs dealt with life on the road. Both communities suffered the perils of touring, that rootless life that debilitates and disorients performers until they don't know where they are or what time of day it is. The Beatles quickly saw that film and television were effective tools to reach mass audiences without the dreadful costs and anxieties of touring. The Beatles were particularly bruised by nasty experiences in 1966 in the Philippines. Somehow, they had offended ruler Ferdinand Marcos and his wife by not attending a state function in their honor, and the band was harassed. Groups such as the Rolling Stones had members with health issues. While Brian Jones was singled out as the group's most notable substance abuser, he also suffered from chronic asthma that reduced the band's ability to play long and extended concert tours. Pop bands bemoaned greedy concert promoters who often tried to renegotiate deals before the band appeared. Famous disputes with record companies and agents erupted over the costs of touring and the expenses incurred. Television not only aided enormously to breaking the British Invasion and helped to secure British acts exposure in the distant frontiers of America, but it allowed touring to be less arduous and long.

For its reach, its influence, its convenience, and its attractiveness to weary touring bands, television became a potent force that influenced the development of the ostentatious qualities of glam rock. The video camera, with its preference for the closeup shot, could prominently focus on makeup costume and broad facial expressions. These were performance characteristics in which glam artists were proficient. Though glams were not prominently featured on video in this country, they exploited their visual qualities on shows such as *Top of the Pops* to great success in England.

SHOW BANDS

It may be derisive to call the bands that predated the glam movement "show bands," but they had an aesthetic that challenged the cool of many of the British invaders, and they transformed them. Perhaps one of the pivotal moments in the creation of glam aesthetics and its influence on the British invasion was the TAMI Show, a program produced in late 1964 and known as the TeenAge (Awards?) Music International. The meaning of the awards themselves is long forgotten, but the spectacle of British and American pop groups colliding produced a melding of very different aesthetics. Famously, James Brown gave a mesmerizing performance of "Please, Please, Please," in which a band member tries to pull the singer off stage, but he won't go. The band member appears as an overwhelmed Brown sings the song's end on his knees. He tries to guide a distraught Brown from the microphone and off stage, covering him in his famous cape. But halfway across the stage, Brown jettisons the cape, cries out, and struggles back to the microphone in time to the music, as the tight band still roars the refrain. Mick Jagger and the Stones were scheduled to follow Brown. But watching him from the side, the band was simultaneously awestruck and terrified. The Stones and other British imports gained enormously from appearing in such extravaganzas with tightly choreographed go-go dancers and brilliantly theatrical American performers like Brown, the Supremes, Ike and Tina Turner, Ray Charles, and Marvin Gaye.

But not just soul groups gave rockers the idea to emphasize performance. Many of the sixties bands had a strong stage presence and superior costuming that led to the styles and costumes of glam. For example, Paul Revere and the Raiders wore Revolutionary War costumes that included eighteenth-century wigs and pony-tail haircuts, frilled French shirts, and velour jackets of red, white, and blue. With Mark Lindsay's energetic singing, varied phrasing, and inspired showmanship, the Raiders performed choreographed dance numbers, partnering a hard charging soul-funk sound with clever, British-influenced pop tunes. Following a succession of hit records, the group hosted *Where the Action Is*, its own carnivalesque afternoon television program geared to a youthful teenage audience. Under the guidance of television programming guru

Dick Clark, the group show ran for two years. Though it was cancelled, Mark Lindsay and Paul Revere of the Raiders hosted another weekly show, *It's Happening*, in 1968–69 and a Saturday-morning music program, *Happening 68*. Throughout the band's career, Lindsay remained the focus, sort of an American counterpoint to the Rolling Stones' Mick Jagger. Like Jagger, Lindsay was an astute student of trends and guided the band through a succession of styles, from pop to country. Though widely criticized for being a merchandized approximation of British-band aesthetics, the Raiders fearlessly pioneered a brand of performance rock that enticed future glammers to dress in costume and perform ecstatically.

THE ROLLING STONES

In England, the Rolling Stones were quick to see the value of an energetic front man. Mick Jagger, though at first simply a white blues singer aping the style of American blues artists, evolved into a ranting, slurring, cavorting, prancing performer. Jagger recognized the frenzied enthusiasm of a swelling throng of adolescent girls, and he emphasized the Elvis-style hip movements, the gesturing to the crowd, and the leering laughter. Jagger was so widely imitated that by the seventies, he had already become simultaneously a legend and a parody. Jagger pioneered a style of singing that merged mannered white-imitation blues with a British-music-hall sense of broad comedy and mischief that was layered with meta-references. In the song "Something Happened to Me Yesterday," Jagger blithers, "Well thank you very much and now I think it's time for us all to go." Again, in "On with the Show" on the Stones' *Their Satanic Majesties Request* album, Jagger slurs, "We'll play your favorite songs while you all soak up the atmosphere." Undeniably, Jagger's lyrics indicate that he already saw his job as show business. Despite a rebel image, Jagger was an accomplished entertainer who could ably work the crowd. Further, the Stones transformed their bad-boy image into playable characters. In the record sleeve for "Have You Seen Your Mother Baby, Standing in the Shadows?" they pose in drag military outfits.

Jagger fancied himself an actor and, on several occasions, sought to transform his magnetic stage presence into an acting career, with mixed results. In *Performance* (1968), Nicholas Roeg's homage to decadent sixties pop culture, Jagger is perfectly cast as an over-the-top and declining pop star addicted to drugs and fame and tied to his own self-invented mythology. Jagger's work is an act of journalistic theatrical self-parody. In the Australian feature *Ned Kelly* (1970), the pop star is less convincing as a nineteenth-century Australian outlaw. But by the 1992 film, *Freejack*, Jagger fits comfortably into the role of a time-tripping body thief/mercenary. At any rate, Jagger was certainly a strong influence on later glam performers, and his early gestures, expressions, rage, dancing, use of props, costumes, and energy all influenced the style of later glam performers. He is particularly a strong influence on David Bowie, who later became a good friend. They performed a memorable version of "Dancing in the Streets" together in the eighties.

THE BEATLES AND PERFORMANCE ROCK

Of course, the Beatles were key figures in the culture of performing rock bands. Strongly influenced by their fifties idols Little Richard, Elvis, Jerry Lee Lewis, and Bill Haley, the Beatles were often very basic, straightforward, and lackluster performers. In the main, their performance consisted of standing in carefully positioned stations, Lennon in front alone, McCartney and Harrison sharing a microphone off to the side, and Ringo in the rear. Their major movements were shaking their heads in time to the music and beat. Their fan base of screaming teenagers made concentration on actual, effective, and correct playing of pivotal importance. However, in carefully staged and blocked performances like those in *A Hard Day's Night* or *Help!* we see the clever, youthful energy of four bright young men who, with a little coaching, became capable performers in a variety of media in a brief time. Their tutelage and learning curve is remarkable when one considers they were Hamburg roughs in 1962 and had progressed to the complexities of feedback and media fame by 1964's "I Feel Fine." It is a remarkable transformation from unkempt, sweaty bar band to eager musical entrepreneurs. During that time, aside from their ever-increasing musical skills, they mastered stage performance, television performance, film acting, and the complicated dialectics of personal interviews. The Beatles were as popular for their opinions and pronouncements as they were for their music. They were wildly amused by the press, and the press adored their accents, their witty responses, and their verbal jabs. Lennon was always the irreverent rebel, and his off-handed replies titillated a press corps that had grown to expect media-savvy celebrities after President Kennedy's warm and often humorous responses to the media. A female reporter asked Lennon, "Are there any subjects you'd prefer not to discuss?" Lennon shot back, "Yes, your husband" (Spitz 2005, 474).

After the 1965 film *Help!* the Beatles quickly saw the power of television as their medium of choice. They began performing a series of impressive promotional videos for their singles to be released on television. Selecting collaborators for television and film projects became an important consideration, because the group could see the potential for reaching millions with a single clip. Unlike Elvis, who appeared on television and also used the media of film to market his recordings, the Beatles adopted a different strategy that placed the music at the center. Starting with "Rain" and "Paperback Writer," the Beatles applied the techniques of avant-garde filmmakers like Antonioni

Though the Beatles were the quintessential "musician's band," their canny use of film, video, and television, starting with the "Rain" video, make them principal precursors to glam. (Courtesy of Photofest.)

and Godard to their promos, sculpting brief but pungent film art works about their musical work. Again, the budding glam artists were a part of this video culture as it was being born, and the image the Beatles presented in these videos emphasized the fun, adoration, and exalted position awarded to pop stars, inspiring the next generation to emphasize performance to even a wider degree.

"RAIN": THE FIRST GLAM VIDEO?

Though it wouldn't seem to rate as such an event at the time, the Beatles' clip for the song "Rain" might today be seen as the first glam video. George Harrison commented, as part of the Beatles Anthology video, that making promo videos like "Rain" inspired the creation of MTV, but the effect on performers was much faster. Elements from the "Rain" video show up later that same year in videos for the Monkees' television program.

The subject of the tune is a thinly veiled reference to nuclear war. Lennon remarked that the song referred to terrible rainy conditions the Beatles had endured in Australia, and how people complained about the weather, but it was easy to interpret underlying messages. The Beatles appear in a British garden, the Chiswick House in London, and children are briefly seen scampering about in the background as the Beatles play the song. Interspersed with shots of the band are images of the individual Beatles in closeup, staring blankly into the camera. There are other shots of the group walking individually or en masse about the garden. For a time, they ramble through a greenhouse. All the while, children are playing about them as they sing the track. The Beatles are subtly costumed in early psychedelic wear, including jackets, turtleneck sweaters, and granny-style wire-rimmed sunglasses. There is an element of nostalgia in the setting and costuming, but a pronounced acidity and alienation in the music. The track ends with the famous early use of backwards tracking of the vocals.

There is a sense of the music progressing backwards as well. The Beatles are portrayed from low angles, and sometimes we see the clipboard indicating the filmmakers are making another take. There is a constant reminder that we are in the midst of watching a band make a short movie about a band making music. The video is hyper-real with this sort of self-referential meta-referencing of the act of making music. Like the best of glam, there is a disconcerting sense of an otherworldly science fiction world being created. This sense is produced not by exotic special effects, but by a cool Kubrick starkness. The characters are costumed, and their movements, though simple, suggest elements of the song's content. The idea of nuclear rain plays off of the dull sunlit sky, in the garden filled with children and life. Though the scene is sunny, a sense of menace is on the horizon. The Beatles continued their television experiments through

Magical Mystery Tour, when the ensemble recorded an elaborate home movie of the musicians on a magical bus trip intercut with clips from the album.

THE STRANGE CASE OF THE MONKEES: THE FIRST GLAM BAND?

Perhaps the most successful pre-glam group was the Monkees, who used the notion of posing as the motive behind their albums and television show. The Monkees were a group of Los Angeles–area actors who auditioned and were cast in a television show that hoped to replicate the success of the Beatles' films in the small-screen format. The Monkees interacted in weekly sitcom plots, played pop tunes mostly penned by others, and mimed to backing tracks played by crack Los Angeles session musicians. The show was a fanciful comic imagining of the life of a rock band. But between the show's first and second season, a remarkable event took place. The performers, seeing themselves manipulated by the mechanics of Hollywood production, decided to wrest control from the Screen Gems studio and create their own albums. As a group of bright and capable young musicians themselves, they used their television success to forge a strong set of songs and began to produce a core of personal and highly theatrical music that rivaled and often surpassed much of what already existed in the rock world. But, like the glam artists who began as a set of groups marketed to youth, the Monkees assaulted their captors, lost their support, and were themselves abandoned by the industry that created them.

Both the Monkees and the glam artists aspired to be more than their controllers had in mind. What the industry doesn't understand is, that notion of artistic progression and growth often leads the industry to destroy the Frankenstein it has created. By their 1967 *Headquarters* album, the Summer of Love had erupted, and the Monkees changed from merely "performing monkeys" to more accomplished and sophisticated pop producers. Their songs were strange and fantastic, and they incorporated the ideas of four bright, diverse minds. Peter Tork and Michael Nesmith were already real songwriters with real musical experience. Micky Dolenz and Davy Jones were both musical performers at a young age, and dynamic singers and performers in the studio. The quartet wedded the weirdness of playing in a rock band with the struggle to become an authentic rock band. The result was a music that expressed a different sense of frustration and anger from much of that launched in the sixties. The Monkees complained about matters of fixed identity that worked against them, a very postmodern theme. As they railed at the sameness of the music business, they created a rich eclectic sound that in many ways rivaled the Beatles' complicated merging of styles.

Working with the best session players, songwriters, and producers in Hollywood, the Monkees produced a wide range of songs. Despite the fact that their time devoted to recording was limited by the enormous demands of an arduous television schedule, promotional appearances, and their own touring, the Monkees accomplished a miraculous amount of important pop work. However, their image as a group of actors crippled their reception. Mike Nesmith described how the Monkees were seen by the media. "The press went into a full scale war against us, talking about how 'The Monkees are four guys who have no credits, no credibility whatsoever and have been trying to trick us into believing they're a rock band'" (Monkees 1995). Much of their output was not released during the band's existence, but Rhino records and MTV re-birthed the band in the eighties and frequent reunions and music video airplay reminded audiences that the Monkees employed a sort of doubling performance long before the glam rockers applied makeup. The Monkees saw themselves as playacting in a bizarre Hollywood parody of a rock band and wished to become that which they played. Later the glams would feel hemmed in being treated only as musicians when indeed many of them felt just as comfortable playacting the role of musicians.

HEAD: THE MONKEES' *SGT. PEPPER*?

Where the Beatles invented an alternative persona in *Sgt. Pepper*, the Monkees began life not as themselves but as an invented TV persona. The Monkees didn't have to create anything fake; they were already saddled with that. Their purpose was to discover their true selves as a performing entity. The glams faced a similar dilemma six years later, when many bands had to determine what characteristics besides the performance elements guided their aesthetic. The film *Head* became the Monkees' rallying cry against their enforced conformity. If individualism and nonconformity were elements of hippie culture, the outcome was often a different kind of conformity to long hair, jeans, and pot culture. The Monkees had a real complaint against a stylistic and corporate hegemonic conformity that deprived a different style of music a position in the marketplace. Theodor Adorno provided a punishing assessment of the need for constant newness in popular music because of its sameness. "Distraction is not only a presupposition but also a product of popular music. The tunes themselves lull the listener to inattention. They tell him not to worry, for he will not miss anything" (Adorno 1998, 206).

Rarely championed, the Monkees were true media rebels of their era, and they paid dearly for it. If their entire career had been a ruse, than *Head* was the Monkees' opportunity to show their true selves. Ironically, whereas the Beatles, a band who had success in films, chose to document their growth in music by a musical work, the Monkees, a group born of television and bred through the television medium, chose to show their progress by the film medium. The subjects addressed in the film were diverse, and the film had key songs that tied to the various themes and sections. At times, the film illustrated the screwball comedy style of their television program, and there is a song in that genre, Harry Nilsson's charming "Daddy's Song." At other times, the film was a pointed commentary and dissection of the television business, and its effect in shaping personas and images, an Adorno-style assault on the "culture industry." Peter Tork's comical but critical "Do I Have to Do This All over Again" lampoons the sameness of television, and examines the nightmarish world of the television actor locked in 18-hour days of endless retakes. At still other times, the film is a philosophical and meditative trip on following one's creative muse, as in the Carole King tune, "As We Go Along." Finally, there is the madness of concerts and the seduction of fame, epitomized by Mike Nesmith's frantic "Circle Sky."

The film has an elegiac tone, and it is tinged with sadness bemoaning the death of the band's television series, the end of the summer of love, and the onset of the drug-addled late sixties. Moreover, like the Beatles' self-revealing *Let It Be* film, the work bluntly states the Monkees' own personal frustration at their tightly constricted roles prescribed by the rules of television. Perhaps the most painful episode presents a fantasy sequence in which Peter Tork, framed as a Christlike figure, caustically rebels against his image as the group's dummy. Tork, a natural and clever comedian, fit comfortably, perhaps too comfortably, into the Harpo Marx/Ringo Starr role of an irrepressible zany and his charming self-effacing personality often led to his marginalization by the show's producers.

Not only was *Head* an expressionistic triumph by a band that had been placed at the margins of pop music; it was an artistic vindication of four producers that had been viciously criticized from within the ranks of the music industry, most notably by Roger McGuinn's powerful indictment of manufactured pop groups, "So You Wanna Be a Rock and Roll Star?" *Head* was a complicated project of filmmaking and an accompanying album with a dizzying mixture of pop rock, nostalgia, jazzy instrumentals, psychedelic broadsides, and freewheeling power rock. In its aural variety, mix of sound clips, and adventuresome music, it falls between *Sgt. Pepper* as a pastiche of pop styles and a prelude to *Dark Side of the Moon* in its liberal use of sound effects.

Commercially, the film was abandoned by the studio, Screen Gems, as a last lark by a dying group. Even executive producer support by the fledgling Jack Nicholson did little to help the film's lackluster reception. With confusing promotion, a marginal debut, and no television exposure, the film and band were left to die. Earlier fans had outgrown the band's prefab pop sound, and though the album's accent was on progressive music, no one at the time was interested in a progressive pop band. Today, the band's output is distinguished compared to much of the product from San Francisco, where tune deaf, pretentious, meandering jam band soloing often presided.

Head stands as an example of sixties art music made within a commercial and performing context and as a decisive prelude to the work of the glam bands a few years later. It also was an early warning that bands that ventured into any performance realm would be viewed suspiciously and would be seen as performers first and pretend musicians. Further, the Monkees' experience of being exalted and abandoned would be a warning to the glam artists who saw their own fortunes undone by the symbolic richness and image sophistication of the short-lived punk movement.

SIXTIES ART CULTURE AND GLAM

But musicians alone did not prompted a society of spectacle obsession. The art world was stirring in the sixties. After the bleak internalness of abstract expressionism, with its lack of a central figurative theme, people were often perplexed and puzzled by modern art. This all changed in the fifties as a group of new, younger artists emerged, taking the title pop artists because much of their content derived from the pop culture. The pop artists went out of their way to upset the public and tinker with images of the status quo. Comic books and cartoons were reengineered for fine art works, and daily newspaper images of disasters could become print themes. Andy Warhol, who had become notorious for painting Campbell's soup can images, made his gallery· workshop, the Factory, an open space for visitors. He turned art events into ways to find new commissions. When selected to do an outdoor mural for the New York World's Fair, he chose to paint the likenesses of several most-wanted criminals from FBI posters. The fair organizers feared that such an image would mar New York's national image and demanded that Warhol alter the image. In the end, he covered the entire work with silver paint. His studio name, the Factory, toyed with the dual nature of a space that looked like a great factory complex lined with metallic aluminum foil and simultaneously aspired to be a workshop where Warhol could mass produce and sell art, a Macy's for the avant-garde. Again, Warhol needed the aspect of spectacle to market his work and himself. But to do that, he had to attract buyers, and he used his lifestyle, his entourage of friends, and his work environment to create a living theatre.

CHELSEA GIRLS: PROTO-GLAM SPECTACLE ART

Warhol was inspirational to artists, particularly glam artists. His contingent of androgynous followers influenced the costuming and cool style of glam. In 1966, Warhol documented his crowd in a series of short vignettes that he pieced together into a longer work, entitled *Chelsea Girls*. The film would mark the apex of Warhol's experimental film phase. Warhol's flamboyant entourage was recorded in various arguments, love affairs, and schemes. The participants made up much of their dialogue, and there is a rough improvisational style to the work. When sparks erupted, it was often because actors were prompted to fight or antagonized before the filming began. As always, Warhol sought to discuss taboo topics like sex and drugs, but in a dull, de-energized fashion that rendered the discussions by turns tedious or campy. The night of the actual showing, Warhol decided to mix up the footage and project the stories concurrently on two screens. The whole experience ran over three hours, with audiences vainly looking for connections between vignettes in one film linking to events in the other. When *Chelsea Girls* was shown, the order was often changed. The project was about watching the characters acting out, not about a coherent story format. Nonetheless, the spectacle of watching the dissipated "residents" perform their anguish and annoyance was fun for audiences. Their odd clothing and outrageous, often cartoonish behavior signaled a new parody form of performance and a self-deprecating "look at oneself" reflexive art. Recently, snippets of various versions of the supposed original *Chelsea Girls* has appeared on the Web, but Warhol's original collage film has long been out of general circulation. The film influenced the glam aesthetic of reinventing oneself as a star, something that artists like Bowie, Ferry, and Bolan explored.

Warhol's famous parties and his quirky group were part of a larger scene in the art world known as Happenings. The Happenings were events sponsored by artists who encouraged performance rather than products. One of the more prolific happening groups was a team called Fluxus, which included ambitious feminist artist Yoko Ono. Ono brought happening art to the mainstream when she met and later married Beatle John Lennon, transforming the character of his work from mere pop music to the style and formats of performance art. Lennon and Ono performed bed-ins where they sat in bed and spoke to reporters about world peace. Their work existed somewhere between art and politics and media. Later, David Bowie would harness media attention by successively announcing his various retirements and reinventions. But Warhol, in his factory, lived a life of constant art projects that captured media attention. In 1965, he announced he was giving up art to make films; he sponsored the pop group the Velvet Underground; he managed a light-show ensemble, the Exploding Plastic Inevitable; and he started a magazine about the media and film, entitled *Interview*. His projects continued the notion of the happening, a series of art events. Tapes that exist of the Exploding Plastic Inevitable chronicle the combination events that Warhol produced in 1966–67, which included the Velvet Underground, Warhol factory regulars dancing, and a light show of patterns and colors that flashed across the screen with little relation to the music played. The sixties art world contributed to the glams' belief that they were making a type of performance art, not just music.

ART SCHOOLS

The convergence of rock music and the visual art world was nothing new, at least in the European tradition. There, college had been an exotic privilege, and only the upper classes were usually destined for college careers. After the Second World War, in Britain particularly, things began to change. Higher education was available to a wider spectrum of society, but social barriers still persisted, and young people that didn't fit the system were given exams at an early age that routed them either towards colleges or trade schools. People like John Lennon and Pete Townshend of the Who found themselves in art schools but spent their nights daydreaming of pop stardom. Many of the professors at these art schools were actually frustrated academics with neither the credentials nor the political clout to land comfortable positions at Oxford and Cambridge. Some were talented artists themselves, and they strongly influenced their young charges. For example, early and influential British pop artist Richard Hamilton taught at an art institute and had Bryan Ferry of Roxy Music as a student. He later referred to Ferry as one of his greatest creations.

Many of the young people in these art schools were strongly influenced by advanced ideas in modernist arts. They learned of Picasso, the Dadaists, and Duchamp, and many were anxious to explore the antics of outrage, unconventional behavior, and scandal that prompted these artists to their successful careers. In their own minds, they saw their pop ambitions as simply another form of art. Bands like the Who thought their act of destroying their instruments at the end of every show was a melding of their teen frustration with a form of aesthetic outrage perpetrated against music. They saw these acts as similar to the 1913 Armory show in New York that was read as an assault against art, or Igor Stravinsky's 1913 Ballet Russe debut of *The Rite of Spring* that was considered an act of sacrilege against ballet and the classical music establishment. They were taking the ideas of the art world (consciously or unconsciously) and applying those ideas to pop music, creating an innovative hybrid form. What audiences didn't quite understand was that these well-educated, literate young men had ingested the ideas of early twentieth-century artists and transformed their ideas into the stuff of the pop culture revolution of the sixties. These art school notions of merging music, shock, and art would, of course, play a large role in the birthing of the glam rock movement.

PSYCHEDELIC SIXTIES

However, beyond Warhol, television, pop groups, and art schools, other factors influenced the glam impulse. The access to television, portable cassette players, Polaroid cameras, and a host of new transistor products made the culture a more portable entity. With that, people saw their lives and, to a large extent, their identities as more portable and disposable devices. A change of outfit could make one a hippie or a straight, and society was reconfiguring codes of dress and behavior. In America and in England, the youth culture was emerging as a subculture or a counterculture. People who listened to music, detested the Vietnam war, mistrusted the government, wore long hair, and spoke out for civil rights were branded as countercultural rebels. For the first time, these bohemian subcultures exercised full rights with the rest of society. More importantly, this subculture had youth's disposable income and a sense of joint unity of purpose that alternately frightened and fascinated the government, the aristocracy, and the press.

This youth counterculture was glamorous, sexy, and popularized as well as scandalized by the press. It was dubbed psychedelia. Contributing to the image was the prevalence of new drug use. Timothy Leary had popularized the use of LSD in the early sixties, and Ken Kesey and the Merry Pranksters had made the rituals of LSD the stuff of novels. This psychedelic era was bathed in bright colors, exotic ahistorical clothing trends, a rich sense of absurdity, a fascination with the past, and a vision of a future socialized democratic paradise. An epitome of the era's music and visuals was the Beatles' *Yellow Submarine*. In this cartoon fantasy, the Beatles portray a pop group/heroes that save Pepperland from an attack of evil, rapacious elves called the Blue Meanies. Interspersed through the film were Beatles songs. When the film arrived at "Lucy in the Sky with Diamonds," a beautiful dancing girl dances through the sky as bright objects emerge from people's heads. The Beatles themselves are portrayed as androgynous boys/men in bright Edwardian outfits. The clever comic scenes with the head Blue Meanie show the demonic elf alternately cloying in his rapport with his minions and violent when ordering his pet Hand to bomb the joy out of Pepperland and turn all things to a dull gray. Such animated images inspired glam dress, fantasy story lines, ornate color schemes, and a playful, surreal sense of the absurd.

MEDIA CULTURE AND CAMP

The sixties was an era in which media not only was more available, it began to be the central occupation of culture. Media began to preoccupy everyone. Comedian/performer Bill Irwin did a standup routine that summarized the problem. In his *Largely New York* stage show, he walks past a person who has been injured and is lying in the street. He goes to someone nearby and tries to get their attention to help the person who is injured. But that person and a crowd of others are fixated on a television in a store window that is showing a video of the person a few feet away lying in the street. Irwin is perplexed that people are more infatuated with the video image than by the actual person. America was awash in a constant, ongoing surplus of media images, and it changed the way youthful Americans saw their country, themselves, and the entire history of the world. The sixties generation moved from slow, quiet, discrete units of media like newspapers, phonograph records, and the radio, to the powerful pervasive media of cinerama movie theaters, 3-D films, stereo FM broadcasting, component sound systems, cassette players, tiny radios and earphones, instant Polaroid cameras, color televisions, and bright magazines and books. This flood of media changed the way people saw the world. When the world could be revisited instantly, the barrier of time, the notion or real and unreal, of past and present, of what was and what is, began to dissipate.

One consequence of this collision of media was camp. Camp was a self-ridiculing type of media that depended on an intimate knowledge of the original source material for its parody of it. Camp put quotes around a thing and flaunted the audience's awareness of the media and culture. If Judy Garland's over-the-top musical performances were grand, they could also be easily transformed into camp because they were memorized, parodied, and reverentially sent up for their extreme and bizarre take on female torch singing. Camp was also a fun way of referencing material you loved. It was more complex than simple parody. It became a popular genre in the sixties as self-awareness of former and extreme styles of performance could still be seen in opera, old movies, or comic books. For example, within a few years of James Bond's hypersexual take on spying, parodies of spy films erupted in works such as *Casino Royale*, *The Man from UNCLE*, and *Get Smart*. Susan Sontag addressed the qualities of camp in her famous essay "Notes on Camp" from *Against Interpretation* in 1966. She wrote that camp had a relationship to certain extreme arts over others, concluding that "for camp, it is often decorative art, emphasizing texture, sensuous surface, and style at the expense of content" (Sontag 1983, 278). In other words, camp is often about marginal or ephemeral art and culture, particularly art that is so extreme and remote that it is highly stylized and thus suspect to a common audience.

Much of sixties pop music appears today to be campy because of its extreme surface appearance. The epitome of sixties camp was the *Batman* television program, which made Batman into a standup routine of ridiculous one-liners ("Come on, Robin . . . to the Bat-pole!"). This mistreatment derailed any serious version of the comic book for another 20 years. In this sense, camp is often seen as an art of bad taste, or a performance form that depends on irony for its humor. Naturally, the self-aware take on show business later influenced the glam aesthetic, making glam constantly self-conscious and superficially affected. Glam's existence in a perpetual hyper-ironic style limited its durability, and much of camp had a short lifespan because irony lost its punch or ironic edge after a time. The *Batman* television program survived only two years. Glam rock, with characters portraying androgynous sexuality and with allusions to golden-age Hollywood glamour, was instantly considered to be camp. Their performances were filled with ironic lyrics and nostalgic images of the past. Perhaps the most specific use of camp in a glam context came in *The Rocky Horror Picture Show*, in which old movie themes (the mad scientist/spooky house movie) meshed with Tim Curry's androgynous Dr. Frankenfurter character.

ROCK MUSICAL

Finally, a new form of theatrical rock debuted at the end of the sixties, elevating the music to more theatrical formats and enlarging the instrumentation and stylistic palette of the times. Broadway saw the power of rock music and looked for a way to incorporate the popularity of hippiedom into traditional Broadway fare. James Rado, Gerome Ragni, and Galt MacDermot wrote *Hair*, a tribal rock opera that told the tale of a young man considering entry into the military and his encounter with a tribe of street-dwelling hippies. The play is a spiritual journey, chronicling his and the tribe's adventures in getting in touch with the spirit and building a community of like-minded free thinkers who are onboard for the Age of Aquarius. The show was performed by Broadway dancers and singers mostly wearing long-haired wigs, but designer Ming Cho Lee's structuralist set, a nude scene, and the rocking score seemed to capture the prevailing spirit of rebellion. The play also showed that rock music could be applied to the musical format (as the Beatles had proved with *A Hard Day's Night*). At the same time, it could produce a plot that was new and quite attractive. The show was a massive hit (over 1,700 performances) and signaled that progressive popular music was a commercial possibility.

It didn't take the rock world long to retaliate with its own new hybrid pop music form. This music called rock theatre or rock opera was pioneered by the Who in their opus *Tommy*, a two-album pop set/song cycle in which lead singer Roger Daltrey sang all the principal parts (mostly the character of Tommy) with some assistance from the other band members. The opera was structured as a complete narrative detailing the birth, trauma, and subsequent cure of the pinball prodigy known as Tommy, or the Pinball Wizard.

The following year, the blending of rock theatre and rock opera was made nearly seamless by Andrew Lloyd Webber and Tim Rice's *Jesus Christ Superstar*. This pop opera detailing the last days of Christ's existence before crucifixion arrived first as a single, "Jesus Christ, Superstar." The title borrowed equally from Andy Warhol's expression about his actors, that they were superstars, and also presented a contemporary time-warped version of an important historical and religious figure, Jesus Christ. The profit from the single allowed the composers to finish the full-scale pop opera, and the music was played by British pop musicians and the London Symphony Orchestra, again setting a precedent for orchestrating pop music, and melding the divergent forms of Britpop and theatrical musical styles. The stage was set for a more theatrical style of pop music that could accommodate the tastes of literate adults and sophisticated youth that appreciated the narrative dimension of rock.

STONEWALL

There is little doubt that the burgeoning gay rights movement was an aspect of glam culture, but how much it impacted the music movement is difficult to determine. Glam performers were excellent at performing gay dress and style codes, but few of the glam performers (Freddie Mercury, Elton John, Jobriath) were actually gay, and very few performers found it acceptable to clarify their sexual orientation. The ambiguity of androgyny was one of glam's best selling points. However, the gay community contributed a sense of rebellion to the glam movement. If civil rights fueled the music of black artists in the sixties, than the struggle of gays to achieve full citizenship was an implicit element in glam's politics, a musical movement that was often criticized for not having political opinions.

In fact, despite the lip service paid to the debt glam owes to gay culture, few studies of glam music spend any real time analyzing the connection between gay culture and glam culture. It is usually given as a truism and dropped with little formal analysis. Still there is a political connection between the two movements. The formal beginning of the modern gay rights movement started on June 28, 1969, when a group of gays at the Stonewall Inn in New York City were raided by the police at 1:30 a.m. Police raids were common in the gay community, as were beatings and harassments that could never be prosecuted in the straight courts of New York City. This night, however, the residents of the bar were numerous, and when several bar patrons were arrested, violence erupted. As people were escorted to a police van, some patrons started throwing rocks and bottles and shouting slogans like, "we are the stonewall girls, we wear our hair in curls," taunting the police. Reinforcements were called, and the evening turned into a full-scale confrontation, with units of police confronting up to 400 rioting, parking-meter-bashing, stone-throwing, fire-setting gays. Weary of years of police brutality, the gays chanted "gay power" and continued the battle all night long. The violence erupted for five long nights, providing a new sense of solidarity in the gay community and abruptly ending unofficial police harassment.

Warhol and his entourage included several gay, transsexual, and bisexual members, and Warhol taunted society with his own ambivalent, androgynous personality. Christopher Castiglia wrote that "it was not just promiscuous sex this culture was inventing, it was promiscuous representation" (Castiglia 2000, 205). Indeed, Warhol and company created the idea that one could quickly and effectively alter one's identity. Warhol made identity portraits (Polaroids with dabs of paint added), created icons from dead film stars, and produced pseudo-superstars with his "screen tests." The glams noted that like artists and gays, they, too, could reinvent their identity and become something more glamorous and more exciting. For strugglers like Bowie, Bolin, and Ferry, such strategies were liberating. If a style or fashion failed, it could be jettisoned, and another method could be employed.

GLAM: THE STAGE IS SET

> There's a new creation, a fabulous sensation.
>
> —Roxy Music, "The Strand"

Many factors encouraged the growth of conditions that allowed the style of glam rock to arrive. Television and new media helped to break new bands and allowed audiences to have an intimacy with bands from far-off countries that had not existed before. Television also marketed bands not only as musicians, but as stage performers, changing the way bands were seen. The hyper-accelerated role of media and the emergence of quick and inexpensive media allowed for a proliferation of bands, tunes, and music to produce an over-whelming exposure to music, past, present, and future. Pop groups like the Beatles began to make promotional films that presented the band as performers as well as musicians. Notably, the Monkees pioneered the notion of a band that consisted of part performers and part musicians. Art culture, psychedelic music, and camp entertainment enlarged the role of self-referential entertainment emphasizing the type of irony that would make glam popular. Finally, gay culture and the suppression of alternative identities gave glams a political edge, emphasizing the notion that people should be free to express their individual identity no matter how unconventional it seemed.

Chapter 3

MR. BOWIE MEETS GLAM

AN ERA OF STRUGGLE

> Any society that allows people like Lou Reed and I to become rampant is really pretty well lost.
>
> —David Bowie (quoted in Carr 1994, 94)

> My performances have got to be theatrical experiences for me as well as for the audience.
>
> —Bowie (quoted in Mendelsohn 1996, 46)

David Bowie may not have originated glam, but he was probably more responsible than anyone for popularizing the format to world audiences. Bad journalism about Bowie claims that he is a chameleon, and that he changes shape and fashion every so many years. Certainly, most artists change to accommodate fashion, but Bowie's changes have always explored the core values of glam—a theatrical, produced, trebly, self-invented, campy, self-aware performance that uses progressive avant-garde themes and musical motifs within the context of a crooner pop-singer style. Glam arose along with postmodernism, and like that term, the number of strategies and styles employed by glam artists is staggering and leads to the perception that the style is rootless and lacks any authentic qualities.

Certainly, Bowie seems to reemerge differently every few years, a reincarnated pop deity; but that is because his essence is so slippery, we only see the actor, not the performer—as in all good theatre. In "Changes," he wrote of his own inability to capture his image in the mirror. Bowie is commenting that before he turns to look at himself, he has moved on to another style. He isn't too concerned that others might see him as a faker, since by then he would be pursuing a different characterization. Bowie is aware that the style of one's performances has to be worn and abandoned, or else they drag the performer down into a dull sameness. If anything, this ability to remain constant while wearing many masks is his strength. Bowie learned this in his 10 years of striving for stardom from 1963 to 1972, and this apprenticeship paid off in his flexible glam style. Bowie was forced to adapt because for so long, he was mostly unsuccessful.

Bowie, like many young British men of limited means, found himself studying in an art school in the early sixties. Though like many of his colleagues, he studied commercial art by day, his dream was of musical fame. Bowie played saxophone in secondary school and envisioned himself as a pop star in the mode of the British Invasion bands. He functioned in several pop bands and worked with Jonathan King as producer, who himself had a pop hit with the tune, "Everyone's Gone to the Moon." Bowie's real name was David Jones, but fearing comparisons to the Monkees' David Jones, he changed his name to David Bowie because he had seen a film about Jim Bowie and his Bowie knife on television, and he thought it had a nice sound to it.

Bowie arrived at an era when pop was in its ascendency, circa 1965–67 when he recorded most of his Deram/London label–period music. It was only later when the harsh tonalities of acid rock and psychedelic bands would attract Bowie's attention. Bowie's interest in his own softer side of his catalogue is reflected in the release of *Iselect*, a CD giveaway with the British newspaper *The Mail on Sunday* that provided the Bowie album as a freebee on Sunday, June 28, 2008. The free compilation focused on album tracks, nearly all ballads with only two real rockers ("Hang on to Yourself," and "Time Will Crawl") being the only up-tempo numbers. The variety of tracks on Iselect ("Life on Mars?" "Sweet Thing," "Fantastic Voyage") remind us that Bowie's voice was always a wide-ranging and supple instrument, and that this voice (along with his keen intellect for writing songs and exploring styles) has kept Bowie a pop music force for over four decades.

Like many students in the art school tradition, the 16-year-old Bowie in 1964 saw himself as a potential aspirant to the model created by the Beatles and the Rolling Stones. Simon Frith and Howard Horne in *Art into Pop* explained that pop artists residing in lowbrow art academies imbued their young charges with a sense of aesthetics and self-importance that translated very neatly into the pop art aesthetics of the mods in early sixties London. Their clothes, their jackets, their hairstyles, their Vespa scooters, and their drugs reflected this aesthetic artistic life. In fashion, Bowie adhered to the mod look with closely shorn hair and brightly colored paisley shirts. He was an attractive, diminutive, charming, poster boy for modism, and he performed (as did many young performers) with a succession of bands looking for the right mix in London's hypercompetitive musical scene.

Bowie realized that real pop stardom eluded him, and he tried a variety of approaches. He continued to paint, draw, and write poetry. He still played guitar, but buoyed by his handsomeness and supple, lithe body, he considered that a theatrical career might better suit his talents. He began taking mime classes. Written performance and stage plays were undergoing an evolution in the late sixties, and acting companies were experimenting with environmental spaces, alternative languages, and nonverbal styles. Bowie saw the stage as a means to live out his artistic ideas and to gain a wide audience in the process. Even at this early stage, it is clear that Bowie identified music, mime, film, culture, and media as all forms of theatre and performance. Even then, Bowie did not compartmentalize these impulses as separate entities. This blurring of distinctions and boundaries would serve him well when rock as a principal means of youth communication was challenged by other media in the seventies. Then, music, television, films, designer clothes, dance crazes, and fads swept audiences more so than the music-centric sixties, and Bowie's mix of music and theatre was a potent force. Youth by that time had been viewed as a market. The media had targeted and commodified youth as a specific demographic market, and listeners were being targeted as specific audiences for specific types of music. If some rockers were not prepared for the transition to the MTV generation over the next decade, Bowie was well ahead of the curve, honing his multidisciplinary skills as an actor, writer, singer, and producer to make himself the type of aesthetic product that Warhol had enthused about to the American press.

Bowie produced a short-lived art collective that he called the Beckenham Arts Lab. "Bowie's intentions were quite clear, he would create an alternative environment to feature new and developing artists, providing a simple showcase for them (Cann 1983, 52). In reality, the lab was nothing more than the back room of the Three Tuns Pub on Beckenham Street, but it did serve as a laboratory for Bowie and a small circle of friends to showcase their work for a small audience of like-minded friends and curiosity seekers.

In July 1969, Bowie was offered an opportunity to record his "Space Oddity" tune and the album that featured the track; *David Bowie, Man of Words and Music* was released in November. Bowie by this time had morphed into a fey, attractive, hippieish, folkie whose most distinguishing qualities was a gregarious smile and a long shock of pretty golden hair. "Space Oddity," gained notoriety and put Bowie on the map when the single release charted in October 1969, due to the moon landing of the American Apollo program.

As the decades changed, Bowie married Angela Barnett, and they quickly had a son, Joe, who would be renamed Zowie to cash in on the Bowie and Ziggy movement. Angela, like David, was also captivated by fame and art. An artist who had studied mime, she poured her ideas and suggestions into her struggling husband's career. It was Angela who suggested that he grow his hair to feminine lengths and pose in a woman's dress for *The Man Who Sold the World* album cover.

We can see at this point that glam was both premediated and an organic arrival. Certainly, there were elements of a plan to create controversy and raise attention, and also an evolution of elements that fell into place. First, Bowie married Angela, and she conspired with Bowie to emphasize the androgynous/bisexual/cross-dressing aspects of his appearance. This part was not difficult. Bowie already was a seasoned performer, was learning to act, was slight in build and stature, and had pronounced cheekbones and attractive girlish hair and features. He could pose as a female and produce credible results. Next, he acquired a new brain trust. He first gained the services of Mick Ronson as a guitarist and arranger. Ronson's power rock and psychedelic inclinations toughened and tightened Bowie's sound. He found a manger in Tony DeFries who was capable of selling his music and freakish appearance and was glad to do it. Finally, he found a sympathetic producer, Ken Scott (and later Tony Visconti), who could articulate a variety of sounds, including psychedelia, nostalgia, music hall, cabaret, crooning pop ambience, hard rock, and avant-garde stylings. The last component in orchestrating all of these parts was the arrival in 1971 of Andy Warhol's touring production of *Pork*, a stage show Warhol had developed in New York in which Warhol and confidante Bridgitte Polk discussed and gossiped about their circle of eccentric friends and their lives. Warhol and Polk's raunchy dialogue was developed into a raunchy stage show, but it pushed Warhol and his ideas out to the road. His company of actors became a sensation in London, where Warhol's theories about popular culture and fame were beginning to gain wide acceptance.

Bowie took away from his meeting with Warhol and his circle some key lessons. First, Warhol gave him the idea that stardom was a self-defined and self-manufactured quality. If you called yourself a star, you became one, and it only took the press to catch up to make your achievement a reality. The trick that Bowie and Warhol mastered was in producing copy-ready material for the press so they would write what was fed them. Second, art was something to be produced like cheese or cars, and that calling attention to the work and attracting an audience to it was far more important than the innate question of authenticity and quality. Third, and perhaps most important in Bowie's case, was the notion that developing a quirky, easily recognizable stage personality was the key to constant media gratification. If you looked like Warhol, you would be undeniably unique, and people would recognize you and photograph you everywhere you went. This would solidify your pretend fame into the real thing. Warhol himself experimented with this notion that look superseded reality. For a time, he sent out a double, a paid actor wearing a wig in his place for a lecture tour in the sixties. The actor was found out, and Warhol had to repay speaker's fees, but he tested the limits of pseudo celebrity.

So, armed with an exotic look sculpted from mime study and bisexual costuming, a strong singing and performance style, a canny production team of Ronson and Visconti, a smart and daring wife, a clever and wily manager who could exploit Bowie's weird look, Warhol's aesthetics of fame and pop culture, and, lest we forget, Bowie's not inconsiderable talent as a singer, musician, songwriter, and performer, Bowie was cocked and loaded to the media.

THE ARTIST WHO WAS SOLD TO THE WORLD

But there were setbacks. His label, Mercury, pulled the female dress look adorning *The Man Who Sold the World* album for fear the controversy might work against their fledgling act. Further, at first, the press didn't know how to take Bowie's mix of gender and science fiction. A strong element of *The Man Who Sold the World* was the use of Bowie's continuing science fiction mania. Bowie was a fan of the genre, and he wrote songs that alluded to the problems of future worlds and civilizations. The song "The Man Who Sold the World" suggests the themes of alienation, fear, and paranoia that populate lots of Bowie's tunes. Bowie roots the tune in Latin beats and rhythms, which provides a slight war between the postapocalyptic subject future and the cliché effect of the pseudo-Brazilian sound that was popular at the time. Bowie sets up an antithesis between the subject and the style of playing regularly to make the listener realize that although the music may sound familiar the subject is anything but familiar.

In the song, Bowie briefly relates the tale of a man who, in his earlier life, had been some corporate raider who had marketed the Earth as a commodity. But now, he is alone and unable to escape the legacy of his dealings. He is a forgotten man who can only stare up into the heavens ("Man Who Sold the World"). The only thing our protagonist has going for him now is a sense of his self-control, his ability to bear the terrible weight of what he has done, to merchandise a planet. He protests that he always had control, and adds: "You're face to face, With the man who sold the world."

The song illustrates the new status and maturity that science fiction had acquired over the years. Not only was it a story about the future and about space travel, but it was complicated by the economics and tragedy of such dealings in a future history. Although there are many precedents for the song, critics have often commented that it resembles Robert A. Heinlein's 1949 future history story "The Man Who Sold the Moon." In it, an obsessive protagonist/capitalist, Delios Harriman, engineers a corporate buyout of the moon. It is a massive and risky venture, and eventually, he is successful. But his dream of actually going to the moon himself is crushed when his peers and coconspirators buy his moon flight company out from under him and determine that he is too important to risk taking such a journey. He is barred from boarding the rocket. Like Bowie for so long, he can see fame in the distance; he just can't reach it himself, a modern Moses. Bowie's storytelling and the driving guitar riff of Mick Ronson make the song an epic tale of woe. As the number closes on a Latin beat, Bowie croons a mournful moan of regret. In recent years, Bowie has complained that many people know the tune only from the live Nirvana cover performed on MTV, and Bowie often has to explain to misguided fans that he wrote the song and, actually, Nirvana copied him.

The album cover was one of Bowie's clearest methods of attracting attention to the album. *The Man Who Sold the World*'s album cover shows Bowie with beautiful, shoulder-length, golden hair sitting on a long Victorian royal-blue satin chaise lounge. He is laid seductively on the couch, stroking his golden locks and shooting his "come and love me" look. Bowie wears a top hat and a silky full-length dress. The dress is provocatively fastened but open at the top, revealing some of Bowie's chest. Bowie wears knee-high boots in the bed. He is draped languorously on the sofa, with a playing card between his index and forefinger. Cards are strewn all over the floor, and Bowie looks like the loser in an all-night game of strip poker at a gay gentleman's club with someone off camera waiting to collect. It was a seductive and smart marketing ploy, enraging some and intriguing most viewers. Though little of real sexuality or menace is present in the picture, there are real implications of provocative gay gesturing, particularly at a time when both British and American society were just learning how to deal with an underground gay subculture that had its own codes and visual symbols for communication.

In August 1971, Andy Warhol's *Pork* arrived in London. The controversial theatre production featured two characters in a gossipy discussion. One character was modeled on Warhol and the other, Pork, was modeled on Warhol's friend and confidante Brigid Polk (a.k.a. Brigid Berlin), herself a prolific artist and a notorious gossip. The evening consisted of the couple's pithy observations on their neurotic and self-destructive friends in Warhol's inner circle. Bowie was enamored of the show, Warhol's aesthetic approach, and the way celebrity, androgyny, and the aura of glamour could be applied, as Warhol suggested, like a disguise or a form of aesthetic makeup. Perhaps more than any other theorist (except maybe Brecht or Nietzsche), Bowie found a substantive game plan for his career in watching Warhol and his entourage operate. Certainly the encounter with *Pork* and Warhol's aesthetic changed Bowie's work and influenced glam for the foreseeable future. Bowie employed many of the Warhol entourage later as front-office workers for his Mainman management organization.

EVERYTHING'S *HUNKY DORY*

Late 1971's *Hunky Dory* is a giant step towards Bowie's mature glam style and perhaps contains his most self-assured pop song craftsmanship. Tony Visconti had left the fold of Bowie's band, and Trevor Bolder had entered, completing the Spiders from Mars backup band. Production on the album was by Ken Scott, who had worked on engineering the Beatles' later albums. The liner notes proclaim "assisted by the actor," a reference to Bowie himself. Bowie by this point considered himself an actor, and he perceived the idea of record production as a kind of auditory script for performance, a kind of total theatre in which Bowie assumes a character and then performs in the guise of the character. Many other rock performers were aware of the theatrical aspect of their work (the Kinks, the Who), but many disdained the idea that they were part of the show business establishment, because it violated their rebel aesthetic. Bowie, however, didn't avoid the tag of performance; he embraced it.

At any rate, the diversity of *Hunky Dory* acts as recorded version of a variety television show. Each song is a different mood and style. The album is perhaps Bowie's greatest achievement as a composer and suggests what Bowie might have become if he had devoted himself only to the craft of songwriting—like a Cole Porter, Rodgers and Hammerstein, or Bernie Taupin/Elton John? Bowie assembles a skillful written assemblage of pop tunes in a single album, a joyful blend of jaunty Beatlesque melodies, torch songs, transgender anthems, commentaries on the artistic life, and aesthetic responses to the Warholian philosophies of self-proclaimed but short-lived celebrity.

Hunky Dory also suggests qualities of a soundtrack, with superb and varied production providing a sonic backdrop to each song. There is a real sense of place and atmosphere to the songs, and there is a richness of a life of the imagination conjured by Bowie's images. This is the journeyman/struggling artist/aesthete finally arriving at the full maturity of his talents. It also suggests that this was a happy period for Bowie: his marriage to Angela; their relative financial well-being; the blooming of Bowie's career; the cohesion of a stable backing band; the arrival of a management team; the relative peace and creative nesting of Haddon Hall, a pleasant flat the couple had rented; the arrival of Bowie's son Zowie (or more plainly, Joe); and a good, creative partnership with Ronson and producer Ken Scott. Bowie was 25, and all the pieces were falling into place. Some of Bowie's work was determined by plan, but much of it was a confluence of elements that fell into order.

One such serendipitous arrival was the short-lived Arnold Corns project. Bowie met and glommed on to Freddie Buretti, who was to be the lead singer for the Arnold Corns group with the core of the band being the Spiders. They only recorded several songs and little came of the project before Bowie went back to recording as a soloist, but Buretti was a great designer, and he created the fabulous costumes that propelled Bowie's early Ziggy Stardust period. Even missteps paid off in remarkable artistic benefits for Bowie at this time.

Serendipity followed Bowie wherever he landed. At Haddon Hall, a kind neighbor donated a grand piano for Bowie's flat, and Bowie became competent composing on the piano. The fact that many of the compositions of *Hunky Dory* are piano-centered, and therefore percussive but melodic, helps increase the tunefulness of the album. Those of Bowie's compositions that seemed to have been written on guitar were decidedly more aggressive and punkish, suggesting that Bowie had angry punk elements in his work going back to his earliest era. Whether it was the piano, the Bowie lifestyle circa 1971, or his marital bliss at the time, the tunes on *Hunky Dory* are rampantly charming, sophisticated, and jazzy. Further, this was the era in which the dominance of the rock guitar was finally challenged by the keyboard, and keyboard wizardry aligned Bowie with the avant-garde leanings in British progressive music. Again, it is no accident that the session keyboardist on *Hunky Dory* and the popular single "Changes" is none other than Rick Wakeman, who would thrive as the featured keyboardist with Yes. He would himself have a remarkable career as a session player and a solo artist.

"Changes" starts the album with a modulation of keys from minor to major, and then moves into a familiar, rocking piano style. But as the title suggests, the song is a clever homage to change, filled with witty key, mood, and tempo changes, and ultimately is textually about the notion of changes. Just as Bowie grasped the idea of the Warhol artist who could change and mold himself, here Bowie extols the virtues of malleability. The verses are taken directly from cabaret singers of the forties and fifties, and there are elements of Judy Garland and Frank Sinatra as torch singers, as well as Roger Daltrey's famous stutter from "my ge-ge-generation," appropriated for the line "cha-cha-cha-changes." The song proclaims the power of changes on us. Though widely suggested as a proclamation of gay awareness, the lyrics point to a more philosophical change in thinking and a more advanced and enlightened way of looking at the world. It is rather more of a pitch for the age of Aquarius than a direct call for gay rights.

Certainly, "Changes" is one of the frankest assessments of the music business ever written. Bowie sang, "Still don't know what I was waiting for, and my time was running wild" ("Changes"). For an artist known for faking it, Bowie's lyric is aesthetically true, and "Changes" truly tells it like it is. In his early career, Bowie ran savagely from one trend to another, and had seemingly arrived nowhere for all of his aggressive work. It must have frustrated him to reflect on the failures of the past 10 years. To him, it must have seemed that he had been waiting around for the wave of fame to scoop him up, and he certainly must have felt passed over for all his attempts at fame. His brushes with fame had been that sweet taste that had ultimately failed him again and again. When Bowie looked in the mirror, he must have pondered long and hard how to turn this career around, how to arouse public interest, and how to finally court long-lasting, sustainable fame. Bowie's song frames the issues of his life and career succinctly. The final three lines situate Bowie's solution. He had not caught a glimpse of himself, and he didn't stick around to see how others were judging his various personas. He refers to himself here as the faker or an actor. And the final line is a validation of his ability to stay ahead of the trends and change to meet the needs of the marketplace. "I'm much too fast." Bowie proved the idea that Brian Eno (first of Roxy Music and later as a soloist) proclaimed that the future would belong to small, mobile units. That is, Bowie and Eno both understood that fast-moving, easily adaptable, quick-to-change personas and careers provided the most agile way to stay ahead of changing fashions.

"Oh! You Pretty Things" is another hymn to Bowie's arriving generation. The second track further develops the themes and obsessions of glam. In fact, *Hunky Dory*, more than any other Bowie album of the era, is really the template, the organum for glam practice. "Oh! You Pretty Things" is not only a paean to the sweet young artists of the glam movement, the youth that idealistically wished to change the music business from the inside, but it is also the story of another cosmic science fiction monster from Bowie's imagination. Here, *the pretty things* are the youth of the human species about to be pushed aside by an even brighter race, *the homo superior*. Bowie explains, "A crack in the sky and a hand reaching down to me, all the nightmares came today." For all the song's charming music-hall buoyancy, there is threat and menace in the lyrics indicating that mysteriously, something is reaching down from the sky. There are many different themes at work. Bowie posits the pretty things as a solution to the sameness of culture while driving their parents wild. The arriving nightmares are about to drive out mankind and replace that species with the homo superior.

"Life on Mars?" is another song suggesting sci-fi themes. People had always wondered if indeed there was real life on Mars, so there is a literal context; but the song also had a social and songwriting context. In the sixties, Bowie wrote lyrics to a French song melody. It was never released, but later Paul Anka bought the French tune, rendering it unusable by Bowie. He rewrote it as "My Way," making it a big hit for Frank Sinatra. Bowie was inspired to write a response to his experience with the business side of the music business. Though the song is a beautiful ballad, it has surreal lyrics and tends to provide a sour view of things, reflecting Bowie's disappointment at losing the tune. Lines like "it's a god awful small affair, to the girl with the mousy hair" ("Life on Mars?") suggests annoyance, with perhaps Bowie as the "girl" with mousy hair. There is a reference to the "Disneyfication" of all art to an acceptable lower level when he writes that America has turned Mickey Mouse into a "cow" ("Life on Mars?").

Bowie's exposure to queens and other cross-gendered personalities was accelerated by his exposure to the cast of Warhol's *Pork*, which hit London like a rocket in August 1971. Bowie apparently was a real groupie to the cast and crew, and he couldn't get enough of Warhol's entourage, breathing in the decadent flavor of Warhol's savants like a graduate student in a research library. Several of the cast and crew wound up working for Bowie and DeFries's Mainman marketing organization as office and publicity assistants. Bowie, always like Warhol a canny businessman, was probably enamored of Warhol's mystique and how he successfully manipulated the press to achieve and maintain his fame. Bowie wanted that power. There was something extraordinarily engaging about the lurid exploits of big-city artists, junkies, queens, and other sorted types that fascinated Bowie. It may have been the big-city allure of urban life after the sleepy existence that he and so many youths grew up with in postindustrial Britain. It was a quiet and morose place because the war, government, business, and economic failures had sapped the country's strength. New York and Warhol were exciting and mysterious.

When Tony DeFries and Bowie arrived in New York in 1971 to sign a contract with RCA Records, Bowie met with Warhol, and the two spent almost an hour not talking. Bored, Warhol left the room for a time, and the only thing that propelled the conversation was Warhol's photo obsession. He kept taking Polaroids of Bowie, instant still pictures that were self-developing and quite remarkable to sixties technogeeks. Warhol was an instant fan of the instant picture camera. It made capturing an image quicker. He noticed and loved the singer's crocodile shoes. Bowie played Warhol a tape of the song he had written about the artist, "Andy Warhol." Warhol later wrote that he loathed it, but on that occasion, he thanked the singer for his efforts and said, "it was great."

The meeting told Bowie little more about the enigmatic Warhol, but Bowie remembered the lesson of being vague and illusory to the media and used it successfully in molding his own public image. Bowie and Warhol both shared a fetishistic rapture about fame and stardom. While both men achieved it, both saw stardom as an aura from the outside, a quality that somehow endowed and anointed the possessor with superhuman abilities of attraction. Warhol was this way because he was shy, ugly, and often tongue-tied, and wished to be the extrovert that stars and performers appeared to be. Bowie was different. He had all the extroverted abilities of a performer and talent, but he had little luck during the first 10 years of his career finding a suitable mechanism to get to stardom.

Critics lauded *Hunky Dory* and encouraged Bowie to take to the road, which he did, mounting a successful tour in 1972 across England. There were accompanying dates in Europe, and by the fall of that year, Bowie was planning an assault on America. He started with a few dates in Cleveland and Memphis, then a triumphant gig at Carnegie Hall in September to a sold-out crowd. In October, he played the jubilant victory lap concert at Santa Monica that was much bootlegged over the years and eventually released as an official live album in 2008.

The year was eventful for Bowie's remarkable productivity, nearly turning anything and anyone he touched to gold. In January, the single "Changes," with the B side "Andy Warhol," neatly combined his twin strategies of androgyny and compulsive fame-seeking. In January, *Melody Maker* released an interview with Bowie in which he admitted he was "gay." He later told another paper, "it was probably the best thing I ever said" (Cann 1983, 85), calling into doubt the entire question of whether Bowie was ever even bisexual. Early in the year, Bowie performed regularly with the Spiders from Mars. Mick Ronson on guitar, Woody Woodmansey on drums, and Trevor Bolder on bass formed the tight core of the band. Constant performing whipped them into a strong performing ensemble, with Bowie shining as the front man and Ronson providing the guitar theatrics with his Jeff Beck–style screaming effect.

ZIGGY AND STARDOM

By June 1972, the next album had arrived, and it was Bowie's blockbuster *The Rise and Fall of Ziggy Stardust and the Spiders from Mars*, a concept album about a wigged-out future rock star self-destructing in a near-future decadent era under the weight of his own ego. Bowie had been at work on the album since June 1971, before *Hunky Dory* was released, so he had plenty of time to hone the songs and integrate the band's vigorous playing into the proceedings. Though a concept album, it had a strong cycle of tunes and produced the effect of one cohesive story. Despite the praise that the work has received, it is more of a group album with strong arrangements from Scott and Ronson, bold singing from Bowie, and some nice psychedelic touches. However, in many ways, it is not an improvement over the stylistically diverse and eclectic writing of *Hunky Dory*, and Bowie quickly saw that the Ziggy character, while it was carrying him to fame was also a confining, limiting role. Like an actor who plays James Bond too long, it limits what you can do. You become typecast in the public's eyes.

In the opening track "Five Years," Bowie confronts a common theme of science fiction literature, a future apocalypse. He describes a future in which Earth has five years until destruction. While we are never told what has marked the planet for destruction, we know it is all coming to an end soon. Bowie writes like a detached newspaper reporter. He describes a girl attacking kids and a black man stopping her from violence. It is a story of sadness at the world's end. Again, Bowie includes his preoccupations with gay identities when he sings that a policeman kneels before a priest and a gay man vomits upon seeing this. He also assails his interest in theatre and performance when he writes, "it was a cold and it rained, so I felt like an actor." With its sparse orchestration of drums, bass, piano, and Bowie on acoustic guitar and vocals, "Five Years" is extremely dramatic and powerful. Bowie's performance and narrative of the end of the world and time carry the song and lend a strong elegiac power to the performance. There is Ronson's strong string arrangement and psychedelic guitar effects that embellish, support, and add to the drama. But at its core, Bowie's marvelous crescendo and vocal performance supports the sentiment beautifully. When on Februrary 8, 1972, Bowie and the Spiders performed "Five Years" minus the strings and Ronson's electric pyrotechnics on guitar, on British television, nothing was lost. Bowie's marvelous vocal, clear performance, and emotional delivery secure the song. Along with "Oh! You Pretty Things" and "Queen Bitch," Bowie's performances for the *Old Grey Whistle Test* television program are a brilliant showcase for Bowie's work circa 1971–72.

While the story of a futuristic pop star's rise, decline, and fall is more hinted at through most of the album than directly proclaimed, "Moonage Daydream" reinforces gender and science fiction issues again with lines like "I'm a space invader, I'll be a rock and roll bitch for you" ("Moonage Daydream"). He also again re-invites themes of fame and paranoia. He tells the world to point their cameras at him, and that his media love affair is a "freakout." Bowie simultaneously likes and wants to be watched while fearing the intimacy and power that voyeur viewers have over him. It takes little reading into the lyrics to suggest that Bowie's description of himself as rock's "bitch" relates to his own strategy for success. It sounds as though Bowie had placed himself on a timeline—that he could endure this rock circus life for maybe five years, "that's all we got." He also suggests he could play this rock-and-roll Perrot for only a brief time. He told *Rolling Stone* magazine in late 1972 that he didn't think being a rock and roller was "much of a vocation" (Cann 1983, 101). Bowie would later see that such a lifestyle would take a heavy toll on his health and personal life.

Scott, Bowie, and Ronson's arrangement on "Daydream" includes an eclectic flute's baroque-ish, playful passage, before returning to the chorus and a string-drenched, echoed, feedback guitar–frenzied outro. Amidst the sound effects, Ronson gives a blistering, astute, self-assured solo, and Bowie echoes, "far out"and other ad libs. It is energized performance music with touches of music hall, progressive rock, and chamber pop. Bowie is clearly building this album for concert performance. There are distinct similarities between this and Bowie's much-later 1983 album *Let's Dance*, which from the title on suggests a concert performance. However, that affair has a plastic hollow sound, while *Ziggy* provides a more engaged, heartfelt sound.

"Hang onto Yourself" is one of Bowie and Ronson's show-stopping rockers, with lyrics that describe Ziggy the star, and his demented fan base following him everywhere. He describes a groupie as "a funky-thigh collector, Layin' on 'lectric dreams." Girls like this groupie are collectors, and the sentiments resemble the tune "Star Collector" on the Monkees' *Pisces Aquarius Capricorn and Jones* album with the lyric "she only aims to please, young celebrities." Again, the distance between the illusory Ziggy and the real problems of pop star Bowie are moving from Bowie's wish fulfillment to a reality. When Bowie was writing *Ziggy*, he was imagining the problems of a prototypical pop star; but by the time he was playing these tracks live, he was himself becoming the real thing, a bona fide pop star.

The album comes to a climax with "Ziggy Stardust," which delivers a ballad of the crazed rocker. "Ziggy really sang, screwed up eyes and screwed down hairdo" ("Ziggy Stardust"). Although describing Ziggy, Bowie deftly describes his own costuming and playacting as a performer. Bowie saw his real talent as a singer/songwriter and as conceptualizer of these theatrical rock pieces. The song is also a martial march, a sort of call to arms for all of Ziggy/Bowie's followers. But the song is a warning. Bowie wistfully explains that the character of Ziggy is absorbed in his ego, a "leather messiah." Bowie ends by claiming that the kids killed the man. Either their adoration or overwhelming expectations were too much for him. Bowie explains that he carried his performance too far, but that he was a gifted musician. Always, Bowie is examining the myth he's creating as he's manufacturing it around the character. In that sense, Bowie's power is self-referential—a meta-reference to the narcissistic energy of rock music. Music feels good because we are creating ourselves, and we are invoking the power in ourselves to make or remake ourselves like the Ziggy character. Bowie sees himself and the constant quest for fame in his audience. These tendencies in pop audiences to want to be the star themselves would manifest itself in punk, disco, the MTV video explosion, grunge, neo-glam, and reality shows like *America's Got Talent*.

The power of *Ziggy*, the album and the production, is that sense of outside perspective that all the players bring to the proceedings. Ken Scott's breathy, spacious production never lets heavy get too heavy. In later non–Ken Scott albums, the mix starts to become murky, and the heavy grinding sounds under Tony Visconti's production lose some of their crisp balance. Bowie's work is so multilayered and murky that a little lightness often helps the mix. But Scott understands in *Ziggy* that to play heavy music and to step back and analyze it, you need space. Every heavy guitar solo is situated in a background of thinner by competing acoustic guitars, tight bass and drum arrangements, and clever and gliding string and piano support. Upper ranges are balanced with lower ones, and the glam sound of the era (under most producers) tends to err on the side of trebly lighter textures and not overly heavy, ponderous ones. In the case of

Bowie, this is likely to clarify the singer's voice in the mix. His clear tenor/baritone range resounds most effectively against a background in which bass sounds are de-emphasized. If Bowie's voice is contrasted with lots of bass backup, it tends to swallow his vocal range and makes his voice seem hollow and shrill. Deepening Bowie's vocals, giving his microphones a very full range, demands that other instruments occupy only very specific registers of their own. Each instrument has a range and situates itself relative to the mix of *Ziggy*. It is a clear plan throughout the album, with strings on the high end, bass and drums confined to a lower midrange, Ronson's crunchy guitars in a midrange-to-high squeal, Bowie's acoustic guitar engineered with lots of bottom, and

Glam's prime mover. A canny, smart musician and a strong performer, David Bowie has a knack for embedding narrative and theatrical elements in his work. Varied and complex, Bowie's works constitute the organum of glam practice. (Courtesy of Photofest.)

finally, Bowie's voice resting comfortably over the mix given a full range of timbres. In essence, Scott works to keep everything else out of Bowie's way.

Further, Bowie's lyrics have a winking quality. One moment he is talking about Ziggy, but also about himself and the business of pop stardom, a strategy that provides multiple levels to the text. This isn't just rock and roll, but drama and music about rock and roll. It is pop music with a very clear subtext about itself. In this sense, it is probably more subtextually poignant about the profession of rock stardom than anything else before or since. It is sort of a rock version of *A Star Is Born*, in which the protagonist is survivor and victim rolled into one, and the villain is the audience and the trappings/seductions of fame.

Perhaps the best way to see Bowie's take on Ziggy is to view it as Brechtian theatre. German philosopher/writer Bertolt Brecht propounded the theory of the *alienation effect*. This theory meant that the actor has to stand at arm's length from a character—not actually embodying the character, but looking at the character from the outside and acting out the character from a distance. It sounds contradictory to say that good acting should be distanced and held at arm's length from the proceedings. The actor literally narrates the character. But Brecht saw the use of this alienation effect in Asian/Chinese performance, and he understood it as a means to provide more subtextual commentary in the material. Brecht wanted to talk about social problems such as greed and injustice, and focusing on the brilliance of the actor's work took away from that social point.

LEAD US INSANE

Aladdin Sane is a clever portrait of touring American cities. It is a strongly Eurocentric portrayal of a foreign, primitive, desperate, and frightening culture, the United States circa 1972. Each song even has an American subtitle to indicate where Bowie was and what inspired him when he wrote the lyrics. The original title was "A Lad in Vein," and references to drug use made that seem too risky. The reference to *Aladdin* and magic genies still suggests pipes, smoking, and drug use but the "insane" saves the pun from total banality. "Watch That Man" is subtitled "New York" and has the sloppy elegance and spontaneity of Lou Reed and the Velvet Underground. It definitely has that slimy urban feel, and the tune works an earthy, organic quality, rising from a fractured, disjointed beginning to a tighter, pounding rocker by the end. At the song's finish, there is a stop and a coda with strong drumming by Woodmansey, a vital chorus of singers, and a spirited guitar outro by Ronson. Throughout, Mike Garson's burning and dissonant piano drives and propels the madness along.

Lyrically, Bowie seems to have mixed emotions about the surroundings. "Watch That Man" describes a party, perhaps one of many Bowie attended, but this wild affair feels like a gig at Warhol's sixties silver Factory. Bowie describes the female or possibly pseudo-female attendants. "The ladies looked bad, but the music was sad." Bowie seems bored and depressed by the band of old married men, the overpainted ladies, and the general surroundings. Like Warhol himself, who usually looked bored at his own parties, Bowie comments, "it was so-so."

The single "Aladdin Sane" is atmospheric and Eastern-tinged, and would later be echoed in Bowie's eighties tune "Loving the Alien." Though different in terms of texture, both songs have an exotic, otherworldly feel. "Aladdin" has the strong dissonant piano solo that colors the song's center. There is the bass riff and the piano ostinato that carries the song, and Bowie's cool, detached vocals. There is a sense of distance and reduced energy, like a current sparking through a wire. The song is subtitled "HMS, Ellinis," describing the boat Bowie took to America. Bowie was a longtime opponent of air travel, having had a few rough flights early in his experience. The song describes the start of a sea voyage as Bowie, or "Aladdin," is off on another trip. "Watching him dash away, swinging an old bouquet—dead roses." The lyrics are much more edgy and surreal. This is a character further gone than Ziggy, living in a solipsistic world of carnal pleasures and strange fascinations. The lyrics are far more ambiguous than previous Bowie tunes, and as a singer, he sounds lost in a revelry drifting away on the boat from the shore. The piano motifs evoke the sense of impressionist floating and key changes. Not particularly dissonant until the middle, just floating outside the conventional tonalities of the song's basic chord structure.

In October 1973, Bowie filmed an episode of *Midnight Special*, a late-night Friday, American pop music series, that was shown in November of the same year. The performance was filmed at London's Marquee club and came as close as any to Bowie's design for a full-fledged musical of the period featuring the Ziggy and Alladin characters. The *1980 Floor Show*, as it was called, had well-orchestrated and choreographed dance numbers and caught Bowie in the midst of the full-fledged glam performance period. In his performance of "Time," he is surrounded by a chorus of male dancers dressed in black spider-webbed leotards. They support him, dance interpretively, and mime behind him performing a choreographed movement routine. At one point, the dancers form a circular couch, and Bowie sits on them. Though the 1973 *Midnight Special* episode has rarely been aired publicly, it is perhaps, along with the 1972 *Old Grey Whistle Test* performance, Bowie's best-controlled example of glam aesthetics: performed, exquisitely played, choreographed, strange, exotic, and campy.

However, overall, *Aladdin Sane* is a much darker affair than *Ziggy*. The arrangements are grim, raunch guitar-esque, furious, and vengeful. Particularly, songs like "Panic in Detroit" and "Cracked Actor" lend a sense that America in the late Nixon era is a shattered land, violent and in tatters. "Cracked Actor," in particular, is a cry for help and warning of things to come for Bowie, who would live for a time in the Los Angeles area with disastrous results.

PIN UPS: REFLECTING THE PAST

After still more touring, Bowie announced his retirement from live performing on July 3, 1973. The retirement was short-lived. He was at work on the *1980 Floor Show* by September and performed that gig in October. He released his sixties tribute album, *Pin Ups*, that features songs that had a special meaning to him during the sixties, and the choices reveal the sides of Bowie's glam philosophy. There is the spacey, avant-garde pop of Pink Floyd's "See Emily Play" and the Yardbird's "Shapes of Things." There is the power-pop modness of the Who's "Can't Explain" and "Anyway, Anyhow, Anywhere." There is the music-hall irony of Ray Davies's "Where Have All the Good Times Gone?" and the sweet crooning of the Pretty Things' epic "Sorrow." Not only is the album a tribute to Bowie's sixties' influences. It is also a statement of how diverse and rich the music of the era really was, and it indicates that much of the sound of glam was in many ways a retro resurgence of the British eclectic pop sound. "Sorrow" was an affectionate tribute to the era. Though slagged as less than the original, on its own merits, it is a properly nostalgic ditty that Bowie makes his own.

Nineteen seventy-three had Bowie in transition. Bowie had disbanded the Spiders in July of that year, and then he "ended" touring and slowly withdrew from Mick Ronson as his cocreator and orchestrator. He contributed a few songs to Ronson's solo album, but mysteriously severed ties with his guitarist, arranger and coconspirator by the time of 1974's *Diamond Dogs*. The resulting *Diamond Dogs* album is the end of Bowie's specifically glam-styled work, although he would return to the glam style in revised formats continually throughout his career because that style was intrinsically the way he saw music. Although he and the press disavowed the glam format, Bowie, whose interest is fame, media, musical styles, camp, filmmaking, and nostalgia, was along with others an originator of the form. He could hardly leave it forever any more than a former Beatle could reject that group's epic past. *Diamond Dogs* has the piano work of Mike Garson but largely is a solo record, with minimal support by a standing band. As such, it is an apotheosis of the glam style ratcheting the themes of fame, future sci-fi worlds, paranoia, fascism, and decadence all into one apocalyptic vision. Bowie had planned the music as the backdrop to a massive stage show around the theme of Orwell's *1984*. Unfortunately, as close as he came was the *1980 Floor Show*, which has strong elements of pop theatre. Bowie had a new set of gowns carefully prepared by Japanese designer Kansai Yamamoto, and during the theme of 1984/Dodo during the *1980 Floor Show*, Bowie has a dramatic costume surprise in mid-song, when the melody switches from "1984" to the interpolated "Dodo." Bowie stands arms outstretched in center stage and his two backup singers tear his long, floor-length frock off to reveal a black slinky outfit with half arm fingerless gloves and a skintight jump suit with no top.

BOWIE'S APOCALYPSE: *DIAMOND DOGS*

The material from *Diamond Dogs* continues in this vein. It is perhaps even more disconcerting, dissonant, and harsh than *Aladdin Sane*, and fans had reason for concern as Bowie seemed to be spiraling into a more doomed and gloomy worldview. The album begins with the swirling, hypnotic, and chaotic "Future Legend" with Bowie in a synth voice setting the stage for the album's world. It is a concept conceit on the level of *Sgt. Pepper*, *Dark Side of the Moon*, and Alan Parsons's *Tales of Mystery and Imagination*. This is a spooky album. It borrows techniques from the progressive rock movement, and there is a lively use of studio effects by Bowie throughout the album to create a lively and expressionistic sonic panorama.

Although only a little over a minute long, "Future Legend" is the keystone work in the same way *Sgt. Pepper*'s brief introduction establishes that album. "Future Legend" is a chilling poem. Bowie later said that William Burroughs's experimental compositional method of writing lyrics, cutting them into pieces, and reassembling them influenced his poetic work here. Still, Bowie's word choice, his rhythms, and his symbol and metaphor systems are all dark and borrow heavily from Romanticism and the nineteenth-century Symbolists. It is a Poe- and Lovecraft-inspired vision of a dystopian tomorrow, when Bowie speaks, "and in the death, As the last few corpses lay rotting on the slimy thoroughfare." The song starts with a mournful cry, and synthesized atonal horns blow a rundown fanfare to an erratic beat. Bowie's voice is clear, but garbled by a synthetic treatment that rises above the din of zombie-like echoing voices. The suggestion is of an out-of-control chorus looking over a desiccated New York in the last phases of its destruction. Bowie lived in New York during this period from April 1974, and his impressions of a decadent city match Gotham's seventies reputation for craziness, violence, and economic disparity, and its eventual bankruptcy a few years later through severe financial mismanagement.

By the time Bowie and his chorus of the dead hit the line "No more big wheels," a flaming electric guitar casts a shadowy version of Rodgers and Hart's classic "Bewitched, Bothered and Bewildered" from the 1940 classic Broadway show *Pal Joey*. Ironically, this was one of the duo's roughest songs, with lyrics that are usually changed or censored. Just, as an example, the last verse is, "Romance-Finis ... Those ants that invaded my pants-finis."

But Bowie's interpolation of the song is a brilliant coup de grâce of rock drama. The stalwart theme of "Bewitched" reminds us of Broadway's (and perhaps, Bowie's?) past glories, and this is contrasted with the dark present. Bowie recalls the nostalgic allure of the city and captures the past glory of the Great White Way stumbling to oblivion. Bowie and the city stand alone. Bowie continues talking of groups of "peoploids," split into tribes and acting like dogs. There is a mocking chorus that parodies when he mentions "Love Me Avenue." (Perhaps another reference to Broadway, or to Bowie's incessant quest for fame?) There are the sounds of animals devouring each other, and Bowie's voice splits into a vocoded chorus as the last strains of "Bewitched" filter out in the background, and "Future Legend" merges with the next song, "Diamond Dogs."

"Diamond Dogs" opens the album proper, and like "Watch That Man," it is a rougher, Stones-style tune. Bowie yells out, "this ain't rock 'n' roll this is genocide." Certainly, like *Ziggy*, this album seems to tell a story of self-destruction. But here Bowie paints a more Brechtian portrayal of a whole society in degeneration, a more lurid portrayal of American in the seventies, post Watergate, mid-disco, and near punk in terms of a music menu. "Diamond Dogs" is a more upbeat affair. If "Future Legend" is elegiac, "Diamond Dogs" is valedictory. It portrays life in a high-partying, wild last binge of this destroyed city, like New York itself, gorging on the remains of its reputation. Bowie's character "Halloween Jack" is a real cool cat who lives on top of Manhattan Chase (a bank), and the denizens are in bad condition but dressed marvelously. "Wrecked up and paralyzed, diamond dogs are sableized." It is a frightening image of the city that certainly would warn anyone away from seventies New York. Bowie inserts elements about his own work as a songwriter and performer, calling his own work future kitsch. "In the year of the scavenger, the season of the bitch" ("Diamond Dogs"). Bowie here sounds like he is also referring to his own hectic partying regime of the era. He even throws in a few howls and "bow-wows," which can be taken as parody or simply fun rock and roll at the city's expense.

MOVING FROM STATION TO STATION: GLAM TO SOMETHING ELSE?

Diamond Dogs marks the official end of Bowie's specific glam work, but his departure from a style that was an intrinsic way for him to see the world was less a conclusion than a respite. Tony Visconti complained that by the time Bowie's white soul statement, *Young Americans*, was ready to wrap, Bowie was so bored with it that he couldn't be bothered to do finish the work on it. By *Station to Station*, a year later, he was reinventing glam by simply widening the parameters and incorporating other styles: punk, metal, pop, and electronica.

In fact, while Bowie was suffering from chronic addictions and was in a severe mental depression, *Station to Station* anticipated his late-seventies glam resurgence and provided the most self-assured, band-oriented work he had produced since *Ziggy*.

The album is an extraordinary blast of balance and shows a real return to core values after the lighter pop of *Young Americans*. *Station* originally only featured six tunes, but all were immaculate. There were the rocking screamers, "Station to Station" and "TVC 15," which still concert favorites to this day. There were two pop numbers, the radio-friendly and soulish "Golden Years" and the hot "Stay"; the ballad "Word on a Wing"; and the Oscar-nominated "Wild Is the Wind" originally recorded by Johnny Mathis, a still-popular crooner. But the real inspiration was Nina Simone, the black jazz singer who delivered a powerhouse version of the tune in 1966. Bowie had met Simone, admired her style, and wanted to pay tribute and emulate her example. Throughout, Bowie and Harry Maslin's production is crisp and clean, and Bowie and the band make up a simple and powerful unit, belting out the tunes in bravura style.

Why this album is not considered a glam work may be due to the fact that it comes after Bowie disavowed what was conceived as a confining style. It may also be that it falls outside the glam period proper (1970–75). Finally, people may see that album as a group album, a musician's album, and not a performance or character piece. But closer analysis reveals it fits the criteria of glam works fairly closely. It has the acidic and rampant energy style of glam. There were concerns with science fiction and fantasy ("TVC 15," "Station to Station"). There were quotations and paeans to previous periods ("Golden Years," "Wild Is the Wind") that reference the fifties. More importantly, when Bowie, still recovering from his health issues, took to the stage in 1976, the numbers from *Station to Station* blended stylistically and seamlessly with "Jean Genie," "Suffragette City," and "Changes," suggesting that *Station* is more a part of Bowie's innate style than the recently concluded aberrational style of *David Live* and *Young Americans*. One might see these albums as works an artist must make to provide a freed perspective from a stylistic straitjacket. Once Bowie knew he could get beyond the confines of the Ziggy character, it was all right to revisit his core conceits.

Another overlooked aspect of Bowie's glam work is his serious work as a producer and shaper of other artists of that era. He took the crumbling Mott the Hoople, a band he had always liked, and resurrected them with "All the Young Dudes," restoring the band's confidence, enlisting them in the ranks of glam bands, and restarting their career with a new recording contract. "All the Young Dudes" is often considered the core Bowie anthem to the glam movement; he himself has rarely performed it, but he was willing to give it to other groups to spread the creed of glam artists. Bowie writes of his generation's concerns and how they compare to the sixties kids. "And my Brother's back at home, With his Beatles and his Stones." He rediscovered Lou Reed through his visits to New York and his contact with Warhol and produced Reed's first solo album, *Transformer*. Bowie gave him the hit record describing the Warhol circle of freaks and transsexuals that put Reed on the map for a long and successful career, "Walk on the Wild Side." This soulish New York–styled number layered Reed's rock style with Bowie's aesthetic influence of period styles and forms. The tune features a marvelous production, an absorbing bass line and a deadpan lyric.

Bowie also found and re-energized proto-punk and hard rocker Iggy Pop's flagging career and worked on Iggy's *Raw Power* album. Amazingly, Bowie toured, secured his American conquest, recorded and released *Ziggy*, and recorded and restored the careers of Mott, Reed, and Pop, all within 12 months. By 1974 he had influenced and supported the careers of singer Marianne Faithfull, who appears with him on the *1980 Floor Show*. He helped Lulu, who recorded several Bowie tracks. He introduced Mainman artist Dana Gillespie, writing two songs for her and producing her album. He even helped former guitarist Mick Ronson, whom he helped produce and provided songs for his first solo effort. Bowie was a titanic force on music of the era, and his retreat from producing was prompted only by the decline in his business relations with RCA and Mainman's Tony DeFries.

The media has made much of Bowie's move from glam to other forms, but as Roy Carr and Charles Shaar Murray pointed out in *Bowie, An Illustrated Record*, the character of Ziggy was a compelling, messianic character that placed Bowie in the position of being a teenage savior. Such a position doesn't last too long. Between Ziggy and Aladdin, the character goes from a punkish-looking guitarist to a mullet, white-makeup-coated, Japanese-adorned freak. By *Diamond Dogs*, the character is melting into a half-man, half-dog hybrid, less human than mutant. Bowie was jettisoning that "character" to take control of the music himself. In a striking interview, British talk show host Richard Harty asked Bowie what character he would play next. Bowie said the character he was going to play next (1975) was going to be himself, and he admitted that he had to "invent himself." Harty corrected him, saying that he would "reinvent himself." Bowie countered, saying that he *really* had to invent himself.

The fact that Bowie made successful forays into films from the eighties on and that he continued to play pop music characters explains that he never left glam. His performances only became more subtle and less perceptible. Perhaps Bowie's best meta-reference to his role-playing glam work is in the video directed by Julian Temple for "Blue Jean." In it, Bowie plays a little fellow, Vic, looking for a date. He tries to wow a girl by lying that he knows a crazy rock star, Screaming Lord Byron. There actually was a pop star named

Screaming Lord Sutch, who played unsuccessfully in the sixties. Byron is a mess; he can barely stand. He has to be given oxygen and injections to be revived, and when he prances on stage, audiences respond like hypnotized supplicants at a cult ritual. Bowie clearly had fun sending up his Ziggy incarnation while performing "Blue Jean," a song that, for all intents and purposes, fits comfortably with his glam-era work.

Bowie's hectic touring schedule, increasing popularity, and strong studio commitments took a toll on the artist. Bowie spent much of 1972 touring to support first *Hunky Dory* and later *Ziggy Stardust*. He toured England and parts of Europe and did an extensive take on the United States. Having had several bad flights, he wished to travel by ground or boat, so touring became slower and more time-consuming. Much of the *Aladdin Sane* work was composed while crossing America. Between 1972 and 1975, Bowie was averaging two major album releases a year. It was a frantic pace, and Bowie, who believed in stardom as a means to his independence and who had craved recognition for so long, did not want the moment to pass him by. So he worked doggedly to secure his fame and not see it flash by as it had for friend and colleague Marc Bolan. But heavy touring, recording, and simply living an unhealthy lifestyle made him dependent on bad foods, smoking, and a variety of drugs including cocaine, amyl nitrate, and other concoctions. By the time *David Live* was released in 1974, even Bowie later commented after looking at the album cover, "My God, it looks as if I've just stepped out of the grave" (Cann 1983, 129).

Bowie's specifically labeled glam period really lasted only about four years. But it was extraordinarily productive, including the releases of *The Man Who Sold the World, Hunky Dory, Ziggy Stardust, Alladin Sane, Pin Ups,* and *Diamond Dogs*. These albums constitute some of the core works of the genre for the songs, the style, the accompanying performances, and their public influence. There is also the *David Live* album, but devotees often see this as a transitional work between Bowie's glam work and his (thankfully) short-lived white plastic soul era. His more progressive experimental late seventies works merge neatly with the earlier glam-period material, and it follows the aesthetics of earlier glam. It uses its method of performance, its use of star-system marketing, its concerns with science fiction and the arcane, and its use of avant-garde, alternative, and nostalgic musical cultures and time periods. About the only thing absent from Bowie's post-glam glam work is the character of Ziggy, who was absorbed into Bowie's broader conception of himself as the actor who dons and controls these alternative personalities. While certainly Bowie marketed himself as making dramatic changes and altering his style severely, truthfully, other works would fit comfortably into his glam career. "Thursday's Child" from the 1999 *Hours* album could conceivably have been written during the *Hunky Dory* sessions. "New Killer Star" could have been a track from *Aladdin Sane*, and "Loving the

Alien" from *Tonight* fits comfortably into the glam obsessions with fame and alien beings.

But the glam period promotes Bowie's core concerns with music performance as an important aspect of rock style. For Bowie and other glam artists, playing pop music was also about applying a character. Another aspect is glam's willingness to sample eclectic musical styles. Particularly in Bowie's work, there is a parallel to the psychedelic artists who sampled other times and styles of music in their song construction. Bowie was equally adept at borrowing Asian-influenced styles, British musical hall, jazzy inflections, hard rock, and trance new-age tonalities to lift the music to a higher level. What has escaped most critics is that Bowie and glam in general encompass a more diverse style than originally thought. Further, artists like Bowie kept those working methodologies clearly in mind when pursuing later work. Part of glam's methodology was to use fashionable guises to market the performers and their work and, in glam's grandest irony, by eschewing the label of glam artists, Bowie and most of the other glam performers were very capable of continuing the tradition under aesthetic aliases.

Chapter 4

ROXY MUSIC: GLAM'S STABLE PROGRESSION

> The artist's object is to appear strange and even surprising to the audience. He achieves this by looking strangely at himself and his work. As a result, everything put forward by him has a touch of the amazing.
>
> —Bertolt Brecht (1992, 92)

It may seem odd to begin a discussion of Roxy Music with a quote from German epic theatre director Bertolt Brecht. But Brecht's notion of the alienation effect closely resembles the techniques employed by Bryan Ferry and the musicians of Roxy Music. Ferry, himself an art school graduate, was taken by the idea of creating a band that acted as an art work, and he was keenly aware of the great lengths that were needed to obtain an audience. Warhol had said that "in the sixties, good trashing was a skill" (1989, 64), and Ferry was a prolific miner of cultural trash. Like Warhol, he was conscious of the synthesis of styles, the collage of images, that was impacting the pop world, and he was determined to ride such an aesthetic to stardom and fame. Like an artist, Ferry thought that you could take snippets and pieces from different musical and visual styles and mesh them in a crazy salad approach to art music. Strange costumes, dancing girls, exaggerated vocal and musical elements, experimental songs, and campy poses made up the musical formula. People might be disturbed and upset by the images and the music, but in Ferry's mind, such a sensory assault was necessary to make the music memorable.

In the end, this experiment in merging art and pop had limitations. Ferry wished to retain the quirky, exotic texture of an alienation effect, that merging of the familiar and the strange that would at once propel Ferry and Roxy to

Bryan Ferry and Roxy Music. Like Bowie, Bryan Ferry was an artist and visionary who saw ways to exploit image and celebrity, using images from film and nostalgia to build a new generation of club/cabaret music. The sensuous romantic heart of glam practice. (Courtesy of Photofest.)

world stardom. But this same effect would ultimately deny them a comfortable position alongside venerable pop artists like the Stones, the Who, or Pink Floyd, who ultimately were far more conservative. Thus Ferry, Brian Eno, and Roxy's story is a tale of begrudging acceptance and fitful success, in which artistic strategies are applied to the business of popular music and culture with mixed results. Indicative of the problems glam had in reaching and sustaining a lasting impression on an audience, Roxy Music stands as an example of glam principles and ideas applied to the contexts of popular music. Roxy was and is an art band that refused to sacrifice their aesthetic for media success. At the same time, their willingness to affect a guise that was at once attractive and distancing distinguishes them as culturally complex and committed to intellectual principles many art and prog bands (such as Yes, Genesis, and David Bowie) long abandoned for more intense media success.

MANUFACTURING ROXY MUSIC: AUTO-GENESIS OF A BAND

While many bands arrive due to an organic series of happenstances, Roxy's origins were the product of clear planning and contrivance, a fact that conservative critics branded as manufacturing a sound and lacking as inauthentic. Bryan Ferry, Roxy's leader and principal architect, himself was an act of creation. Ferry was a child of the post war, the third of four children born to a horse steward for the Newcastle mining operations. Life in Newcastle was hard, but Ferry as a young man was given piano lessons. He was only moderately proficient, and his sister rebuked his efforts to learn proper keyboard technique. As a youth, he was influenced by jazz musicians, particularly Charlie Parker. He was also enamored of the wild, exaggerated solo style of fifties bebop and cool jazz musicians. His vocal and pop tastes veered towards rhythm and blues and soul records. There is no doubt that an interest in jazz riffing and the baroque sounds of soul influenced his later singing style, itself a combination of crazed soul experimentation, diva-affected vocal tones, and strange wails and rumbles.

In the sixties, Newcastle birthed the working-class rhythm-and-blues sound of the Animals. Aptly, Eric Burden wrote songs like "We Gotta Get out of This Place." Ferry felt similarly compelled to move on. The manufacturing and industrial scene was Ferry's origin, but he was interested in using manufacturing and the industrial scheme in a far different way, to produce a series of musical images that could be marketed and popularized. Ferry formed the Gas Board, a covers band, with himself as musical leader and lead singer. But his viewing of the 1967 Stax Records package tour of Europe changed many of his ideas about performing pop music. In tow were many of the company's strongest performers, and Ferry was greatly impressed by Booker T and MGs. Booker T's group was a smooth soul machine of instrumental players with plenty of funky strut moves and a strong, determined groove line. The ensemble played tight little tunes and could break into explosive solo sections, only to return to tight ensemble arrangements. Ferry was moved by their professional demeanor and their excellent playing. Film director Mike Figgis (*Leaving Las Vegas*) who was actually a member of the Gas Board remarked that "he wasn't a very good soul singer, he had that tremble" (Buckley 2004, 28). But it was precisely due to soul music and that Stax tour that Ferry adopted such affectations. Ferry said, "I think that was like my sort of vision on the road to Damascus ... I saw Otis Redding, Sam and Dave, Steve Cropper, all these people on stage in their splendid suits and it was the best thing I've ever seen" (Buckley 2004, 27). The tour marked him for life, and you can see the reminiscence of sixties soul singers in his vocal stylings even now.

Ferry may have been born into a working-class mining family, but his family understood and supported his goal to avoid a life in the pits. Ferry majored in Fine Arts at Newcastle University. Ferry himself described his existence as art by day and music by night. While he was at Newcastle, popular and influential British pop artist Richard Hamilton was a guest lecturer, spreading the mantra of popism. Hamilton wrote that the fine arts needed the energy of pop culture to survive. He said, "if the artist is not to lose much of his ancient purpose he may have to plunder the popular arts to recover the imagery which is his rightful inheritance" (Hamilton 1985, 144). Ferry was in the throes of the pop art explosion that rose in the late fifties and early sixties. He was a devotee to Hamilton's creed and an avid student of pop art and its attendant culture and inspiration. As a movement, popism wasn't just the appropriation of pop art symbols; it was a violent reaction against the bleak and colorless world of the abstract expressionists. As their name suggested, these artists were abstract painters with no regard for the figure or recognizable forms, and they focused on their own heightened emotional states, their emotional reaction to the world.

Confronted with a seemingly chaotic world destroyed by World War II, the nuclear bomb, and the nihilistic philosophies of absurdism and existentialism, abstract expressionism seemed relentlessly bleak to the next generation of artists. Popism revived fun and looking at the outside world. Simultaneously, it wasn't a frivolous art movement as it is sometimes characterized as being. Popism was heavily critical of consumer culture and appropriated pop symbols to reexamine them and their iconic value. Further, pop discussed the problems of modern consumer culture in which choices were made only about consumption, not production. By opting to be served and given things, popists would say that modern consumers had lost many of their freedoms to examine and participate in their culture in a real and meaningful way.

This perspective shared elements of a Marxist critique of culture. The materialist side of popism suggested, like the Marxists, that powerful companies manipulated fashion, creating Theodore Adorno's notion of a *culture industry* that hegemonically manipulated desires and images of success. Hamilton emphasized the sense that pop was modern and dealt with modern items and objects. It was a strongly American movement because America was the home of the most consumer-oriented material products. Further, in his collage art where multiple objects were placed together, often one on top of each other, these objects were merged or collaged into a complex series of icons—a body-builder, a home stereo, a tape deck, a suburban dream house. Hamilton's visions praise the impact of consumer society to bring us riches, but simultaneously, the insidious images suggest that there is something dead, empty, and unnatural about all the elements of consumer society. In some way, consumers are disconnected from all the wealth they have acquired; and despite their vast richness, consumers exist in a hollow, otherworldly ghost world of possessions that symbolize nothing, values that represent nothing, and places that are filled with meaningless minutia.

Ferry picked up on Hamilton's collages and incorporated those images in his own songwriting. In "In Every Dream House, a Heartache," Ferry sings a love song to a fetishist's plastic love doll. In "Virginia Plain," he euphorically spouts, "make me a deal and make it fast," sounding like a game show host. Further, Ferry's juxtaposition of this critique of consumer culture with his own austere upbringing made the critique even more personal. Ferry was no novice to hard work and hustling for money. He explained in a BBC Four documentary called "The Roxy Music Story" that he had played in a band called "The Banshees that played working man's clubs, so it was a good sort of apprenticeship" (BBC Four 2008). But Ferry's year with Richard Hamilton changed his outlook on the image of popular culture and consumer society, making him a composer capable of tackling theories and social issues. Few composers could entitle songs "Remake/Remodel" or "Editions of You" or "The Bogus Man." Each tune held within it some critique of a consumer culture that slowly was turning people into Baudrillard's dreaded simulacra. It was flattering when years later Richard Hamilton remarked, "Bryan Ferry, my greatest creation!" (Buckley 2004, 24).

But Ferry was no idle theorist, and he quickly put what he had learned into practical guise. Ferry immediately gathered that the look was the means to sell. Just as American industrialization had placed supermarkets with variously brightly packaged products in front of consumers for quick decisions, Ferry deduced that being a brightly packaged band would induce people to buy him and the package. Ferry wore sharkskin suits. He found a good tailor and adopted the notion from Cary Grant that good tailoring would keep him in style and fashion regardless of the prevailing trends and styles. He bought clothes by Marcus Pryce, the guru of mod fashions of the sixties. Ferry's well-groomed appearance made him appear decidedly out of place in late-sixties London. That was precisely his plan, to avoid looking like another hippie musician. He bought a Studebaker, not because it was the best car, but because it was fashionably designed and had a look. But Ferry wasn't banking entirely on his musical career. He finished his degree at Newcastle. Even his guru Hamilton thought Ferry would go on to be an artist. Indeed, Ferry did produce several art shows, exhibiting at Durham University in 1967. But by

1968 he journeyed to London to seek his fortune, and within a few weeks he was fortunate to find a position as a ceramics instructor at the Hammersmith Mary Bow's School for Girls, a middle-class college prep school where young women could be safely exposed to the arts. It wasn't the top of the world, but it was a start.

Bryan Ferry tried to create a variety of bands and sought to enter the field of entertainment as a singer, even auditioning for King Crimson in 1970. Robert Fripp, the band's leader, was looking for a different sound, but he was impressed by Ferry's unique vocal quality and drive and recommended Ferry to his record label, EG records. Ferry had been composing since 1969 and had amassed a body of tunes, some obscure and some pop-oriented. He already had product to market.

Ferry's composing style always featured the vocal and melody line strongly, if oddly. In standard musical progressions, Ferry would often drop the third chord in the progression, making the progression simpler and often more modal, repetitious, and atmospheric. Ferry argued that his lyrical content was often complicated by an interest in surrealism and automatic writing. Ferry wrote that he liked to place clichés and common phrases in his lyrics, but in odd settings so that these phrases stand out in a new way. Ferry explained in 1972, "we want to get through to different people on different levels so that whereas one person, maybe a Hampstead intellectual, would say, 'How camp!' A kid would respond by saying, 'That's weird!' The kid would probably get the bigger kick" (Williams 1972). In later songs, such as "The Thrill of It All," Ferry inserts expressions like "something's got to give," or "oye vey," into an otherwise edgy song with a driving, manic beat. These phrases provoke the Brechtian alienation effect, immediately prompting a sense of commonness and placing something disconcerting and out of place together with the everyday. For Ferry, music wasn't just music, but a form of visual theatre in which the familiar and the surprising compete.

Ferry was older, had a day job, and recognized that the window for achieving anything in music was rapidly closing. He had to work quickly to break in. He wasn't looking for the traditional pub band; he was seeking a group of inspired amateurs and intellectually like-minded experimenters. He hobnobbed in the music scene, ran ads in the trade journals, and began to amass a band.

One of Ferry's coconspirators was Andrew Mackay, also a schoolteacher. When Ferry advertised for a synthesizer player, he ran into Mackay, who was classically trained on oboe but also owned a VSC3 synthesizer, a rare and expensive item in that era. Later, Mackay would become enamored of the saxophone, and this would become one of his primary contributions to the band's sound. Ferry and Mackay had similar art school backgrounds, and both expressed an interest in the intersection of art and music. Mackay had worked in a performance art group called Sunshine while at Reading University.

They performed their offbeat blend of music and happenings at the school. Mackay served as an English teacher by day and moonlighted in pop and blues bands by night. He had experimented with the avant-garde and appeared at the London Arts Lab.

Mackay suggested his colleague and former schoolmate Brian Eno as a technician and tape operator. Eno also brought a host of unique qualities to the band. He was technically proficient and could manipulate tape, produce unusual sound effects, and operate the synthesizer to extreme effect. Like Mackay, Eno had an abiding interest in the works of modern composer John Cage, who was a strong proponent of chance in music and prescribed pieces in which accidents would inspire the musical event. So far, Ferry had created a band that had more interest in theory, chance music, atmosphere, and effects than in a substantial performance unit.

Phil Manzanera was a guitarist who auditioned for the guitar job in the band but lost out to the more famous David O'List. O'List had been important to Ferry's recruiting. Ferry thought that he needed at least a few musicians in the band with name value that could help to obtain a recording contract. O'List had been the lead guitarist in a successful British band called the Nice. Their lead keyboardist, Keith Emerson, had lately spun off into his own successful outfit, Emerson, Lake, and Palmer. Ferry was sure O'List's name value would benefit the band. But Manzanera had also given a capable audition of neo-psychedelic guitar playing, and he got on well with the band. David Buckley wrote that "as a lead guitarist, Manzanera was neither strong nor dominant. Rather his slightly fey and undeniably eccentric guitar parts seemed to interweave themselves with the general pattern of the group sound" (Buckley 2004, 62). Manzanera had a day job at a travel agency, and he had worked with a minor progressive band called Quiet Sun. After the band lost a sound engineer for a gig, Ferry called him to run sound at a Roxy gig.

Manzanera was born Phillip Targett-Adams (and took his mother's name Manzanera when it came to performing because he thought it sounded more like a guitarist's name). His father was a globetrotting executive for BOAC and his mother hailed from Colombia. After living in Cuba, Venezuela, and other areas in South America, his family returned to England, and there he discovered pop and psychedelic music. Like his later bandmates in Roxy Music, he had been exposed to so many ethnic and obscure musical traditions around the world that the Roxy Music concept, a music without traditional boundaries, seemed like a fascinating idea to the young musician. Also like his peers, he saw few musical limits and felt empowered to experiment with a wide range of sounds. When guitarist David O'List became embroiled in an angry exchange with drummer Paul Thompson at the band's pivotal audition, O'List's days were numbered, and Manzanera quickly filled the empty slot.

Perhaps next to the pivotal influence of Bryan Ferry, Brian Eno was another strong influence in concocting the Roxy sound. He was born in Woodbridge, Suffolk, in 1948. His dad was a postal worker, and he was educated in a Catholic school by nuns and priests. He studied at the Ipswich Art School from 1964 to 1966 and graduated with a diploma in fine art from the Winchester Art School in 1969. In their influential *Art into Pop*, Frith and Horne argued that something about an art school education altered the way rock was seen and produced in Britain. They wrote that, "what British musicians have added is style, image, self-consciousness—an attitude to what commercial music could and should be" (Frith and Horne 1989, 1). Certainly that seems to be the case in terms of Roxy Music.

In particular, Eno had an extremely eclectic relationship to music. He seemed to absorb a variety of musical influences, and Eric Tamm, in his book on Eno, suggests that he typifies, "a new type of composer whose musical background is astonishingly diverse: he has exposed himself to a variety of traditions ranging from rock to classical, from avant-garde to experimental, as well as to a variety of non-Western musics such as Arabic, African, and Bulgarian" (Tamm 1995, 16). Eno lived near two U.S. Army bases, and as a youth, his sister brought back American rock-and-roll records from the army PX store. He was excited by echo chambers and effects on songs like Elvis's "Heartbreak Hotel." He also liked to repeat songs over and over again on his parents' automatic record player. He would turn on the family's old player piano and listen to hymns like "Jerusalem" repetitively. His uncle left a collection of Ray Conniff Singers pop records at his house, and he absorbed these bland elements of American pop recordings as well. As a teen, he was influenced by the Who and by Warhol's experiments with the Velvet Underground's noise art. Later, he became excited by John Cage's musical experiments with silence and chance music and the minimalists. Eno had flirted with music, performance, and art in school, but Roxy allowed him a full vent for his burgeoning interests. He could work with a group, help in crafting its sound, learn the synthesizer, and participate in composing. It was a golden opportunity for a self-professed "non-musician" to find a place in the music business.

Ferry referred to Eno as "a mad boffin" because he would cavort madly across the stage performing on synthesizer and wiring multitudinous devices to each other. Eno had originally been a backstage element, but his pronounced tinkering with the sonic elements of the band led to his appearance on stage. At first, Ferry felt such disparate elements lent themselves to the common madness of the band. But after a time, Ferry believed that Eno had become a distraction and was pulling focus from him and the band's music. Eno had a strong performance and marketing background himself. He headed the student union at the Winchester School of Art and was around visiting artists and acts at the school. Eno's gifts were his interesting musical theories, his varied musical ideas, his attractiveness to women, and his ability to play a musical catalyst to everyone from Roxy to later David Bowie, Talking Heads, U2, and Coldplay. After he left Roxy Music, he purveyed his own brand of glam experimental pop music. Eventually, Eno would incorporate some of Cage's thinking into his more outré musical experiments and performances of the seventies and beyond. Without him, Roxy lost a key musical innovator, but also could solidify a dense imaginative sound that coalesced around Ferry's, Manzanera's, and Mackay's songwriting. Behind this nucleus, they were able to gain the support of a wide range of external players. The band learned experimentation from Eno, and he learned about image and the value of excellent tunes.

The glue of the band was Paul Thompson, a drummer who like Ferry was a Geordie. He had a solid backbeat and had the most professional experience, having played in a variety of local and pub bands. He was also a solidifying influence. He got on well with Ferry and the others, and he provided a rock-solid foundation to an otherwise flighty and flaming musical style. But unlike some drummers who were pragmatic and dull, Thompson quickly grasped Ferry's dress-up manifesto and donned outrageous gear, including a caveman/Fred Flintstone attire to add to the band's wardrobe high jinks. Thompson confessed to a wide range of musical tastes; anything from Dionne Warwick to Frank Zappa to the Beatles impressed him, so he was wide open to the band's increasingly eclectic approaches.

The band may have stayed simply an interesting idea, but Ferry spent considerable time and energy marketing the band to agents, record companies, and radio stations. Ferry, the well-dressed, well-coifed, handsome young man, was an impressive sales figure. His sharp outfits, articulate voice, and shy and somewhat quiet demeanor made him a more compelling salesman than your common huckster. Further, though he acted as an agent, he was the band, too—the concept, and the complete package. He courted Richard Williams of the BBC's *Old Grey Whistle Test*, a popular musical showcase program, and he raved about them. He talked them up to the BBC, wrote a rave review of their recent London performances for the influential British music magazine *Melody Maker*, and had them perform a series of tunes for the popular Radio One underground show hosted by the leading DJ, John Peel. Williams cited their diverse musical interests, their flaming style, and their exuberance in making them the next big thing.

Initially, though, other critics, press, and record companies were disinterested. Ferry had racked up piles of rejections. But Bryan Ferry's master plan for success was indeed masterful. First, Ferry accepted a common fact: that with an average age of 27, most of the band members were too old to start gigging and build a reputation for themselves through the traditional band/club circuit. It would take too long; they all needed income, and the chances of success were slim. None of the members, save Thompson, had ever performed in the band circuit. Most of the members had barely played, and they had little knowledge of audiences and the hit clubs. Ferry also recognized that this band was strong in theory. Ferry and Mackay had backgrounds as teachers, and Eno and Manzanera were technically savvy with equipment and electronics. They were a bright and articulate team. None of them were particularly interested in the routine interests of pop bands, girls and drugs, although Eno seemed to make up for the rest of the band in his voracious appetite for girls and wild sex. Ferry instead was determined to debut his brand of pop by writing music, making demo tapes, and ushering those tapes to various radio stations for play. Despite a lack of concrete success, the band was building a buzz. John Walters of the BBC was intrigued by Ferry's "Larry the Lamb" vocal mannerisms (Rigby 2005, 22), and Richard Williams described their demo tape as having influences that stretch "from Ethel Merman to The Velvet Underground to Jazz and they want to bring all these elements into the music" (Rigby 2005, 19).

Ferry was more interested in recording than live performance, although he quickly became adept at both. He felt that film, video, and recorded material was potentially more rewarding than a gig at a time. Ferry also realized that stardom was often an acquired status, and Ferry was quick to acquire star players to make his band more popular. For some months, he courted and finally engaged David O'List, former guitarist of the Nice, to join the group and add some nice psychedelic guitar touches à la Syd Barrett. Ferry did use the party and society scene to advantage. He met and courted Anthony Price, London fashion guru, and engaged him as costume designer for Roxy events and album covers. Price's images would become the early Roxy style.

When Ferry did agree to perform a gig, it was usually with a canny eye to events that could propel the band forward. One early eye-catching event was a benefit party for the London Tate Gallery, singularly combining Ferry's interest in art and music. The band also played the posh 100 Club in downtown London, a trendy nightclub hotspot. Through selected gigs like these, Ferry found the last ingredient in his recipe for success, good buzz about the band.

Ferry explained his approach. The band members were older, and breaking into the business needed craft. Ferry presented to the management groups and record companies that he was a packager and had put together a band, a sound, a look, and a style that could be marketed as a complete whole. Ferry's angle was that a complete package was a much easier sale for the record company and the record-buying public than a band and management team having to craft a package, an image, a look, and a sound. Ferry had done that all for them. Like Warhol, Ferry understood the relationship of market capitalism to the market of music and thought cold-bloodedly and rather cynically about ways to bend that system to his ideas. Warhol phrased it this way: "Business art is the step that comes after Art" (Crone 1987, 14).

Ferry's perception of the business—the methods of production, appropriation, and adoption—were taken directly from Theodor Adorno and his famous phrasing of the "culture industry." Adorno had said that in capitalism, culture markets drive consumption of premanufactured industry ideas of normalcy, beauty, and coolness. Adorno feared these culture industry marketers because he was concerned that such industries could manipulate people as certainly as Nazi propaganda had galvanized the German people to an evil purpose.

Ferry's marketing acumen also adheres to Simon Frith and Howard Horne's thesis about the simultaneous occurrence of pop music and pop art in English art schools in the fifties and sixties. Such institutions sponsored a form of pop art that extended into all elements of pop culture. Graduates of such schools saw their canvas as the world, and they applied the art school idea to the production of music. Frith and Horne argued convincingly that groups such as Roxy Music found a comfortable meeting place in music for the ideas of pop art. A group could take notions of collage, expressionism, and abstraction and translate those concepts into musical equivalents. Frith and Horne wrote that such ideas were clearly marketed by art institutions, and the students saw little difference between the application of these methods to art or to music or popular culture in general. Indeed, there were aspects of Marxist theory here, but as Adorno and others saw it, Marxist thinking was now being applied to culture, not necessarily the economic structure.

Finally, Roxy auditioned for the management team of David Enthoven and John Gaydon, otherwise known as EG Management. They had already propelled ELP, T Rex, and King Crimson to prominence, and they expressed an interest in the tape Ferry had diligently marketed. On Tuesday, February 1, 1972, the band assembled at a closed theatre, the Granada, and performed a set for the team. They went down well, and EG agreed to sponsor their first album and an advance. The band recorded their first album for £5,000 in 10 days. Roxy exploded with the single "Virginia Plain" and carved a career with strong, aggressive, and diverse musical styles. Ferry sang in a wild parody of pop singers, and the band thrashed through a strong assortment of self-penned material. Eno's synth attack on "Virginia Plain" added just the right touch of avant-garde obscurity.

Ferry had done his marketing job well, and EG offered him a separate contract as a solo performer. Ferry quickly obliged, releasing *These Foolish Things* in 1973. Ferry appeared in Brando/James Dean/Elvis regalia, a dark T-shirt. For 1974's *Another Time, Another Place*, Ferry is featured in a white dinner jacket at a swank party. What a difference a year makes. Ferry's solo work was just as wild as Roxy's take on pop rock. When the singer assailed Dylan's

"A Hard Rain's a-Gonna Fall," there was an obvious quality of sending up the serious folk singer's work. A roaring chorus and a rousing rock band behind Ferry's demented vocal work made the song a sing-a-long rather than a battle cry. In a single track, Ferry undercut the pomposity of America's most lauded singer/poet. For the Leslie Gore teen tear jerker, "It's My Party (and I'll Cry if I Want to)" Ferry retains the girl's point of view for the entire song, appealing to the band's gay following. Ferry's solo work would continue during the Roxy years and become the centerpiece of Ferry's work in the years when Roxy was mothballed.

THE THREE STAGES OF ROXY MUSIC

Roxy's sound was continually changing, but the band's glam work falls into three distinct periods. There is the early Roxy sound of the first two albums with the jagged anger and explosive force of Eno's keyboards and sonic embellishments. Ferry, Eno, and the band were attracted to the Velvet Underground, a strongly influential pre-glam group noted for an arty image, pre-punk noise levels, and a close association with Andy Warhol and the later work of members Lou Reed, John Cale, and Nico. Clearly, in songs like "Virginia Plain," there is a sense of the band emulating the Velvets' bashing approach. Mackay is bleating on oboe and sax, while Manzanera's guitar is wailing through chords. Ferry's voice is over the top and quirky. He places emphasis on all the wrong syllables to make the words stand out. By turns, the music is serious, threatening, annoying, and parodic. All the musicians are playing to their most extreme nature. Every sequence seems dipped in irony, filled with loud, aggressive, and angry sounds. It is largely an unfocused wall of sound until the break and Eno's synth solo bring the tune to a climax. The ending is sudden and unexpected, with Ferry closing on the final vocal phrase, "what's her name, Virginia Plain?" Peter Sinfield's production places it all up front, and Ferry's vocals are obscured by the rich and crowded mix of instruments. Were it not for Ferry's insistent phrasing, there would be little focus.

Starting with Eno's departure, the entry of Chris Thomas, and a stronger focus on Ferry's unique vocal qualities, the sound begins to change to a tighter ensemble. In Ferry's canny "Street Life," there is a more professional and focused sound. There are strange keyboard tonalities, string synths, and effects, but they are mixed into the arrangement, and the rich palette of sounds is mixed around the melody. The focus is on Ferry's voice and Manzanera's riff-loaded guitars. The sense of song structure is emphasized. The verse, chorus, and solos are differentiated parts. Sounds are separated and compartmentalized in the mix. When "Street Life" erupts into its middle break, it is clearly Ferry's warble of "street life" that connects the parts, while Manzanera's, Mackay's, and

Jobson's solo bits are contained neatly in the solo section. The melody line receives more attention, and Ferry has an opportunity to sing as a singer, and not like another soloist vying for attention. The dynamics and resolution are sharper, with a real crescendo, ending (as in "Virginia Plain") on a vocal phrase. Continuing in *Country Life* and *Siren*, the band distills a strong group identity, and the playing is focused around well-crafted pop tunes such as "All I Want Is You," "Out of the Blue," and the band's only stateside-charting tune, "Love Is the Drug."

While "Drug" seemed to hint at disco, it was pub rock compared to what was arriving in European dance clubs. There, complex remixes and atmospheric effects were turning beat-oriented tunes into extended operettas of instrumental variety, rhythmic complexity, and production genius. Ferry was keen to take the band to that next level. In its final phase, from 1978 to 1982, Roxy began to experiment with Euro-disco and boldly neglected the American market dominated by the Eagles and Fleetwood Mac clones. The group morphed into a performance style partially influenced by disco, club music, and German trance, while still retaining a love of rock and melody. Producer Rhett Davies played a key role in the band's sound, adding a cleaner, more Germanic Kraftwerkian sheen. In *The All Music Guide to Rock*, Jason Anthony credited Kraftwerk, a German synthesizer quartet, with "hypnotically minimal, obliquely rhythmic music . . . [that] resonates to virtually every new development to impact the contemporary pop scene of the late 20th century" (Anthony 2002, 632). Having worked with Eno after his departure from Roxy Music, Davies was keenly aware of sonic experimentation, ambience, and texture.

Ferry and the band took a two-year hiatus from 1976 to 1978 while pursuing other projects, and came back with the strong *Manifesto* album in 1979. The music was haunted by the spirit of Eno, with tunes more languid and ethereal, and Davies's production lent the band some of Eno's distanced electronicism. It is as if the band had been listening to his work in his absence and had developed as a unit along similar lines. The songs were markedly less rocking and more atmospheric. Davies replaced hard sounds with beautiful washes of keyboards. There was a progression from Germanic, frenzied fury to impressionistic, floating tone colors and atmospheres. Here, the variety of sounds in the mix was decorative and suggestive. Ferry and crew had become adept players, and the Roxy crew made Eno's theories about soundscapes palpable. The mix became the key aspect, and placement in the sonic environment mattered more in a song such as *Manifesto*'s "Dance Away" than in 1972's "Virginia Plain." Anarchy was replaced by a theme of lost romantic languid longing. Paul Thompson had been replaced, and many fans complained that the new band was more of a backup group for Ferry and did not strongly feature the various members of Roxy in solo parts.

Keyboard sounds and Ferry's voice were dominant. Critic Simon Reynolds said as much in BBC's *The Roxy Music Story*, when he argued that the later Roxy Music sounded like a disgruntled and world-weary Bryan Ferry who had arrived at fame and fortune and didn't like what he found in such a place. He was more lost amongst riches and wealth than he had been when struggling. Ferry's voice is at his most sincere when speaking of crushed love affairs. The music has both a lush quality imparted by beautiful synth parts and a spare quality provided by cleaner simpler drum parts engineered by Davis and devoid of Thompson's bash style. The overall feel of the later albums is distanced music composed in space.

COUNTRY LIFE: COOL FIRE

Certainly a high point for Roxy Music was the *Country Life* album of 1974. Glam had passed its apex and was rising to baroque excesses, and bands like Roxy were stung by the criticisms that they were all flash and no substance. Roxy sought to reverse that impression by creating a detailed, complicated work that presented glam values in succinct terms. This album focused the band's fascination with glam ideas into a series of meditations on the media, pop culture, political theatre, and genre fiction. The playing is tight and dramatic, Ferry's vocals impassioned, and the album exists as a totality not common to most Roxy or glam albums.

Though Roxy would have been loath to call the album *a concept work*, there are underlying thematic conceits. The title *Country Life* refers to a British magazine that reflects the elegant lifestyle of country estates owned by the British aristocracy. Like *Architectural Digest* in the United States, *Country Life* was the ultimate coffee-table magazine of posh British society of the seventies. You could find it in the House of Lords, Buckingham Palace, or any place royal watchers and wannabes frequented. A spread in country life was what every Tory Party member dreamed of (along with a knighthood). It was a sign you had made it.

With true style, Roxy lampooned the pompous, decorative covers with their own version of country life. Usually, *Country Life* featured wealthy debutantes in riding gear enjoying the majestic English countryside. But Roxy featured two nearly naked models in heavy makeup and eye liner, making the sort of pun that Shakespeare would appreciate suggesting the two meanings of "country life" (cunt and country). Here, the two glamorous models appear semi-nude (one topless, and one in a see-through bra). Both are wearing only underwear. The country aspect, of course, refers to feminine parts, but also the girls are blandly staged in front of what appears to be a forest scene. So there is a semblance of sexuality and the high and vulgar life of the rich and famous simultaneously. Shakespeare made a joke mixing country and cunt in *Hamlet*:

Hamlet: Lady, shall I lie in your lap?

Ophelia: No, my lord.

Hamlet: I mean, my head upon your lap?

Ophelia: Ay, my lord.

Hamlet: Do you think I meant country matters? (Act II, Scene 2)

Sonically, the album is anything but organic and country sounding. The only track that has any semblance of a folk sound is the coy "Prairie Rose," a riff on Zane Grey transposed into a space-stomping war chant. Producer John Punter (who would later produce the Roxy clone band Japan) gets a dense sound that provides bite and a sense of space and creepy atmosphere.

The album begins with the tantalizing "The Thrill of It All." This paean to a desperate lover calling out to his amour is so over the top as to seem parodic. Ferry moans and cries, "I can't speak, I couldn't take more than another week." The figure seems to be completely intoxicated by love. The driving rhythm of Paul Thompson, the churning, blazing guitars of Phil Manzanera, the wailing sax of Andrew Mackay, the howling voice of Ferry, and the atmospheric keyboards of Eddie Jobson make a throbbing wall of sound that is alternately chaotic and threatening. This is clearly a love song in which the singer is at wit's end. It is a desperate rocker filled with Dionysian strains of ecstasy and anguish, characteristic of the best glam work. Emotions dominate over technique, although Jobson's keyboard emulation of escalating strings at the end are strangely reminiscent of the psychedelic cathartic conclusion of the Beatles' *I Am the Walrus*. Roxy only borrowed from the best. It is such an invigorating and draining album by turns that the listener almost can't continue.

But Roxy's members are masters of content, moving to the restrained and modest pop rocker, "Three and Nine." The lyrics here are far more cryptic and suggest images of three—images of 3-D, or three screens, or three lovers. Nine exists as a multiplication of three, and the song's cowriters, Ferry and Mackay, toy with additions of those numbers throughout. The lyrics suggest some Dada configuring of language, and the playful instrumentation and lighter tone suggest a song about self-amusement and pensive suggestions of life lived in the margins. Ferry sings "I'm a misfit too," suggesting that for him, a threesome might be a better configuration of partners than a mere mate—"3 and 9 could show you any fantasy." He also discusses three and nine as 12 and permutations such as two and six. Mackay's influence as co-songwriter is evident in the strong presence of oboe accompaniment, with light and airy tones brightening and lightening the Roxy sound as his sax solos could make the band sound crashing and loud. Almost the exact opposite of "Thrill," "Three and Nine" is restrained, playful, lilting, and consistently bouncy and charming. Ferry contributes a light harmonica wail, harmonizes with himself, while the oboe and synth double each other. The breathy quality suggests French chanson. In 2009, Ferry saluted French song writing legend, Charles Aznavour at the Cannes Film Festival with a version of Aznavour's classic tune "She." Here, Ferry is similarly lyrical.

The album's leadoff single, "All I Want Is You," is similarly driven and demonic like "Thrill." But here, instead of a frantic driving rhythm, the band opts for a military stomp. The tune starts with Manzanera's roaring guitars, fiercely distorted and vigorously announcing the main riff. Thompson's drums kick in with a grand stomp. Ferry's vocals plead, "somebody told me just the other day, that you're leaving me we're through." Ferry's handsomeness mocks the lyric. It would be hard to imagine girls leaving this behind (although a few years later, model Jerry Hall would leave Ferry for Mick Jagger). Ferry croons that other girls are just boring. Manzanera wrenches uni-notes and chords from his guitar in staccato bursts, raising the emotions of the song higher. Ferry dives into a second verse complaining that all his girlfriend wants is cheap sex, "cut price souvenirs." Ferry here seems to be the serious one in the relationship, looking for love, not titillation. The band erupts with Jobson and Ferry providing a set of crunching chords, Mackay roaring on the saxophone and Thompson rolling through the drums in dramatic fashion. Manzanera soars through one of his best solos, pouring back into the main verse. Ferry breaks into the middle eight again, spouting French, for "Love, always, love." Ferry rolls down into his lower register. He gives his former love a verbal spanking. He scolds, saying he won't change his diction for her. He isn't planning to change because she is shallow.

Ferry seems to be coding a message to glam rockers as well. He argues that images can start to be confusing. Ferry's scold is also saying that image and guise has limits. There is a need for some ultimate substance, some real stability, some underlying values to hold the notion of glam together. If image is simply built on image and with no foundation, there is nothing to hold up the glam industry.

Throughout, *Country Life* is varied and covers a mercurial blend of styles from medieval dirge to frantic careening rock apocalypse, but the album ends on a clever and comical high note, parodying the idea of Western cowboy anthems. Manzarera's brisling guitars and Mackay's fat sax sound fill the track "Prairie Rose," with a tinny fifties, B-movie Western ambience. When Ferry enters with a whisper of the word "Texas," he follows up with "That's where I belong." Could anything be more unlikely than the Euro-fashionista Ferry in Dallas? Ferry is singing to a girl (Prairie Rose?) and invoking the spirit of the prairie and the Old West. As the song stomps to a mighty conclusion, Roxy Music raves up to a crescendo with Thompson's thundering drums, Manzanera's screeching guitars, throbbing and bobbing bass, and sax riffs competing for attention. It is an exhilarating sendout to a transcendent album. Roxy's main competitor David Bowie put out the dark and ominous *Diamond Dogs*. By comparison, *Country Life* from the same year was dense, varied, excessive, and acidic. Both Roxy's and Bowie's work mirrored the perplexing complexity of glam, where in an album the mood could range from serious and bleak, while another artist might opt for mad and overwrought.

THEORY OF LOOKING: DEDICATED FOLLOWERS OF FASHION

Roxy, and particularly Ferry, was convinced that the visual statement would sustain the group and demand attention. In their earliest appearance in 1972, the band had well-defined style ideas. Ferry sang "Virginia Plain" in a black sequined outfit, with jet-black hair defying gravity and swept up. Phil Manzanera wore a black jumpsuit and bug-eyed glasses. Andy Mackay wore a green-and-blue space suit that resembled something from the fifties sci-fi epic *The Day the Earth Stood Still*. Eno hovered over the VSC3 synthesizer wearing a silver-fringed, lame fur jacket and high-waisted bolero pants in full makeup. Later, Manzanera would argue that the band dressed up in outrageous gear simply to outdo one another and to freak each other out. It became a contest to see who could be more outrageous than the last guy.

The costumes changed for nearly every show. After Eno's departure, Ferry took center stage, and his stage entrances were always hotly anticipated. In 1974's "All I Want Is You," Ferry lurked at the rear of the stage in the song's introduction and sauntered out like a cheap, hip Nazi in a brown shirt, military tie, and boots. Andy Mackay looked like a member of the Stax records horn section dressed in a baby-blue, oversized, zoot-suit tux and tails. Manzanera wore a flowing red peasant shirt, and Eddie Jobson is rail thin in a black-pants-and-silver-vest ensemble. By 1979's promotional film for "Angel Eyes," there are dancing girls miming the harp sounds and dressed like silver and gold angels. Ferry is in a pink oversized suit, white shoes, and gray tie. With his slick, black hair, most singers would look like a Good and Plenty box, but Ferry makes the ensemble a classy choice. Manzanera, in bug-eyed spectacles and shorter hair, wears a yellow double-breasted waist jacket with gray pants. A drummer is wearing a klattu-style, science-fiction jump suit resembling something from the movie *Alien*, making him also appear angelic. Andy Mackay is wearing a baby-blue Nehru-collared/band jacket and light pants that set off his sax beautifully. Bassist Gary Tibbs wears a light-blue dinner jacket, thin bowtie, and pink pants that work well against his blonde hair.

While critics would argue that the attention to costuming detracted from their musical gifts, Ferry believed, like Motown's Berry Gordy, that the art of performing was intrinsically tied to presentation, and this image simply aided the showmanship and reception of the work.

ROXY VERSUS BOWIE

Although in many ways arriving exactly at the same time as Bowie, Roxy's formula for success was quite different. Whereas Bowie always embraced change and aggressive alteration of his sound, even when things were going well, Roxy thrived on the refinement and perfection of an ever-more exotic and otherworldly vision. Whereas Bowie would employ shrieks and outrageous vocal gyrations for effect, Ferry was a more subtle audiophile, caressing the microphone and coaxing another strange tone from his fragile-sounding vocal instrument. Finally, whereas Bowie started trends and fads and sometimes followed them, Roxy steered a middle course away from trendy singing and writing towards materials that more and more took on an ethnographic and otherworldly absorbed sound.

FERRY'S SOLO CAREER

Ferry's solo work has been similarly conceptual to the band that he started as Roxy. When he was marketing the band, the EG Management company offered him a solo deal, instead, and he argued that Roxy was a package deal; but wisely, he also negotiated a side solo deal for himself. In his solo records, he provided a compelling image of elegance. His *These Foolish Things* album sees him in tuxedo singing strange versions of "It's My Party" and "Smoke Gets in Your Eyes," sort of love songs sung by a bizarre Bill Murray–Andy Kaufman sendup of crooners. After Roxy's departure, Ferry's "Slave to Love" and other solo outings explored lounge and disco styles. *Bete Noire* further explored the club scene. In these albums, he merged the theatricality of the pop song with darker, ambient readings of his former material. On these albums, Ferry worked with ace sessions guitarists David Gilmour, Johnny Marr, Robin Trower, and Chris Spedding.

In the *Taxi* album from 1993, Ferry crafted an eerie techno version of the old Fontilla Bass hit "Rescue Me." *Mamouna*, released in 1994 was nearly a fairy tale to lost love, with songs such as "Your Painted Smile" and "Mamouna" that could easily have constituted a post-*Avalon* Roxy album. A more recent covers album, 2003's *As Time Goes By*, sees Ferry perform famous songs from the past in an authentic and respectful manner although using elements of glam style to make them still distinctive. *Frantic*, released in 2004, saw Ferry working with Dave Stewart, Spedding, and Trower to craft an album that embraced a harder rock sound.

While crafting a new Roxy album, Ferry returned to solo work with 2007's *Dylanesque*, a straight ahead set of Dylan covers recorded in a brief period. Gone was Ferry's need for extensive artifice to produce interesting versions of classic tunes. What began as hopeless and sometimes laughable parody has morphed into reality, as Ferry has now become the master showman and romantic artist that he once seemed to perceive humorously.

ENO AND ENOSCIFICATION

Eno was a complicated figure who extolled elements of glam experimentation and chance in pop music. Although only in Roxy for two years, he contributed to outside Roxy projects (notably with Manzanera and Mackay but also in supporting Ferry's solo works) and has worked fitfully in variants of the glam style over the years. Throughout his career, Eno pursued a rabid interest in theory and performance, and participated in a wide range of musical and nonmusical art experiments. His installations, gallery shows, and influential musical theories have been manifested and developed through live settings and albums of material.

Of note are the oblique strategies, a set of tarot cards for music manipulation that served as instrumental glue for many of his coconspirators to the present day. The oblique strategy cards are simply a series of printed cards with musical and operative suggestions inscribed on the back. For example, a card might tell a producer to "emphasize the flaws" or ask, "Is there something missing?" The interpretation of what is meant is left up to the actual reader, but the cards are sufficiently open to encourage wild and varied approaches to working in the studio. Many of Eno's colleagues have been impressed by the application of such chance strategies in the creation of music. In fact, the cards became mythically popular. Today, you can download a free "Oblique Strategies" widget for most computer systems that allow use of a hypertext version of the cards. The cards are particularly useful when a creative block defies rational, straightforward, logical means. Eno's other "oblique" techniques have included mixing musicians and nonmusicians in the same project to advantage a final product.

Finally, Eno was able to parlay his peripheral status as a nonmusician and achieve deep influence like Roxy. As George Melly wrote in *Revolt into Style*, "they knew that, in the pop world, the moment of total universal hysteria is the harbinger of complete rejection" (Melly 1989, 78). Both Eno and Roxy understood that temporary fame was fleeting, but a significant role in the business was the product of craft and interesting ideas. Neither Roxy nor

Eno were icons at the level of Bowie, but their work was consistently valued and considered.

ROXY, FERRY, AND ENO INTO THE MILLENNIUM: PROJECTING GLAM

As the nineties waned, the separate elements of Roxy Music began to reappear. Ferry's covers album, *As Time Goes By*, paid tribute to midcentury crooning, and his 2004 album *Frantic* provided blistering and searing songs in the style of early Roxy. Roxy's back catalogue had been remastered, and recent bands including Scissor Sisters, Franz Ferdinand, Suede, and Pulp praised the band and cited them as a serious influence.

Even the differences between Eno and Roxy lessened. Eno joked in the BBC's *Roxy Music Story* that band chemistry had not changed in 35 years. The band and Eno had always kept in touch, with Roxy members participating on Eno albums, and Eno doing session duties for various configurations of the group. The similarities between the two are striking. Ferry affected the guise of the bored, sullen, dissolute romantic, spurned by love and grappling with a sense of ennui. Eno played the dandy gad-about intellectual being dubbed "Professor Eno" by members of the media for his endless pontificating and extrapolating of complex ideas. Both Roxy and Eno followed similar experimental music agendas. Though Eno became famous for coining genres like ambient music, it was Roxy in *Avalon* and Ferry in *Boys and Girls* that made ambient and atmospheric rock a staple of the eighties and beyond. Both continued to perform sonic experiments in music, and both became more conservative in their craft over the years. Eno supported veteran hitmakers U2 in their album ventures, and Ferry recently tackled a conservative group of Bob Dylan covers. Further, in recent times, both Eno and Roxy have championed melodic rock. Eno has come back to writing actual pop songs and singing (with U2, David Byrne, and John Cale).

Also, Roxy and Eno have continually existed as style icons and gurus of fashion. After his fitful career as a rocker, Eno dropped the punky furs and makeup for a sober and stately look as an elder statesman of rock aesthetics. Ferry, always associated with well-groomed tailoring, has been a perennial fashion icon, and was a model for the fashionable London clothing company Marks and Spencer.

Beyond fashion, both Roxy and Eno have been adept at transforming clichés into working methods. Ferry and company subverted musical clichés as divergent as ambient trance or pastiches of fifties dance bands. Eno has deconstructed prog rock, noise music, muzak, and ambience, and recently championed generative music that creates itself. Eno said on the British television program *Pioneers* that "my contribution was I think to do with threading in a lot of the stranger sonic and conceptual experiments that were going on in conceptual music . . . trying to make those a part of what could be done in music at the time" (*Pioneers: Brian Eno* 1991).

Ferry is rarely associated with lofty theories like Eno, but like Warhol, he was more than adept at putting them in action. Believing that the artist had to do something novel to capture the public's attention, Ferry applied strategic adaptations of classic material by adding alienation effects, reasoning he could make the material new again. Emulating the Chinese actor that was at once the character and not the character, Ferry's Brecthian effect stylized the work, adding unusual future retro costumes. Ferry explained that "we were going on stage thinking that on-stage was for dressing and making up— to intensify the whole experience" (Stump 1998, 48).

But Ferry's theatrical inclinations didn't stop there. The music couldn't be simply pop in funny costumes, although for a time, that's what critics suggested. Ferry was as musically adventurous as he was "costume-ly" courageous. Singing in an exaggerated falsetto, crooning in a whine that overaccentuated many tones and decreased the beauty and tenderness of ballads, Ferry collided with the material. He knowingly stripped the familiar of its associations and inserted himself into the crooning profession, revealing it for all of its naked exaggerations and swarmy cut-rate pandering of romantic tropes. This wasn't an easy task, and Ferry's approach was the subject of derision and ridicule until later voices such as those of Robert Smith and Stephen Morrissey made Ferry seem natural. In his 1974 rendition of the torch song "Smoke Gets in Your Eyes" Ferry solos on piano wearing a Casablanca-era Bogart tuxedo . He snarls some lines, wails others, and moans ecstatically in a humorous and affectionate parody of the singing styles of 30 years earlier. Susan Sontag called this form of clearly intentional exaggeration *camp*, and that style expresses Ferry's art. Sontag wrote that camp is "the love of the exaggerated, the 'off' of things-being-what-they-are-not" (Sontag 1983, 108). She explained that camp objects contain strong artifice, and in people, camp "responds to the markedly attenuated and the strongly exaggerated" (Ibid.).

THE ROXY INFLUENCE

Roxy burst onto the scene in 1972 with a string of hit singles and popular albums, including "Virginia Plain," "Do the Strand," "Pyjamarama," "Street Life," and "All I Want Is You." The band was only marginally popular in the United States, and Ferry and Roxy struggled for acceptance in this venue. They achieved their highest success long after glam had peaked with the unlikely coupling of New Romantic music and ambient sounds that characterized the *Avalon* album. But *Avalon*, though brilliantly shimmering and mesmerizing as a sonic landscape, was not altogether different from earlier Roxy albums.

Unlike Bowie, who performed radical shifts in direction, Ferry and Roxy simply refined their process to make the band sound strange but smooth all at once. Even when Roxy approached disco in "Love Is the Drug," they performed disco in their own Roxy style, parodying the form and making fun of the drug-propelled disco craze. Utilizing different forms of music, such as ballad, German music hall, hard rock, soul, and film music, the band explored different costumes and instrumentation, but produced very unified and holistic albums expressing a preference for the decadent club scene. Pausing in the mid-seventies to rethink their direction, the band came back stronger for the menacing and club-based trilogy, *Manifesto*, *Flesh & Blood*, and *Avalon*. By *Avalon*, the band had embraced new-age instruments and imagery, and the sound had lightened. At the same time, their image evolved into themes of decadence, self-absorption, and "me-ness." Lyrics from *Avalon* told tales of late-night drinking bouts, burnt-out lounge society, and lovers too distracted to focus their attention on the beloved. "When the samba takes you, Out of nowhere, And the backgrounds fading, Out of focus" ("Avalon"). There is a sense of pop impressionism as the music glides over the listener, becoming more spacious and ephemeral. "You run through here with your words of sand, I can nearly understand," sings Bryan Ferry in "The Main Thing." We have little idea of what Ferry is describing, and in the video, we see disconnected images of an amusement park and a chorus of women's legs dancing in the air. The beats dissolve into mystery. Roxy parted in the early eighties, but Ferry's *Boys and Girls* sank deeper into beat-drenched club sounds, with Ferry still exploring decadent club environments. The music was very programmatic, with images of southern sambas in "Limbo," seaside tales in "Windswept," and hidden kingdoms in "Mamouna."

Roxy was a key influence on New Romantic bands such as Culture Club, Duran Duran, the Smiths, Japan, and Heaven 17. By the nineties, the band was nearly enshrined with Britpop stars such as Elastica, Suede, Pulp, Pet Shop Boys, and Morrissey aping their catalogue.

At the dawn of the millennium, Ferry reformed Roxy, and the band has toured and slowly crafted a comeback album. Fashion guru Anthony Price joked in the *Roxy Music Story*, "it's about time ladies!" But by the millennium, many contemporary groups were acknowledging the band's influence, including Franz Ferdinand, Scissor Sisters, and My Chemical Romance. Meanwhile, the hyperactive Ferry still performs impressions of crooners, explores other artists (*Dylanesque*) and produces his own unique song cycles (*Frantic*). Roxy staked out classical themes of nightclub culture, decadence, and a continuing fascination with pop culture. If a glam act could feel at home in a Weimar-era cabaret, a soundstage from *Casablanca*, or a seedy sci-fi B-movie set, that act was always Roxy Music.

Chapter 5

GLAM'S CASUALTIES AND RESURGENCE

THE "PROBLEM" WITH GLAM

Glam had many perceived problems that were enhanced by its rampant media exposure. Marshall McLuhan had a theory that media was an extension of man, but that media could easily be overextended and betray mankind. For example, television could extend our eyes and our vision, but trusting everything we saw and witnessed on television could very easily overextend the medium. We could wind up believing everything from McCarthyism, celebrity scandals, to Saddam Hussein's weapons of mass destruction. We could even believe that people cared about the lives and deaths of celebrities.

Such was the problem of glam's overextension into the media. Everything about glam and glam artists became overreported, and people became quickly tired of them. Roger Crimlis and Alwyn Turner said, "lipstick was essentially what the best of 1970s rock was about" (Crimlis and Turner 2006, 11). More than lipstick, the sense of exaggeration that was glam was a quality that could overwhelm people. Yet simultaneously, this obsession with a public visual culture would ultimately sustain the genre. Crimlis and Turner explained that "this strange new genre nevertheless announced the arrival of a visually literate strand in rock that was to set the agenda for the next decade and beyond" (Ibid.).

While media saturation turned people away from glam, there was also a fear that the style would become repetitive. If the music was just rock in costumes, then bizarre costumes had their limits. Marc Bolan's work reflected repetitious ideas for a time, and Gary Glitter careened into self-parody almost overnight.

Further, the tendency towards camp encouraged excesses and insincerity that persisted. Some groups didn't know when to turn irony off or at least down, and the prevailing image was that glam took nothing serious and placed quotes around everything, including "rock." The ironic posture was perceived as a limitation, and punk suffered a similar fate as every musical statement had to be an anguished, bitter rant.

Beyond camp, some groups began to indulge in self-mockery. Queen had a sense of humor about themselves, but when Freddie Mercury began to appear in biker machismo, people believed he was ridiculing gay icons, a large part of the band's base. Such gestures could be seen as pandering to a public once cherished through revered feminized images of long hair and pretty posturings. Photographer Mick Rock helped to furnish the public images of glam icons like Bowie and Queen, and even modeled his famous "Bohemian Rhapsody" images of Queen upon a thirties image of screen diva Marlene Dietrich. Alice Cooper's horror shows devolved from thrilling escapades into the arcane to critiques of bad horror film clichés. When hair metal bands became indistinguishable from one another, the crowds began to drift away. Was that Slayer or Def Leppard? Further, the theatrical spark that animated early glam bands lacked any development. The shock value of costume and dress up needed to develop and expand. Many of these bands kept doing the same tired costumes and schtick. Like endless sequels to minor slasher films, there was no advancement to the plot; it remained superficial. Even more deadly was static music. You could change the show and visuals, but if the music remained neutral or regressive, there was no dialectic, no progression.

JOBRIATH

Jobriath was a Bowie clone, dressing in a feminine manner and playing an epic glam theatrical rock. In his rogue/rock songs like "I'm a Man," he played with Bowie clichés and wore theatrical costumes. He had an attractive voice and clever theatrical gestures. In real life, he was gay, and quickly his star was eclipsed by the superior marketing of Bowie. His balletic movements and fey dancing was ridiculed at the time. Sadly, his work was not appreciated for a theatrical cabaret statement. Everything about Jobriath was just as engaging as David Johannson and the New York Dolls parody of a glam group, but Jobriath's career never took off. His record company could see that this mix of theatrical costumes, a spacey hard rock, and theatrical gesturing was not having the effect it wanted, and they pulled the plug after two albums. The albums were received by a puzzled American press.

Was Jobriath a put on, or a lamer version of Bowie's schtick? Journalists were suspicious, but had no way to judge the vitality of a form of music that wallowed in artifice. Jobriath was equally depressed and stunned by the reversal.

His songs were not as spectacular as Bowie's, but if Bowie had faded from the scene after *The Man Who Sold the World*, it is doubtful he would be remembered. Jobriath retreated into the bizarre alternative persona of Cole Berlin, a lounge lizard like David Johannson's (New York Dolls) alter ego, Buster Poindexter. He changed his performing name to Cole Berlin, an amalgam of Cole Porter and Irving Berlin. He wrote plays and lived in a pyramid, which he claimed gave him inspiration and energy. His work in that format was charming and engaging. As Cole Berlin, Jobriath performed on piano a quixotic mix of music hall and overly theatrical pop standards. He literally became the languid lounge lizard that he had described in glam tunes. He never performed his own Jobriath songs again. By 1983, he contracted AIDS and died forgotten, sadly, as a footnote to rock and theatrical rock history.

T. REX-CSTACY

Now his lovers have left him, and his youth's ill spent.
—T. Rex, "Dandy in the Underworld"

Marc Bolan's search for fame was similar to other glam performers. He grew up in a lower middle-class home. His mother worked at a fruit stand, and his father sold cosmetics and drove a truck. By all accounts, the family doted on Bolan and encouraged his musical interests. When he was eight, they bought him a drum kit, and he was fascinated by films, particularly horror films. By age 14, he was kicked out of school for truancy, but as Nicholas Schaffner reports, he had already developed a fascination with "Greek mythology, British romantic poetry, and the French teenage prodigy Arthur Rimbaud" (Schaffner 1983, 151). Though these elements played a strong role in his later writing and formulation of artistic principles, Bolan did not directly benefit from the art school education that like-minded musical innovators Lennon, Bowie, and Ferry had endured. John Walker acknowledges that if art schools didn't create better pop musicians, it did help them along, because, "at the very least it is a place where budding Pop musicians can meet like-minded people, and form a band" (Walker 1987, 15). But also, art schools provided a laboratory to try things out and find out what was ineffective. Frith and Horne pointed out that "punk rock was the ultimate art school music movement" (Frith and Horne 1989, 124), and artists like Bolan followed that dangerously experimental credo.

Bolan found that being a handsome young mod had challenges. He was pretty, had a long, attractive shock of hair, and an impish body. He thought he would experiment in the pop business. He began writing songs with a local student, Keith Reid, who would later become the pivotal/surreal poet/lyricist for the successful Procol Harum. Bolan attracted local attention for his style, flashy wardrobe, and come-hither, sexy look and was featured in Britain's *Town Magazine*.

He performed modeling gigs for men's suits. With a small profit from modeling, Bolan disembarked for Paris and claimed to live with wizards, and witnessed paranormal events such as levitation, occult ceremonies, and demon summonings. Throughout, Bolan was a master of self-hype, mythologizing his own origins and producing charming patter to the press. He would hang out at the right pubs to meet music journalists. He began writing songs furiously, and he stockpiled a series of tunes that would last him through the first few years of his fame. His music associates thought he was a crazy but clever young loon. Bolan lived with an ultimate belief in his own talent and eventual success. He said in 1971, "I see no reason why freaks shouldn't be in the charts, but then they turn around and resent you for it" (Murray 1991, 26). Bolan was always aware that his innovations could make him loved and damned.

He fell under the sway of Simon Napier-Bell, the producer of the Yardbirds. Bolan was impressed by watching the Yardbirds' style of working, and he appreciated the improvisational ability for band members to interact. Bolan never had that. He decided to form his own band, creating Tyrannosaurus Rex with his sole musical accomplice, Steve Peregrine Took (his real name was Porter, but he changed it to sound like a character from *Lord of the Rings*). Took was an undisciplined but occasionally brilliant percussionist with a gift for singing harmonies. Eventually, their instruments were either repossessed or sold to pay the rent so they regressed to acoustic guitar and bongos before long.

Like so many London musicians before and after, T. Rex was fortunate to bump into the influential BBC DJ John Peel. Peel was a remnant of the sixties pirate radio movement in England, and when the pirate illegal radio stations were closed, the BBC hired Peel as their resident freak DJ. He gave the BBC street credibility, and they in turn obtained an entry to hipper sounds. Over the next 30 years, his infallible ear for new talent would break some of the best artists/bands of British pop. He was the resident DJ at the hip London club Middle Earth, and with a shared natural affinity for woodland fairy tales and *Lord of the Rings* mythology, Peel advocated T. Rex's sound and installed them as Middle Earth's house troubadours. This effectively launched the band. Music industry types visited, and Tony Visconti, a minor assistant producer, was amongst the people smitten with Bolan's attractive stage persona and magnetic singing style.

Visconti's label thought the band had little commercial potential, but with Visconti's support, they were signed. For £400, they produced their first album, the long-titled, *My People Were Fair and Had Sky in Their Hair ... but Now They're Content to War Stars on Their Brows*. During that same year, Bolan had two non-album singles that caught cult attention. There was the riffing, clever, and repetitive "Debora," and the seductive "One Inch Rock." Though the title suggested sexuality, according to Bolan, the story was actually about an enchantress that transformed a hapless lover down to a one-inch size.

Bolan's early style was anarchic, psychedelic, folky, and definitely geared for eccentric tastes. Bolan suggested that T. Rex was influenced by early Syd Barrett and Pink Floyd, and he argued that Barrett was one of the "few people I'd actually call a genius" (Schaffner 1983, 154). When T. Rex performed at some outdoor festivals, David Bowie actually performed a pantomime act at some of their shows, trying desperately himself to break into the rock circuit. The 1969 *Unicorn* album began to exploit the magic of studio technology and gave the band a fuller more vibrant sound. But Bolan's bandmate Took began to behave erratically, beating himself with a belt and stripping on stage. Bolan consoled himself by writing a book of poetry, *Warlock of Love*, a chapbook of verse and fairytale images. Bolan recruited marginal bongo player/percussionist and helpmate Mickey Finn. The pair had chemistry and were mutually supportive. T. Rex was off in a new direction.

Bolan strapped on an electric guitar and began to guide the band in a more electric style. With *Beard of Stars* and the simply titled *T. Rex* album, Bolan was placing himself into a more commercial guise. Bolan said, "I wanted people to look at things in a new light, and the only was to do that was to . . . change the music, and change the name, but not lose identity in any way" (Murray 1991, 25). He wrote and performed another hummable and shuffling tune, "Ride a White Swan," which had patented mannerisms of Bolan's low-key rhythm guitar work, chanty vocal style, a poppy rhythm, and a penchant for myth-based lyrics. The vocal rides on top, some atmospheric background vocals add dimension, and a subtle string support makes the song enchanting. Visconti later said that Bolan and T. Rex were always his number-one responsibility. Even after Bowie had become a regular collaborator, he felt wedded to T. Rex and their work. This time, the production was tight and clean, and the elements, the crackling guitar, the shuffle beat, and particularly Bolan's voice stood out in sharp contrast.

The song ignited a firestorm of interest. The following T. Rex album of 1970 was fueled by moderated hippie/fairy motifs framed in a more rocking format. Bolan began to wear some glitter makeup and stars on his cheeks along with gold and silver jackets. The term "glitter rock" was coined derisively to describe him and his appearance. But Bolan's sound was catching on; the *T. Rex* record was released in the United States by Reprise, and the usually American rootsy *Rolling Stone* even managed a positive notice. Bolan was quick to capitalize on the attention and wrote a personal letter to *Rolling Stone* editor Jann Wenner, saying, "I've enclosed some poems & pictures in case there [*sic*] of use to you" (Schaffner 1983, 157).

Bolan had larger ambitions. A track on *T. Rex*, "Children of Rarn," was to form the basis of an unrealized Bolan magnum opus, a song cycle along the lines of *Tommy* or *Sgt. Pepper*. Unfortunately, Bolan never went beyond demos of the longer musical theatrical endeavor. His work as a pop megastar was just beginning, and he felt he had to apply himself to that work.

Part of the problem all the glam performers had was the rush to fame. In the seventies, the movement from peripheral figure to star was very quick, and the road to ruin was just as rapid. As the industry had accelerated, the artists had to adapt. Bolan felt compelled to follow the business imperative rather than an aesthetic one. Bolan, like Bowie and Ferry, had been on the outskirts for over five years, and he was hungry to solidify his opportunity for fame and fortune. But simultaneously, Bolan's rise was accompanied by a requisite amount of blather and self-aggrandizement, something that would approach ego mania over time. "I've suddenly turned into that mental channel which makes a record a hit and I feel at present as though I could go on writing number ones forever" (Sinclair 1982, 37). The quote aptly summarizes Bolan's intellectual and career problems. Like Bowie, Ferry, Alice Cooper, and Sparks, there was enormous pressure to be productive, and this sense of having to make hit records according to an assembly line model induced a false pressure for quantity over quality. In truth, albums and longer, more complex works were the new frontier; but Bolan was slow to accept that art albums were the road to critical success. At the same time, Bolan believed in a punk aesthetic in which he would engender an idea and quickly translate it to tape with little studio sophistication. This stood in stark contrast to progressive groups, who labored for years over a single work. Bolan refined his ideas, but remained true to his subject matter rooted in fairy tales, imaginary worlds, and images of pop culture fame. Bolan said, "I'm now living my fantasy . . . I am what I used to write about on those old albums—I am that" (Sinclair 1982, 41).

Bolan was touring extensively, had prepared a stronger stage band with bass and drums, and was about to change record labels, but he needed one single and album to finish out a previous contract with Fly Records. The single was "Get It On," and the album was *Electric Warrior*, both big sellers for Bolan in the States. By July 1971, Bolan had several top singles, and by the end of the year, the album was at the top of the British charts. Charles Shaar Murray wrote that in 1972, this "solo act has sold sixteen million records in fourteen months . . . Bolan sells three out of every hundred singles in this country" (Murray 1991, 32). Bolan dutifully toured the United States as a support act, and audiences were either rude or indifferent to his sound. Bolan cried out to the front row crowd, "we could be at home playing to people who want to see us" (Schaffner 1983, 158).

As Bolan's fame grew, so did his self-destructive nature. In his chronology of Bolan's life and career, Cliff McLenehan commented that "Bolan was no angel and he often deliberately baited the press with a series of provocative statements" (McLenehan 2002, viii). He often said, "I'm very self-destructive" (Schaffner 1983, 158), and he seemed to delight in weaving fantastic arabesques of what he would do with his newfound fame. One problem was that he kept switching band members and had few musical peers on board. Took and later

Mickey Finn existed mostly as side men, and other players were hired on a contract basis.

Much of the engineering and planning for Bolan's career was done by his wife, the creative Jane Child. She did everything from select clothing and styles for him to listening to his songs and sorting out the better material. It was Child who picked up on the quality of "Ride a White Swan" and encouraged Bolan to record it quickly. Child had been a secretary at the talent agency that handled Syd Barrett, not an easy case, and she was accustomed to handling difficult artist types. She helped Bolan (much as Angela Bowie helped David Bowie) to navigate the troubling waters of the music business. Few realized the influence June Child had on Marc. She even sewed his capes to give him a wizard appearance. But eventually, Bolan became alienated from her and preferred the company of his backup singer Gloria Jones, a personality enthralled by Bolan, and a less astute student of business. Bolan's widow June died of a heart ailment in 1994, and her memorial mentioned that "Marc was so very impractical, all he lived for was his writing. Poetry, lyrics and music were all that ever mattered to him then. She had to take care of everything else in such a manner that Marc often didn't realize she was doing it" ("In Memoriam: June Feld").

But Bolan was catching the wave of the time. He performed and hung out with Elton John and Ringo Starr. Both were enthusiastic about the young singer, and Elton performed almost as a backup player on a live version of Bolan's "Children of the Revolution." But many of Bolan's best moments were either forgotten or not revealed at the time. Rumors abound that he played on Alice Cooper sessions in Morgan studios ("Bolan People") performing on tracks "Hello, Hooray" and "Slick Black Limousine" in London in 1972 and that he contributed guitar to Jeff Lynn and Electric Light Orchestra's megablaster "Ma-Ma-Ma Belle" in 1973. None of these apocryphal performances are officially documented.

Electric Warrior was a crowning effort, inspired by old rock and roll and representing Bolan's myth concerns. The record merged folk, rock, shuffle, and pop conceits into a mesmerizing blend of styles that created a template for later power pop groups. His flashy guitar work signified his style. There were some brilliant strokes, but Bolan was an impressionist, painting broadly and providing little detail. His lighter sound was an alternative to heavy metal and ponderous prog rock. He was into pop music, fashion, flashy images, and most importantly, fun. There was still an essence of a hippie woodland elf who delighted in rousing people in a communal orgy of commonality. Michael Jackson applied a similar technique in his performances centered around himself in the eighties. Like Jim Morrison earlier, performers like Bolan and Jackson were seeking to return pop music to the sort of cathartic tribal ritual that had united African and Greek clans centuries before. Although critics argued that Bolan had sold out his hippie roots, Bolan gleefully reported, "I am my own fantasy" (Schaffner 1983, 159). Indeed, Bolan had exceeded his own expectations, and had little inclination where to go next.

Despite the problems Bolan had with acceptance in the United States, his style had become sharply defined. He wrote lyrics dependent on images from romantic poetry, horror, fantasy, and mythological symbolism; he used an ethereal, lilting, cooing voice that was distinctive; and he merged a sense of techno-primitivism with the sounds that were current in the rock scene. Bolan wrote fun pop ditties such as "Cosmic Dancer," which described the singer as a dancer at a very early age. "I was dancing when I was twelve, I was dancing when I was aaah, I danced myself right out the womb, Is it strange to dance so soon?" Further, Bolan's partying spirit and libidinous odes explored a strain of pre-punk rebellion that seemed to have gotten lost in the ponderous self-important music of the seventies. People from James Taylor to Yes were striving for *meaning* while ignoring the superficial elements of image and spectacle. But Bolan saw a different aesthetic, and his rise could be likened to Dylan's transition from folk to electric pop in 1966. Purists were horrified, but eclectic listeners who wanted a real poet in pop music saw Dylan as joining in the pop movement. Bolan saw himself in this light.

Although Bolan enjoyed the trappings of stardom, he had a rough time adapting to this new found power and spent much of 1974–75 in a funk. First, he was unable to conquer America. Despite a string of British hit singles, he remained a second-bill act in America, and no amount of promoting by his strong American label (Warner Brothers) could move record buyers. Second, he was a sloppy performer producing sloppy theatrics, self-indulgent jumps, goofy cavorting, and bashing on stage. He banged tambourine on the guitars, danced, and focused on entertaining the crowd over performing to the service of the overall sound. Ironically, there are no live T. Rex concert albums, in an era suffused with self-indulgent two- and three-record live albums. Bolan was more comfortable creating in the studio, when he was being creative. He viewed the live experience as a celebration.

After *Electric Warrior* and "Get It On," his contract came up for renewal. He made large demands and attempted to handle negotiations himself, usually an unfortunate choice since artists are rarely capable managers. He did have money for a time and bought a fashionable office building in downtown London, where he managed his empire, a new record label all to himself, and rented parts of the facility to other artists and musicians. But immediately, the money and influence went to Bolan's head, and *The Slider* album already showed signs of tiredness. Charles Shaar Murray with NME winced, saying Bolan's lyrics were "lame, slipshod, and flabby" (Murray 1991, 161). Although there were still echoes of Tolkien in the lyrics and a notable nod to H. P. Lovecraft, it was as if Bolan had stopped reading books except the book of himself.

Bolan's troubles were compounded by drugs, drink, and an unhealthy preoccupation with David Bowie's career. The press had called Bowie, "the thinking man's Bolan," and Bolan was stung by the negative comparisons. Bowie had mimed at T. Rex concerts in the early days, and Bolan had guested on early Bowie tracks such as "The Prettiest Star."

But Bolan's atrophy contained elements of a different movement. Bolan's same sound and repetition was often a motif, a choice. Bolan's work was a portent of the frustration and tedium with rock that would emerge into the punk rock movement. Like the punks, Bolan plowed through rock clichés and repeated infectious chugging riffs with abandon. But real dangers erupted in the bloated *Tanx* album that featured what Nicholas Schaffner called Bolan's "heavy metal sludge" and "boozy growl" (Schaffner 1983, 164). Bolan stopped listening to talented advisors such as his wife June or his loyal producer Tony Visconti and instead followed wild impulses, made more erratic by his bad diet and drinking habits. He made bad recording decisions, determining to set every impulse down on vinyl, and coined new absurd subgenres for every new form of music he supposedly invented. There was "erection rock" and the dubious "cock rock," but critics dubbed Bolan's motley stew "feeble rock." Warner Brothers cancelled his recording contract in the United States, citing that Bolan cost the company more in promotion than he produced in sold product. An artist that billed himself as the ultimate product was liquidated for lacking sales potential. By all accounts, Bolan was starting to live his mythology, an Icarus character who flew too close to the sun, or a Narcissus blinded by his own reflection.

Gloria Jones, Bolan's new amore, was a deft soul singer, and she encouraged Bolan to a funkier, soul influence, but by 1974, Bolan's concerts were a shambles. He appeared fat and bloated. The stage show consisted of a mechanical star, with Bolan popping out surrounded by the other musicians. At the end of the long jam of "Get It On," he pulled out a whip and beat his guitar. For the finale, the guitar was thrown at a prepared/fake amp that exploded. The show was a limp cross section of Who frenzy and Hendrix excess, but blander. In his last American tour in 1974, he played second billing to Three Dog Night. A performance clip from British television to promote the single "Teenage Dream" shows the problems. Wearing a black-and-gray jumper tunic, Bolan mugs his way through the song, straining with uncomfortable gestures and leaving the guitar part for what seems like minutes to bleed pseudo-emotion from his voice and body language. He overdressed. His gestures seem an odd parody of Gary Glitter (himself the biggest self-parody in the business). Gloria Jones's vocals are mixed high in the background. Kids in the audience that are blocked around Bolan look completely bored in his presence. The tune is a lifeless retread of Bolan's *Electric Warrior* form.

Bolan's *Light of Love* (1974) is certainly not perfect, but indicates a new direction with the help of Jones. Bolan and band perform in white with

Bolan singing, "Won't you Burn for me light of love," almost endlessly through the song. Despite the dull and repetitive lyric, the sound is cleaner, there is a decent clavinet sound, and a funkier sense of rhythm. The band is dancing on what looks like a white transparent disco floor, and colorful phased-lighting effects make Bolan's gestures more fluid and less hammy. Bolan's vocal is also cleaner, and despite repetitive lyrics, strutting, and gestures that ape Glitter, the ensemble looks like a journeyman entry from *Soul Train*.

Bolan was having other career reversals. He was a tax exile from 1974 to 1975, living in America but missing London and his popularity base. From 1974 to 1977, he had no record distribution deal or tours in America, worsening his economic status and deteriorating his popularity further. He was perceived as a failure in the United States—a one-hit wonder, a Bowie clone who ironically had been a Bowie inspiration.

Future Pretenders front woman Chrissie Hynde was a journalist at the time, and she rose to Bolan's defense in print, claiming he asserted the punk ethic before punk. But in 1975, Bolan began a long and slow rehabilitation. He ventured into television production, a natural adjunct to rock stardom, and perfect for the fresh-faced pop rock star. He interviewed several pop celebrities, including Marvel Comics' Stan Lee, and suggested that a Marc Bolan/T. Rex comic could be forthcoming. In 1976, declining fortunes decreased his tax burden, thus allowing him to return to England. He began writing a regular column on other artists for the *Record Mirror*. Always an easy and gregarious conversationalist, Bolan was beginning to find his muse again through other communication mediums.

His 1975 release, *Futuristic Dragon*, has some weak material, but started with interesting chanted, spoken mythic verse lyrics sung over a series of sounds, tones, sound effects, and vaguely disco-esque rhythms that suggested a mash-up of Isaac Hayes's "Shaft" versus David Bowie's "Future Legend." It was a rough mixture, but Bolan's experiments showed maturity.

The year 1977 brought positive changes. Bolan was cast in a short-term pop show called simply *Marc*, and he was popular as a host and performer in an environment he could control, surrounded by professional helpmates. The series was a hit. Cliff McLenehan wrote, "A camp kitsch classic or crap? You decide" (McLenehan 2002, 230). He had secured a new band of professional sidemen including Herbie Flowers and Tony Newman, two previous Bowie session players who helped to streamline Bolan's rhythm section, giving the singer/guitarist the strong underpinning he needed to perform consistently. Further, the shows were deemed professional and tight, and those who saw them explained that Bolan looked slim and fit. His health had improved, and he seemed to be moving to secure control of his downward-spiraling career.

On top of this, he had recorded a bright new album, *Dandy in the Underworld*, a work that suggested Bolan was spending more time in writing and music production. The title song reflects the mythic story of Orpheus descending to hell to save his lover Eurydice. The lyrics are clearly autobiographical, with Bolan discussing his own descent. With haunting lines like, "now he forever stalks the ancient mansions of hell," sung in a style that was not only listenable but clear and audible, Bolan seemed on the verge of recapturing his old swagger. He had just finished the first season of *Marc*, had dueted with old buddy/rival David Bowie (performing "Heroes" on the television program), and was anticipating a new television season and planning a series of tours in Europe. Suddenly, he was dead, killed before his 30th birthday when girlfriend Gloria Jones drove his Mini Cooper into a tree. The semi-conscious Bolan was not wearing his seat belt, Jones was exhausted and had likely fallen asleep, and the car drifted off the road just a few miles from their mansion. What was to come next was snuffed out.

QUEEN: RAGE IN METAL

If any single glam group inspired hair metal for the next decade, it must have been Queen. Unlike Jobriath or Marc Bolan, Queen was a solidly managed group, and their tale is similar to Bowie and Roxy's odyssey. The crucial difference is the untimely death of irreplaceable lead singer Freddie Mercury. Mercury was a charming and talkative extrovert, songwriter, performer, and catalyst who helped catapult the band to the stratosphere of pop stardom.

Queen was a well-educated group of students who played pop music at night. Their education and their association with art schools, universities, and technology made them especially adept at using glam techniques and parlaying these formulas to massive success. Roger Deacon and Brian May worked in a psychedelic pop band named Smile. Freddie Mercury sang in a succession of bands and played backup for Smile in bands named Ibex and Wreckage. May was a science student working on a degree in physics, Deacon was majoring in electronics, and Roger Taylor was studying biology (hoping for a career in dentistry).

Only Mercury had a background in the arts, obtaining a diploma in Art from the Ealing College of Art, but his experience in design, image, costuming, and performance was pivotal to the band's success. He designed the band's regal crest, with lions on both sides, two virgins, a crab, and a fierce eagle above waging a war over a crown. The image is quite striking and suggests the band's power, noble bearing, and internal conflicts, a creature that for all its power could tear itself apart. The symbol derived from the various members' astrological signs (an Aries, two Leos, and a Virgo) and Mercury's interest in mythological themes. From 1967 to 1971, the band played bars, clubs, and college gigs. When Smile's lead singer quit in 1971, Mercury saw the potential in Smile's guitarist and drummer (May and Taylor) to form a strong musical partnership, and he signed on with his signature extrovert moves.

Mercury performed with a regular microphone stand until one day while lifting it, the heavy base of the stand broke loose. Mercury realized he could carry the far lighter whole stand around with him wherever he went, using it as an extension, a pointer, or a penis. The microphone antics were endless. Mercury would jam the object between his legs, thrust it to the sky, and ride it like a witch's broom. He used it as projectile, weapon, sexual appliance, and object of anger. Mercury's stage presence was so much larger than life, it is no surprise that few fans troubled him off stage. He looked aggressive and tough, probably owing to the boxing training he took in prep school. Mercury might have been average-sized, but on stage, he looked tough and formidable. Stephen Thomas Erlewine, writing for the online *All Music Guide*, wrote that, "Queen's music was a bizarre, yet highly accessible fusion of the macho and the fey" (Erlewine). It was hard to take Queen's posturing as guitar gods, and it was also difficult to see the members as pretty-dressed poofs. They were an enigma riding on the crest of the dislodged gender wars.

After slogging through the pub band circuit, Queen's members determined that to break into the music business, they needed a strategy. Like Bowie and Ferry, they opted for choice gigs, producing demos, and securing the support of wealthy patrons, a record label, and management company. Queen's game plan was honed in a series of years. Between 1970 and 1971, the band played few gigs and a small uneventful tour in the summer of 1971. At that time, Terry Yeaton, a friend of Brian May's, invited the band to the newly completed De Lane Lea studios. The owners wanted the band to test out the state-of-the-art equipment and to determine if the studio would attract paying customers. In return for tuning the equipment, the band was allowed to record when the facility wasn't being used. This gave the band an erratic recording schedule, but the opportunity to use a first-rate base station when the facility was not in rental to a paying customer. But being around the action had its benefits, and when producers Roy Thomas Baker and John Anthony dropped by to check out the equipment, they were impressed by the band performing inside. They suggested the band visit and use Trident studios, another watering hole for current and aspiring British pop musicians. The band found friendly owners at Trident and were again allowed free studio time when others were not performing. This time was invaluable for the band in shaping material and learning studio production techniques. Both would come in handy during their next 20 years as performing and recording artists.

Though Queen could take months to produce an album, by turns they could produce very quickly and on location. Both elements were vital to their busy touring schedule. By the fall of 1972, the band was given a small salary for playing at Trident, members of the band were performing on outside recordings, and by 1973, their first album was completed. Things began to accelerate when the band performed a session for the BBC. Influential disc jockey John Peel played the band's work on his "Sounds of the Seventies" radio show. By March, EMI signed the group. Songs like "My Fairy King," and "Seven Seas of Rhye" illustrated Mercury's fascination with mythological fantasy themes. The band had learned many studio tricks and had mastered complex overdubs and sound effects. Brian May took great pride in engineering an album that obtained complex sonics without the use of synthesizers to get extreme atmospheres. He and the band boasted on the cover, "No synthesizers appear on this album." The band believed they had made a better, more vibrant record without the technology of synthesizers. At this point, synthesizers seemed to be dominant in rock music. *Time Out* magazine wrote that their record was a "thrusting, dynamic forceful . . . debut" (Rock 2007, 180).

Things grew faster as the year wore on. The band worked on a second album, *Queen II*, and this time they were booked as proper clients. The songs were stronger and more focused. The sound was more atmospheric. They toured with Mott the Hoople, fresh from a David Bowie–engineered rebirth. In 1974, they scored a lucky appearance on the British institution *Top of the Pops*—lucky because David Bowie pulled out of an appearance a day before filming was to begin. Queen entered the studio to make a background track for "Seven Seas of Rhye" (a song on the first album), since the rule on *Top* was that background tracks (minus vocals) were the format. Bands played on tape and simply mimed along with the prerecorded track. Queen gave a strong performance. Mercury shook his hair, and the band dressed in black jumpsuits and sequins. Their hair was immaculate, long, and beautiful. The vocals were high and theatrical. Brian May's guitar was filled with rock star riffs. Mercury posed with his microphone and gestured across the stage. He turned his back to the camera. Mercury's lyrics told of a medieval land invaded by a dream demon who would "challenge the mighty titan and his troubadours." Mercury performs the song seriously with little humor. Mercury was sensitive to audiences who were serious or wished to indulge in fun. Here, the myth fairy tale is played straight. There is something already faintly operatic in his strong falsetto and harsh vocal tone. To be a singer in a hard rock band is a difficult job, but Mercury blasted through May's dense mix, screaming guitars, and a full sound.

FREDDIE'S COSTUMES

While all the members of Queen wore costumes, as the band progressed, more attention was thrust on Mercury, and he went from wearing feminine batwings to pseudo-Elizabethan frocks to more outrageous garb. Mercury sent himself up in the video for Queen's 1986 tune "The Miracle." Here, children perform as Mercury, first with his long hairstyle and an open-breasted harlequin dance/tights outfit. Then the singer transforms into a short-haired *Sgt. Pepper* yellow band jacket façade. This is replaced by a mustachioed Mercury in a black leather biker ensemble. Then he moves to a muscle T-shirt and high-waisted construction worker pants with a wide black belt. Mercury's costumes flirted with gay imagery, the Village People biker ensemble, and bare-chested red-and-white suspenders with hot pants. But Mercury's bold costumes were so obvious and humorously displayed that audiences couldn't parse whether they were humorous homages to these styles, or actual symbols of his affiliation with gay groups. On occasion, he came adorned in a 12-foot royal cape and a crown. The symbolism of rock royalty, or the "gay queen," was always ambiguously posited.

Yet unlike Bowie or Alice Cooper, few of Mercury's outfits caused outrage or even much notice. Mercury had established himself as a larger-than-life icon, and like Elton John, the wild outfits were assumed to be part of a baroque show. Mercury said that "glamour is a part of us, and we want to be dandy . . . and it was really the dandy thing we were into: dressing up, fooling around" (Rock 2007, 49). Mercury and the band's blasé approach to glam fashion made it less of an issue as the band neatly segued into prog, hard, and retro rock styles.

The group always had fun with popular culture, and those images are rarely covered by the press, who focused solely on Mercury's performances. The band's video for "The Invisible Man" was an exercise in funky electro tones with riffing beats and blurts of sound effects. The members are creatures in a fake house on an early video game console, and a little boy goes about the game/video zapping the cartoonish band as the music percolates through the process. The group ridiculed themselves and video game culture.

QUEEN'S APPROACH

Queen approached pop with theatrics, a sense of mystical awe, a dose of heavy-metal riffing, and a self-deprecating sense of humor. They balanced the pompous silken costumes, the long hair, and the songs containing fairies and elves with guitar overload. Later videos critiqued the band's image and rock culture itself. Mercury's "I'm Going Slightly Mad" illustrated the band's sense of humor with Mercury in fright wig lampooning himself.

Although there were plenty of rockers on Queen's debut, little distinguished them from other heavy metal bands. But in *Queen II*, Mercury asserted a powerful melodic influence over the Brian May tune "Father to Son." Mercury's vocals are controlled and authoritative. The song sets up a strong melody, explores a lengthy solo, and triumphantly returns to the earlier anthem like core themes. May said later that "we wanted to make hard rock music that still had the power of, like, The Who or Led Zeppelin, but with more melody, more harmony, and more texture than had been done before" ("BBC Radio One" 1983). They succeeded brilliantly with a dense sound that could contain elements of music hall, heavy metal, progressive rock bombast, and rock-and-roll silliness.

"Killer Queen" was the surprise radio hit from the band's third album, *Sheer Heart Attack*. Mercury claimed the song came to him in a single night, and it flowed very smoothly. Clearly, Mercury's sharp and literate lyrics are a triumph of political whimsy, discussing a "killer queen" who can take out enemies with laser beams. "Gunpowder gelatin, dynamite with a laser beam." The song has a bouncy, jaunty, music-hall feel but a gritty, driving beat. Roger Taylor's drumming is alternately ornate, delicate, and furious, and Brian May stomps in with another articulate and nimble solo. The band crashes to a furious crescendo and then sends the whole thing home with echo and guitar feedback. This is a hit single that owes nothing to half measures. It is compressed hard rock, skilled songwriting, and smooth production.

Queen's next big hit, "Bohemian Rhapsody" from 1974, was the band's biggest and best-known song and sets in motion the reaction to glam that forced the band and other glam artists to work for versatility. Here, Mercury used his strong background in classical and international music to craft a diverse and knowing piece of pop fantasia. Mercury, the pop artist, mythologer, and clever reflector of the current scene, starts with the question, "Is this the real life, is this just fantasy?" What follows is a mini opera of overwhelming voices, powerful guitar figures, and complex musical movements. At six minutes, the song exceeded the usual single playing time by double. The classical elements seemed guaranteed to drive teens away, and the complexity would drive rock fans to simpler fare. Remarkably, the single was a watershed experience, liberating the band, providing a worldwide hit, and giving them the clout to do whatever they wanted to do for the rest of their careers.

The aftermath of "Bohemian Rhapsody" said more about the band. There were no excessive concept albums, great demands, or ego trips. The band played more dates and commanded higher fees, but stayed extremely loyal to their fan base and remained extremely focused on the types of core pop tunes and metal melodies that they pioneered. Their next album, *A Day at the Races*, continued the soaring tunes of *Night*, and they had another big smash single in "Somebody to Love." But for every pop hit the band produced, there was chilling, angry rock in the next tune. *Night at the Opera*'s leadoff track, "Death on Two Legs," was a bitter, violent attack on someone who had angered Mercury. "You suck my blood like leech, you've taken all my money, and you want more." These blazing vocal parts on Queen's records were compiled and recorded mostly by Mercury.

The band ranked as one of the most theatrical groups in the field. They were exciting and exacting in concert, they utilized video to make their songs more programmatic, and they wrote music for two films, *Flash* and *Highlander*. Director Duncan Mulcahy said, "Queen's music was just right for the [*Highlander*] film. They have a very keen sense of visuals. They wrote very powerful, anthem-type songs, and the film needed just that type of energy" (Rider 1994, 208).

They spent 10 years perfecting a stage persona with Mercury's theatrics, occasional set pieces, and the odd video backdrop. They toured new venues including Eastern Europe and South America, where they were hugely popular. Part of this international appeal might have derived from Freddie Mercury's (a.k.a. Farouk Bulsara) lineage as an Asian, his background as the son of diplomats, and a man who was well traveled and comfortable in world cultures while retaining his Englishness. In fact, from 1974 to 1986, Queen maintained an intense touring schedule, paralleling the trajectory of Led Zeppelin and the Who as a great stadium band. Although their performances were clearly hard work, Queen was immaculately rehearsed and gave the impression of a natural and spontaneous show. They appeared to be genuinely enjoying themselves.

Mercury was a strong front man. Gregarious, but a bit shy offstage, he was a cheerleader in front of thousands. He had an athletic and lithe stage persona who grimaced, delivered, and insinuated the songs with gusto. He bounced around the stage in athletic shoes and tights, dragging his microphone across the stage. Mercury was adept at posturing and striking strategic poses in key parts of each song. Although he occasionally had vocal problems from voice strain, Mercury was one of rock's most durable singers. The persona and loudness of the butch stage performer (emphasized in the title of their live album, *Live Killers*) belied the fact that Mercury was always a strong and sensitive performer of more introspective material. Particularly in songs from *The Miracle* and *Innuendo*, Mercury shines. The band's final live gigs at Knebworth and Wembley Stadium in 1986 scored with fans. Over 120,000 attended the Wembley show, and the band boasted the best lighting and video effects of the era. Queen was always about staging a good show.

Videos for songs like "Bohemian Rhapsody" (1974) filled with complex (at the time) special effects made the group popularizers of the video format. They were often credited with the invention of MTV. In fact, as the eighties loomed, their video work was often brilliant and cleverly rendered. Even the controversial and provocative "I Want to Break Free" from *The Works* illustrated their commitment to theatrical forms. All the members wore drag and played caricatures from the popular British soap opera *Coronation Street*. The hammy performance of the whimsical song showed the group assailing pop as quaintly as the Beatles. Guitarist Brian May thought it may have hurt the band's reputation, but the band continued to produce spirited videos up until Mercury's demise. The video for "The Miracle" featured a charming assortment of child doppelgangers for the band, and there is goofy amusement at watching Brian May play next to pint-sized version of himself, or a child Mercury thrusting his libidinous microphone stand into the air. The song's Beatle-ish style and anthem/nature added to the sense of fun. "The Invisible Man" from the same album mocked video game culture, with the band playing characters in a Donkey Kong house being zapped by a young video gamer.

Mercury and company are wearing VR visors like something out of eighties computer-culture movies like *War Games*.

The band's videos for *Innuendo* are quite inventive. While Mercury's declining health presented problems, the straight-ahead rock of "Headlong" is brimming with traditional Queen energy and bravado—lots of pelvic thrusting in that one. Mercury indulges his theatrical loon side in "I'm Going Slightly Mad." He covers his thinning hair with an outlandish Warholish wig and prances about like the Mad Hatter. Despite Mercury's poor health, in these last videos he gives signature performances. "Days of Our Lives" is heartfelt and plaintive. "Mother Love," from the album *Made in Heaven* and completed after Mercury's death, has a splendid *Alien*-ish science fiction video, with Mercury's melancholy tune framing a dangerous space battle between astronaut and alien.

The band members were accomplished. All functioned as a strong touring ensemble—sensible and gentlemanly business professionals, clever video designers, adroit songwriters with clever melodies and hook-ridden tunes. When performing live, they were a blazing unit, with May's processional rock riffs authoritative and commanding. He held the songs together with a winning attack of distorted guitar fury. Deacon and Taylor placed the rhythm section as a pounding, throbbing machine unit. Even in a later synth-oriented track like "Radio Ga Ga," the powerful thunder of Taylor and Deacon prevent the sameness of synthesized sound from depriving the music of life. Mercury understood the use of the voice, did strengthening exercises like an opera singer to strengthen his instrument, and studied with opera singer, Montserrat Caballé. He even performed an album with her to show his appreciation for the operatic form.

AFTER

The memorial to Freddie Mercury at Montreux describes the singer as a "lover of life and singer of songs." One of the last recordings by Mercury, "Mother Love," ends with a collage of Mercury's voice and vocals, including an early recording of Mercury singing Carole King's classic, "Goin' Back" with Freddie singing, "I think I'm goin' back to the things I loved so well." But true to their theatrical impetus, the band made Mercury's last recording theatrical and not maudlin. They gave the clip to Jim Gillespie, who fashioned a creepy science fiction story around the premise of *Alien*. A lone astronaut fights desperately to keep an alien from taking over the ship. The shape-shifting intruder (actress Alice Krige) finds a picture of the astronaut's wife and inhabits that form. The astronaut must exit the ship via a life pod, with a surprising resolution. Mercury rarely took himself too seriously and, in an interview, joked, "King Mercury, long may she reign" (*Queen: The Days of Our Lives* 1991).

The careers of Queen and Marc Bolan illustrate the complex problems that glam had. Maintaining a postmodern audience was difficult, and continual change was expected. Performers such as Bowie and Roxy learned that, but acts like T. Rex and Queen had to fight for success and had to cope with problems of retooling for new audiences.

THE GABRIEL SOLUTION

Peter Gabriel broke many glam stylistic roadblocks, continually elevating the form, the complexity, and the variety of music. When Gabriel saw that Genesis could become stale and rudimentary, he ventured on a solo career. Combining the winsome songs and personas he crafted with Genesis with a newfound interest in world beat music, Gabriel pioneered new hybrids with glam. He enlisted Robert Fripp of King Crimson, played blends of glam and progressive music, explored intricate rhythms and textures with the help on synthesist Larry Fast on keyboards, and produced Eno-esque sound sculptures in instrumental albums like the *Passion* soundtrack for Martin Scorsese's *Last Temptation of Christ*.

Lastly, Gabriel stepped outside the confines of purely egoistic pop to embrace not only world music, but world concerns (South African apartheid, world hunger, world peace). Though embracing world politics, Gabriel never abandoned politics of identity and disguise. In powerful videos such as the MTV hit "Shock the Monkey," Gabriel deftly combined issues of world culture, Western hegemony, and the crisis of identity for Western peoples. In the video, a wide assortment of guitar and vocal textures compete with flaring keyboard flourishes and staccato rhythms to produce an otherworldly and unsettling effect. Gabriel sings, "cover me, when I sleep." The images illustrate a business man in a suit (Gabriel), confined to a claustrophobic office inhabited by bills and gyrating fluorescent lights. In another room, a monkey sits, an intended victim of medical experiments. The monkey jumps about, but by stages looks oddly calm. As the video progresses, the Western businessman becomes, like the monkey, more agitated as the business equipment and swirling lights become more animated, consuming him. Gabriel moves from conventional dress to tribal African face makeup. He begins to resemble the monkey, and by the frantic end, Gabriel leaps on to his desk, wrestles demonic midgets, and pounds his desk; we aren't certain who is in a cage.

Despite public resistance, Gabriel triumphed over the confinements that glam artists had endured and managed to overcome the trivializing image of glams as merely self-absorbed narcissists. By 1987's mega-platinum *So* album, Gabriel had carved a secure niche for himself as a respectable world artist. He plunged his own money into a comprehensive recording facility in the English resort town of Bath, the Real World studios. He started the successful and insightful

Real World record label that discovered and featured artists from around the globe. He translated the internal search for identity that glam artists pursued in the seventies into a broader global mandate for world identity in the eighties, making musical artists aware that there were many ways to approach the theatrical impulse.

Artists as diverse as Bowie, Eno, Roxy, Madonna, and Gorillaz were involved in these transglobal pastiches of glam theatrics wedded with nationalistic tribal music. Gabriel himself began to work with an assortment of world popsters and continued making complicated music videos featuring himself and a creative ensemble of performers. "Sledgehammer" used the exciting style of clay animation in a video in which Gabriel merges with a plastic cyber-self and transmutes his essence into a dancing cavorting animated character. "Don't Give Up" is a thoughtful meditative ode to artistic integrity produced with longtime friend and associate Kate Bush. "Digging in the Dirt" is a psychoanalytic parable of finding self, at once a personal exploration of honest feelings and emotions, and at the same time, an existential analysis of man's place in a larger context of planets and ecological settings.

Despite the pitfall that confronted many glam artists, Gabriel maintained images of identity politics and role playing while merging aspects of art rock, progressive music, world music, and pop into a dialectical synthesis that kept glam fresh, while refocusing the style on issues outside individuals. For Gabriel, theatre was a world cultural enterprise, not simply the dreams of stardom confined to an ambitious individual. Artists with insight like Gabriel's saw glam and its aesthetic on a larger stage and overcame self-centered, narcissistic, and negative media depictions to allow the form to flower as a natural part of the media-enriched landscape during later decades.

Chapter 6

GLAM IN THE MARGINS

By the time Fried wrote about the dangers of art's degeneration towards theatre in 1967, the process was well under way.

—Michael Archer (1997)

Archer's prejudice against the theatricalization of art in the sixties also reflects the prejudices that affected glam rock. Pop's progressive theatricalization was a means of making pop vital again in the seventies era of increasing fragmentation. Far from delegitimizing pop, acting pop was an acceptance of pop's native theatrical bent. David Pattie wrote that "we should be very wary about any assumption that an easy line between the real and the theatrical can be drawn" (Pattie 2007, 83). Pattie goes further, saying that there is no reason to assume because something is theatricalized, it must necessarily be less authentic. Painters like Warhol who seemed to praise surface over depth were recognizing the new image-based reality of seventies postmodern society, a place where the image predominated. Music was also replacing musical codes with style codes. Metal, soft rock, funk, glam, and punk each had a distinguishing look, and John Walker wrote that, "in the twentieth century, the most popular cultural forms—the cinema, rock concerts, stage musicals, television—have tended to be mixed-media" (Walker 1987, 9). By the seventies, image and music were inseparable.

Art and music both turned to appropriation to make sense of the complex image world. Richard Appignanesi and David Garratt have said Madonna is the "'queen of appropriation,' taking on the personae of Hollywood superstars and even presenting herself as an all-purpose porn sex symbol" (Appignanesi and Garratt 2003, 148). Like music, art had lost direction as well. Michael Archer argued that "there was no preferred way of working that would cover all circumstances and requirements, and the idea that an artist should have a signature style, as Newman had his zips and Mark Rothko his fuzzy rectangles ... ceased to make much sense" (Archer 1997, 62). Consequently, glams shed styles like layers of skin. If music was their passion, then performance became the vehicle for delivering that music.

But as glams continually changed their performance methods, audiences often could not keep up. As glam artists proliferated and used a wider palette of performance styles, audiences became more confused. Where did the fantasy of the role end, and the reality of the performer begin? Edward Lucie-Smith commented that a problem with seventies art was that "one must hold the whole history of modern art in one's head in order to comprehend it" (Lucie-Smith 1980, 7). The chaotic art scene dictated that glams would have a difficult time maintaining a connection with an audience, who like the performers themselves, held identities in constant flux.

POP AND ELTON JOHN

Glam not only arrived as a style unto itself, but also was cannibalized by other styles. The dawning postmodern era provided massive media choices, and the explosion of various options allowed constant and continuing reinvention of pop stars. Still others adopted glam as a strategy for a brief time. Different formats interacted with glam over time, borrowing techniques from the glam style to accentuate a performer. Pop and glam had a wide convergence in the early seventies, with everyone from Elvis to Abba to Sonny and Cher wearing skintight sequined outfits and featuring choreography prominently.

One popster who dabbled in the glam style and has returned to it fitfully is Elton John. Though not considered totally a part of the glam movement, Elton John, like David Bowie, was a veteran of the sixties pop scene, and like Bowie, he understood the need to move with the times. Born Reginald Dwight, John started his career as an aspiring songwriter and bluesy pianist, who won fame in the early seventies with a series of sensitive singer/songwriter albums that birthed hits such as "Your Song" and "Border Song." There was a touch of gospel and American soul, and Elton howled like his blues heroes. But as the glam movement accelerated, John quickly jumped on board, turning himself into a living spectacle. He wore outrageous outfits, and he bought hundreds of outlandish glasses—some had over 70 lights, others were diamond-studded, and some spelled out his name. To cover his thinning hair, he wore a wide range of hats and comedy costumes, including a Donald Duck suit, drag dresses, military regalia, and track suits. He bounced and pounded on his piano imitating Jerry Lee Lewis, and he composed songs in everything from retro rock

("Crocodile Rock") to symphonic prog ("Funeral for a Friend") to dark, gothic tomes dealing with perversity and homosexuality ("All the Girls Love Alice"). Despite the fact the John was principally the writer of the melody and collaborator Bernie Taupin wrote the lyrics, it is clear that Taupin wrote detailed stories that told Elton's story and interests as well as his own. But Elton continued to work in glam style long after the form was widely dismissed. He dressed in Mozart-style classical wear for "Live in Australia" and wore a twenties-style straw hat ensemble for "I'm Still Standing." In 2008, he performed in Las Vegas with a massive female body set complete with a 20-foot lipstick tube. At the end of "Saturday Night's Alright," two giant breasts hanging above the stage squirted white confetti on the crowd from their nipples.

John and Taupin were dubious about John as a performer. Mostly, John had been a shy and retiring pianist with a bluesy R & B–influenced voice. Taupin's lyrics showed a decided interest in American pop culture. *Tumbleweed Connections* strongly favors the South and old Wild West, while *Goodbye Yellow Brick Road* features Hollywood icons in songs like "The Ballad of Danny Bailey" (John and Taupin's take on gangster films), "All the Young Girls Love Alice" (a tribute to the era of women's films), and "Candle in the Wind," Taupin's stirring tribute to the legend of Marilyn Monroe. Together, their music was beginning to illustrate a theatrical cinematic flare. John's score supported the romantic film *Friends*. Judy Parkinson wrote, "Elton's stage costumes were the armor under which he could hide, and the more elaborate they became, the more he could conceal his real self, and more fun he had with his audience" (Parkinson 2003, 61).

DISCO AND GRACE JONES

> Models are there to look like mannequins, not like real people. Art and illusion are supposed to be fantasy.
>
> —Grace Jones

Other genres interacted with glam, notably disco. Like glam, disco was involved with presentation, façade, and artifice. Disco's insistent beat, focus on dance culture, and lure of narcissistic pleasure prevented most people from taking it as a serious musical form. But European producers, bored by staccato beats, repetitive lyrics, and blasé themes, determined to lift the form from its cultural ghetto towards new heights. Glam had highlighted the theatrical, used narrative structures, interrogated themes about media, and questioned issues of gender, culture, and identity. The genre needed artists who were similarly adventuresome in their ability to hybridize forms. Such a creature was Grace Jones, who herself grew up an outsider, a visitor in various cultures, and a symbol of the disparity between visual culture and substance.

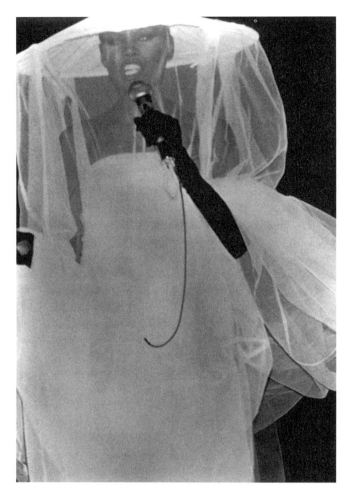

Grace Jones broke color and aesthetic barriers, seamlessly merging the worlds of disco, fashion, and art rock with the theatricality of glam. Still a potent force, Jones merges ethnic styles, incandescent singing, and sonic atmospheres in an intoxicating brew. (Courtesy of Photofest.)

Grace Jones was born in 1948 as Grace Mendoza in Jamaica, one of seven children of a seamstress and fundamentalist preacher. Her family moved to Syracuse, New York, and for a time Grace attended college there and majored in theatre. From an early age, the music of the islands was in her blood. By 1968, she had left college to seek fame as a model, performer, and nightclub entertainer in Philadelphia and New York. She began to get modeling contracts for appearances in magazines due to her striking features: chiseled cheekbones; piercing eyes; a lithe, sinewy, androgynous body; and a smirking, campy attitude towards life. She refers to her early career as a "campaign" for attention, and she spent years dancing on tables, wearing bizarre outfits, and scandalizing society in Manhattan. On occasion, she would appear topless and create a spectacle. Finally, *Elle* magazine reported her as a feature story, and her career as a model, singer, and actress was launched. She posed for *Elle*, *Vogue*, and *Pravada*, and proved to be as popular in Europe as in the United States. While pretending to be a singer for a photo session, someone suggested (to the photography community's surprise) that Jones could sing. She quickly acquired a record contract with Island Records and had a disco hit with the ironic tune "I Need a Man." She debuted at the *Les Mouches* (The Flies) disco to a crowd of mostly gay, adoring fans. As others have written, Jones made a complicated statement, striding to the stage in her manly garb, singing "I Need a Man" to a room of mostly homosexuals. Without knowing it, Jones had made the gender questioning that was subtextual in much of glam overt in disco.

An astute student of the disco scene, Jones could see that lengthy beat tracks were aesthetically unfulfilling. She was determined to remake herself. As a daughter of a large household of children, Jones was used to finding ways to stand out. As a black woman, she was aware that makeup intended for white models did little to accentuate her bark-colored skin. She designed her own makeup and techniques to augment her vibrant flesh tones with flattering colors. She wore outrageous costumes that bolstered her nearly six-foot stature. Jones also approached music as performance. She was friends with Warhol, who had made show, pretense, and surface an art form. She was married for a time to photographer Jean-Paul Goode, who arranged her intricate and cleverly choreographed shows and staged her as a photographer would stage a model. She assailed Edith Piaf's "La Vie en Rose" in a disco version complete with a prop accordion draped across her frame.

Jones did not avoid controversy, and her performances to gay audiences, dancing to a group of sweaty gay men at discos while she herself wore a very butch, close-cropped, symmetrical, geometric hairstyle, drew criticism that Jones lionized the gay community. She went further, puzzling civil rights groups by appearing as a panther in a cage. These controversial images seemed to signal to the black community that Jones was willing to confront dehumanizing stereotypes of African Americans as less than human. But at the same time, such portrayals troubled groups who saw her as simply another caricature of the black-faced entertainer. Clearly, the sexual ambiguity of her look and her stage presence made her a popular icon for gay audiences. Though Jones was principally heterosexual, she understood the growth of the gay audiences, and this prompted her to play with sexual and taboo images that society had wished to avoid.

In *Nightclubbing*, Jones began to experiment with more rocking rhythms and grander pop structures. Her brooding and atmospheric "Walking in the Rain" featured not only a disco beat, but also suggested a subdued dynamics, a threat of menace not previously seen in disco, and a palpable aura of drama. Jones's version of The Police's "Demolition Man" is chaotic and trumps the original with its masterful sense of anger and authority. Throughout her career, Jones suggested the strong crossover possibilities for glam and disco. Though glam focused on performance, rock, and electronic instrumentation, disco's movement from mere rhythm to electro-digital technology and a coldly inhuman beat explored the post-human themes of glam, providing a capable vehicle to mix theatre and pop sensibilities in the burgeoning digital era.

In her one-woman show, entitled *One Man Show* for ironic reasons, Jones pursues a wide range of video and stage effects to produce a memorable event. At one point, she steps across the stage in short Kabuki footfalls, filmed in fast motion that gives her the appearance of a cartoon figure. She stops and stands on the edge of an oversized stage staircase and pulls out a large trombone. She appears to blow into it, but instead a loud, percussive sound effect signals the start of "Demolition Man." As the rough instrumental takes shape, Jones stares at the audience in robotic poses, like a female Terminator. She shouts and declaims the lines of the song like a political despot. Behind her stand, a chorus of Grace Jones clones (produced in rear-screen digital projection), all adorned in smart sharkskin business suits and dark glasses, march in time to the music's military beat. In "Libertango," a tune that conflates liberation with the restraining power of a tango beat, Jones appears wearing a set of geometric face appliances, cones, triangles, and squares that cover her head, her mouth, and her nose. As the tune begins, a pair of disembodied hands wearing gloves pulls the appliances from her face (attached by rubber bands) and cuts them free. She is ironically "freed" by the tango. As Jones, wearing black and an accordion, finishes the song, a series of disembodied hands applaud the diva (*Diva* is also one of her album titles). The entire program is a piece of performance art and works as a tightly choreographed spectacle against state-of-the-art lighting effects.

Jones continued through the eighties working with a series of experimental music producers that straddled pop, disco, prog, and theatrical genres. In 1986, she worked with Trevor Horn (Yes, Seal, Frankie Goes to Hollywood) on the *Slave to the Rhythm* album. In essence one tune endlessly remixed, the album was a massive experiment in transforming a single composition into different guises. Jones also used the controversial title of "slave" to suggest that there was an issue of bondage to the music in the same way African Americans were actually in real slavery. The album is drenched in complicated audio production work, and actor Ian McShane contributes his voice to the proceedings as a narrator and links the various cuts together. The album is a concept piece showing the variety of Jones's voices and her link to aesthetic art rock and glam rock gestures, and it broadens her grasp of rock idioms. Her next album, *True Story*, featured the rough-and-tumble rocker "Crush" with a strong beat, and a rousing instrumental track. The single "I'm Not Perfect (but I'm Perfect for You)" illustrated more of Jones's over-the-top performance style and sense of humor. In the video, she plays a giant singer, towering above the backup singers and her fan base. Jones is joking about her size, both figurative and real. As she sings about her lack of perfection, commentators including Andy Warhol deadpan that "Grace is perfect!" In the background, artist Keith Haring is painting a variety of symbols on a large canvas, and soon Jones is wearing the giant 20-foot canvas as a skirt. There are bright colors and elements of African tribal wear, and Jones's cosmopolitan assemblage suggests complex video montage, years before that became practical.

Through this album, we catch glimpses of the real Grace Jones. A funny and charming person, she uses her larger-than-life persona to project media images. Her 1989 *Bulletproof Heart* was another album of tough rockers. After that, Jones took 20 years off, married, focused on family life, reorganized her finances, performed in a few films, lent her image to a video game, released an occasional single, and appeared on stage fitfully. She returned in 2008, having lost none of her ferocious bite, with the album *Hurricane* that showed new maturity and tenderness. This was a more autobiographical tome about her family life in Jamaica. "The Williams Blood" talks about her blood line. In the video, she sings in a giant hat in a gay club with a chorus of gay men behind her. In "Corporate Cannibal," she discusses the practice of companies devouring each other, and she starts off in a threatening tone saying, "Pleased to meet you, pleased to have you on my plate." Through the track, Jones repeats that her job is to be a man-eating, killing machine. Jones performs against a wildly distorted background in which her head and body become progressively violated by video synthesis. In "This is Life," Jones works against a stark rhythm machine track. The work is diverse, and Jones also delivers powerful rockers and quiet touching ballads.

Jones retains her theatrical bent, and in Jon Caramanica's review of her recent live show, he describes Jones as still a stage performer, "during 'I've Seen That Face Before (Libertango),' Ms. Jones danced an improvised tango with a mannequin head, then kissed it and held it to her breast" (Caramanica 2009). Jones uses the irony of working with a mannequin to illustrate that the images are all manipulated, all contrived, and all disposable. Before Madonna was synthesizing dance performance and choreographed shows, Jones had mixed glam, dance, and theatre sensibilities, producing wild shows that showcased elaborate costume changes and stage effects.

METAL AND ALICE COOPER

When we did "School's Out," I knew we had just done the national anthem. I've become the Francis Scott Key of the last day of school.
—Alice Cooper (quoted in Fussman 2009)

Glam wasn't able to survive without partnerships. The music hall tradition, the cross-dressing comedy of England, and the transgressive spirit was absent in America. What the colonies wanted was naked aggression, and the rock concert, the wrestling arena, and the Wild West show presented the American audience with their form of vulgar, debased, and proletarian theatre. If glam was to reach America, it had to rip victory from the acid-crunch chords of heavy metal. Ian Christie, in *Sound of the Beast: The Complete Headbanging History of Heavy Metal*, argued that groups like Black Sabbath arose from "the downside of English society, the unemployed . . . people regarded as morally suspect and of negligible social worth" (Christie 2004, 1). Metal was born in the industrial wastes of Northern England by groups like Deep Purple, Black Sabbath, and Led Zeppelin. Whereas John Lennon moaned to Chuck Berry, Robert Plant wailed to Howlin' Wolf behind the sounds of Jimmy Page's thousand guitar productions. The sheer volume and distorted cacophony of metal was a scream against the brutality of a socialist society that promised much but gave little to English citizens. All they could look forward to was a life on the dole and a sense of no future. Metal was an angry, raging, rebellious cry against such a fate, and the music fed upon the ravaged feelings of hopeless young people who needed heroes that shared their plight. This was a music of anger and bitterness.

But metal went further than mere rebellion and elevated the struggle of youth to allegorical levels. Christie writes that "a resonating echo from a distance of long ago, the music dramatized the conflicts of humans on earth not as current event news stories but as mythic struggles" (Christie 2004, 5). For heavy-metal enthusiasts, the story of modern suffering and economic blight had parallels in the history of the world. Heavy metallers dressed in grim medieval garb, like renaissance wizards and knights. They perceived their struggle as universal and eternal.

Alice Cooper was destined to life in mythology. Born Vince Furnier to a family of Pentecostal preachers, grown in the rugged old West of Phoenix, Arizona, and schooled in the theatrics of Saturday afternoon wrestling programming, Cooper believed America was saturated with myth images. The Cooper band, formed at Cortez High School, was roughly modeled on the Rolling Stones. Cooper understood that rock was transforming rebellion into a marketable commodity. He commented that "what we do is make sure that if some kid pays $6 to see a show he's not just going to see some guy playing guitar. He is going to see something he will never forget" ("Schlock Rock's Godzilla" 1973). Cooper elevated the glam content in the shows. He delighted in a close rapport with the audience, and he sparred with them in raucous displays of camaraderie and raunch. In one concert, he yelled into the crowd, "Do you want to kiss me?" and when a boy replied "Yes," Cooper dismissed him meanly, calling out provocatively, "faggots are all alike."

Cooper realized that performing any sort of theatrical show suggested to some a queer guise, and Cooper found ways to maintain theatricality while projecting strong gender messages. In early shows, working with limited budgets, Cooper would simply drape the band and audience members in white sheets. Cooper commented that "I think that sometimes those things make a creepier show than elaborate props" ("Livewire's One on One" 2001). Cooper's strategy was to be outrageous and to provide a freak show, and the press dubbed his act *shock rock* due to his use of exotic and violent props, liberal borrowing from old horror films, and vaudeville schtick. The band journeyed to Los Angeles and was signed by Frank Zappa to his Straight label. After performing two lackluster hard rock albums, they met producer Bob Ezrin, who urged them to move to a more theatrical pop/metal position.

Cooper and guitarist Michael Bruce were keen to be successful and wrote a series of pop concept songs that established the group as a rebellious, gothic, metal, performance band. Their breakthrough came in the song "I'm Eighteen," in which they sang of a youth that "just don't know what I want." In the Ezrin-produced album *Love It to Death* (1971), the band began to transform their psychedelic, rambling rock into a tighter, focused structure. *Love It to Death*'s cover featured Alice and the band wearing bright polyester dresses, long hair, and makeup, setting up many features of glam and hair metal bands. Always the provocateur, Cooper sticks a finger out of his pants to resemble a penis. The band affected a sick, stoned, and menacing bad-boy pose. When Cooper was interviewed for a Finnish television station in 1973, he explained that "when audiences see someone named Alice Cooper they expect to see a blonde folk singer, but what they see is me! I like to do things like that" ("Alice Cooper Interview").

Cooper personally adopted a character that was a master of ceremonies, horror icon, drunken lout, and devilish prankster. The band produced a blistering set of cinematic rock albums. *Killer* held the dark and sensuous "Desperado," a song inspired by actor Robert Vaughn's performance in *The Magnificent Seven*. *School's Out* had the anti-education anthem of the same name. *Billion Dollar Babies* was an epic portrayal of mid-seventies America beset by rising fuel prices, bad wars, and corrupt politics. Cooper commented that the sixties rockers were people who "died of excess" (Fussman 2009). He saw himself as the tail end of a society infatuated with overindulgence. He told *Time* magazine, "all I do is project fantasies. I don't preach. The only message is here I am and what are you going to do about me? I'm sort of a spit in the face" ("Schlock Rock's Godzilla" 1973).

Cooper masterfully helmed a raucous stage review in the *Billion Dollar Babies* tour, and a strong record of the tour, *Good to See You Again* exists as a powerful documentary of the concert/band experience. Cooper wears a white leotard and sings "Raped and Freezin" while petting a mannequin torso. He drools spit on it and licks it off. But beyond goofy pop schtick, Cooper starts the film with a standard dance number in a pink tuxedo and a Hollywood setting reminiscent of *Gentlemen Prefer Blondes* and fifties Technicolor MGM musicals. He dances down an all-pink staircase and set and sidles up to a bewigged lounge pianist, while the Cooper band, all playing orchestral instruments, sit uncomfortably in short-haired wigs and pink tuxedoes. Eventually, Cooper and the band become annoyed with the directorial concept, tear off their clothes, and smash the piano. Arguing that the film is their work, and they have no obligation to conform, they storm out. It is classic meta-theatre, with Cooper the showman using a theatrical gimmick reminiscent of a *Monkees* episode to proclaim his own vile theatricality. Later in the film, in "Under My Wheels," the song grinds to a halt, a frame around the drummer drops, and an American flag pops out. Cooper grabs it and carries it around the stage, while the band lights sparklers and fireworks to proudly proclaim their patriotism. They stand off to the side and a Richard Nixon clone enters. The band begins to beat him senseless. The crowd explodes into laughter and cheers.

In a 1975 performance of "Steven," Cooper mourns a dead dancer on stage, and then is grabbed and chased by an eight-foot Cyclops with a headlamp eyeball. Cooper eventually cuts off the monster's head and parades it around the stage. The dead dancer is now a blood-lusting vampire. Cooper ends her with a stake through the heart. Meanwhile, a variety of spider-costumed dancers swarm across the stage and occupy a large spider web that has dropped across the proscenium.

Cooper in recent years has argued that audiences are more difficult to shock. He told *Livewire*, "you know I don't know if they can be (shocked) anymore. I think television does more shocking things" ("Livewire's One on One" 2001). Cooper branched out in the late seventies/eighties, embracing everything from children's programming to metal music, focusing on a rough, less theatrical delivery. But occasionally, he reached back to his horror show bag of tricks. In an appearance on the *Muppet Show* in 1978, Cooper emerged from a coffin in full Dracula regalia and sang "Welcome to My Nightmare" to a chorus of Muppet dancers and musicians. He projected animated ghouls and ghosts from his arms and eventually disappeared in a puff of smoke.

Videos for 1994's *The Last Temptation* cast him again as ringmaster in top hat, with images of flame-throwing freaks, snakes, clocks, spiders, hypnotists and beautiful dead damsels littering the landscape. The epic production was a horror tale montaged in a Freudian/Salvador Dali dreamscape.

In a later show, Cooper is featured as a mugger singing "Wicked Young Man" while throttling a nurse walking by with a baby carriage. For 2000's Brutal Planet tour, the concert opens with a cyborg in a box warning the audience to leave before the evil master, Alice Cooper, arrives. Too late—Cooper enters in silhouette from the top of a long staircase. He parades to the front of the stage dressed in red leather and sporting Japanese sticks in his hair. On his back, he has a long-sheathed Samurai sword, which he employs to threaten the audience. A girl walks by, and Cooper shoves her into the trunk of a burned-out derelict car. With Cooper in charge, it is a brutal planet. The *Along Came a Spider* video in 2008 continues the grim images and dark ideas. This time featuring metal guitarist Slash, in the video, Cooper is committed to a hospital. He sings, "they tried so hard to bury me, but I survived it every time." The song, "Vengeance Is Mine," suggests that Cooper doesn't need a comeback as much as simply some new victims. While Slash solos away, Cooper gleefully garrotes a slutty nurse in green bra, maroon hair, and overly painted nails. Things go from bad to worse as Cooper and company sing amongst the disabled and psychotic inmates of the asylum. Again, Cooper strangles several women and then is dragged away. In the morgue, he sings, "Killed by Love" as he unpacks a variety of medical scalpels and saws. He prepares to dismantle a beautiful blonde female corpse in a purple satin party dress. As the video ends, Cooper has more homicidal fantasies as the attendants drag him back to his cell.

While many other glam acts have worried that theatrical aspects might alienate fans, over the decades, Cooper has embraced his style more fervently. He explained that, "I don't mind being the Vincent Price of rock and roll ... I always thought that Vincent Price movies were scary but funny ... I think that's what the Alice Cooper Show should be" ("Livewire's One on One" 2001).

GOTH, SIOUXSIE, THE BANSHEES, AND THE CURE

> The gothic and the Grotesque applied to the visual arts, as to literature, remain fluid types that transcend formal categorization and resist definite conceptualization through a multiplicity of metaphorical meanings.
> —"Unsolved Mysteries," Christoph Grunenberg (1997, 170)

Though performers like Alice Cooper and David Bowie had already invited gothic images into the glam world, the darkness of rock began to evolve in different directions. After glam was eclipsed by the burgeoning punk movement, the Sex Pistols became a raging phenomenon and practiced their own rock theatre of outrage. Malcolm McLaren, the Sex Pistols' manager and the intellectual stimulus to the band remarked that, "as soon as something became good—a shirt, a dress, a design, a shop, the group—I'd destroy it immediately and start something else" (McLaren 1998, 1077). Indeed, punk flamed brightly for an instant, but beyond outrage, the punks offered little musical innovation. In a sense, punk went beyond glam but rejected elements of glam's culture and sophistication. But there were others who took the outrage of the seventies in a direction that merged the ferocity of punk with the whimsy and mood swings of glam. They were the goths. As Grunenberg pointed out, gothic influences are porous and filter into other art forms but often are hard to define in themselves. Goth's influence on glam is similarly complex. Goths were so named for their infatuation with "gothic" culture.

The Goths were a notorious and destructive tribe who roamed Europe near the end of the Roman Empire, causing destruction and chaos. The form in architecture referred to French architecture of the twelfth century and was deemed "Gothic" by high-minded Italian artists who saw it as loathsome and inferior, and "thus the style was labeled 'Gothic,' with a decidedly derogatory intent" (Benton and DiYanni 2008, 271). The style was revived in the nineteenth century, influencing British art, literature and fashion, and "was designed to evoke the spiritual and ethical values of the Middle Ages" (Benton and DiYanni 2008, 457).

Many theories have been suggested for the style's return in the seventies. One idea is that postmodern artists, in attempting to flush modernist ideas from experimentation began using more far-reaching sources and sought the medieval era for inspiration. Hebdige points out that, "subcultures represent 'noise' (as opposed to sound): interference in the orderly sequence which leads from real events and phenomena to their representation in the media" (Hebdige 1979, 90). For theorists, Goths were, like glams, a strong dissonant chord in society. Goodlad and Bibby commented that "goth's costume code is conspicuous for its eclectic historical references including the Renaissance, the eighteenth century and especially the nineteenth century Gothic revival and Victorian styles" (Goodlad and Bibby 2007, 138). Goodlad and Bibby conclude that the Goth dress code continued to pick up cues from Hollywood horror films and dystopian science fiction. Another explanation was simply a lack of satisfaction with the progressive West, which provided little romance, visual splendor, or baroque embellishments to daily life. Comparatively, goth, with its throwback to medieval fashions, dirge-like melodies, and undead makeup, gave everyday life the glamour of playing dress up, and transporting its adherents to another time and place, a distinctly glam concept.

One of the Sex Pistols' principal fans was Siouxsie Sioux, who evolved from the torn and tattered punk shamble to an elegant, teased hairstyle, Asian-influenced clothing, and Kabuki-style makeup. Her fan band ventured into the goth category, cherishing darker feelings and emotions. Siouxsie appeared on a British talk show as part of the fan brigade for the Pistols. She wore revealing outfits and wild eye makeup in an effort to establish her own fame. Eventually, the nascent band landed a gig at London's 100 Club. Few of the original members knew anything about playing instruments, and they had to borrow equipment from the more professional band the Clash. Their first performance featured a 20-minute droning version of "The Lord's Prayer," described as "unbearable" (Bracewell 2005). Whereas the Sex Pistols boasted expressionistic outrage, the spirit that anyone should be free to make music, Siouxsie Sioux and Steve Severin transformed that undirected rage into darkly melodic, psychedelic strains that reflected the hysteria of teen angst but also projected an aesthetic façade of fatalistic dread. John Doran of the BBC writes that, "their first Peel session . . . shows a band who still had trace elements of glam rock, were strangely psychedelic, tribal, and stentorian" (Doran 2009).

The band worked with neo-psychedelia producer Steve Lillywhite, who had worked with Gary Numan and Ultravox. For their first work, they focused their energies on a zombie/postapocalyptic sound. Siouxsie noted, "there was a healthy fear of our appearance" (Bracewell 2005). They named their album *The Scream*, which people thought reflected an interest in the dark expressionistic art of Edvard Munch, the Norwegian painter who drew women as vampires and images of desolation, depression, and depravity. Also, Frank Perry's seventies film *The Swimmer*, with its story of an alienated, mentally disturbed man swimming his way across neighborhood pools, was a source. *The Scream*'s cover shows seemingly drowning men and women struggling under turbulent, black water. The glam aesthetics of goth groups was the result of visual images, and the Banshees sought a performance that served as a cultural event. Their first hit single was the charming and friendly "Hong Kong Garden," which used chiming percussive sounds and xylophone to create the brittle tone of chopsticks and Asian instruments. Michael Bracewell of the *Guardian* called it, "one of those records that immediately summoned up a world view—dark, tense, eerily erotic" (Bracewell 2005). Siouxsie wore dark leather costumes, exposed parts of her body, often performed in a trance-like focused mantra, or danced wildly and frenzied. On *The Scream*, Siouxsie and the band exhibited a sound that far exceeded the limitations of punk. Siouxsie commented that "the labeling of 'punk' . . . (was) the death of its vital energy" (Ibid.). Siouxsie and the band knew they had to journey in a different direction for inspiration. Severin said, "we, perversely, saw ourselves as taking on the baton of glamorous art rock—Bowie and Roxy Music" (Ibid.). The linear notes to the reissued *Scream* (2005) denoted that the Banshees were "not so much a band as an idea, this first Banshees prototype was little more than a violent tempest of social disaffection looking for a focus" (liner notes, *The Scream* reissue, 2005).

In 2004, Siouxsie and Budgie returned to London to play the Royal Festival Hall on October 16 for the elegant *Siouxsie/Dreamshow* performance. The band even arranged a playful warmup gig in the tiny 100 Club in London, the place they first played as the Banshees nearly 30 years earlier. In a video documentary of the event, Siouxsie explained that "the show was a dream come true to work with a fifteen piece orchestra" (*Siouxsie/Dreamshow* 2005). Here Budgie and Siouxsie reorchestrated and produced glamorous, sophisticated versions of their work as the Banshees and their other incarnations. Siouxsie said that, "as a performer, I have a lot of material to draw from including material from the Banshees and The Creatures (her offshoot rhythm band with Budgie)" (*Siouxsie/Dreamshow* 2005). Siouxsie conceived the evening as a retrospective of her 30-plus-year career, including 27 songs from all stages in her evolution. The backup group was a simple four-piece band, including keyboards plus two backup singers. Augmenting the sound, the band was supported by a 15-piece orchestra, the Millennia Ensemble, including a brass-and-string section to provide a variety of orchestral textures to Siouxsie's often edgy, brittle compositions. Budgie's blazing drum work was supported and supplemented by Taiko drum performer Leonard Eto, who added a furious energy to the performance. The drumming complexity added a manic and multicultural identity to the show, making Siouxsie's already exotic stylings deeply intercultural. Siouxsie entered in a long black-and-red gown appearing like a wild kabuki dancer and danced her way to center stage. In Japanese regalia and makeup, Siouxsie performed an incantatory version of "Say Yes!" a piece that was more a tribal invocation than an actual melody. This was merged with "Around the World," an opening that seemed closer to a call to worship, a ceremony of dark rituals than an actual series of songs. The brooding "Seven Tears" focused the ensemble on a dark, mournful mood, with lyrics describing "raging horses and tsumanis." By "Standing There," the show had evolved into a mutated big band ensemble. The powerful horn section had given the unit a strong suggestion of nostalgia, and the Banshees' music slid into a time warp recalling the loud and raucous dance hall music of the World War II period. The program featured drum ensemble, orchestral music, light show, and Sioux playacting a vamp, harlot, injured soul, and harsh dominatrix to the crowd. Siouxsie even purred her lyrics in a low growl alto voice that she used seductively on the audience. As she entered her fifties, Siouxsie still portrayed a wide range of characters, acts, dances like someone 20 years younger, and still relishes the roles that glam gave her. She told Bracewell that "someone asked me how it felt to be the queen of goth . . . but I would much rather be known as the Ice Queen" (Bracewell 2005).

MOODY GLAM, GOTH, AND THE CURE

Bands like the Banshees personalized the goth sound to reflect inner turmoil. Others saw goth as an expression of the disruption and disharmony in modern postindustrial society. Csaba Toth argued that goth reflected "the postindustrial disappearance of the laboring body against the backdrop of vacant factory yards, deserted farms, bleak downtowns, a polluted environment, and ever-present television screens. In this Gothic land of the end of the long cycle (of the post-war boom), boundaries between the 'normal' and pathologized 'other' collapse, and the 'normal' is often more dreadful than its unnatural opposite" (Toth 1997, 88). Many goth groups agreed with Toth; the normal of modern society was more frightening than the abnormal. At least the suffering, anguished, and moaning sound of a human meant you were alive, or at least undead. Such a believer was Robert Smith, who said that at 14, he wanted to "sit on top of a mountain and just die" (Thompson 2000, 5). For Smith and his peers, pop music was a way to relieve the angst of living in a disturbing world. Nancy Kilpatrick, in *The Goth Bible*, wrote that, "most people concur that goth is a darker offspring of punk, and the bastard pansexual cousin of glam emerging from the mists in England sometime n the mid-1970s" (Kilpatrick 2004, 79). Smith was one of those early innovators. The later founder of the Cure decided to start a group with his brother and sister and school friends. The aptly named the Group performed a strange amalgam of songs by the Sensational Alex Harvey Band, David Bowie, and Jimi Hendrix in their own warped and bizarre way. Part of the structure of their style was the odd assemblage of influences. Harvey and Bowie brought an audacious mix of theatricality, self-confession, and music-hall madness to the music. Hendrix's wild style brought a rough, experimental, psychedelic flavor to their sound, and of course, Smith brought his own teenage neuroses to the brew.

In the aftermath of the first glam era, Smith mixed a morose blend of melody and melancholy in goth music. Like other youth disgusted with bleak postin-dustrial England, Smith longed for a romantic blend of images and fantasy. Goth was a place to channel mystic past worlds. But the world of gothic fantasy was itself a fantasy from the fevered pens of T. E. White's *Once and Future King* and *Book of Merlin*, Tennyson's "Morte d'Arthur," and Sir Walter Scott's *Ivanhoe*. The Pre-Raphaelite brotherhood concocted beautiful medieval maidens and pretty mythic representations of the medieval period, again prompting more romantic, wrong-headed views of the gothic period. Illustrations by medievalist Arthur Rackham that pictured delirious fairies and more modern craftsmen like Reg Kelly (*Prince Valiant*) and Frank Frazetta conjured a beautiful but nightmarish world of castles, stalwart knights, and fetching princesses. Still, Hollywood compounded the misimpressions of a feudal romantic era with *Knights of the Round Table*, *Ivanhoe*, *Prince Valiant*, *Monty Python and the Holy Grail*, *Camelot*, *Ladyhawk*, *First Knight*, and a host of other films that propagandized the Middle Ages as a glamorous, costumed spectacular.

By 1981, they were playing a music that was evolving from raw punk roots to a more sophisticated atmospheric blend of horror movie sensibilities. "Other Voices" from the *Faith* album showed the group performing in a misty room that seemed to be composed of a spider cage of ceiling beams. Smith moaned/cried the lyrics to "Other Voices": "you brush past my skin, as soft as fur." Smith's pervasive moan sounded like the longings of a 15-year-old boy for some girl and sexual adventure. Nancy Kilpatrick referred to his brand of singing as the story of Dracula as told "from Mina Harker's viewpoint" (Kilpatrick 2004, 81). In truth, Smith did a lot to feminize and civilize the sounds of punk and glam. Gone was the consistent anger and bile of punk goth pioneered by Siouxsie Sioux. Smith replaced Sioux's energy with a mournful, melancholic warble, a wispy, moaning, sad revelry. In fact, at 50, Smith sounded relatively unchanged, but there is no condescension or pandering to teen emotions. In fact, the thing that distinguishes the Cure's act and Smith's theatricality is the completeness of his identification with these childish emotions. He isn't that child anymore, but he continues to deliver and appear to feel the longings and anxieties of youth in a very real way.

In the Cure's fourth album, *Pornography*, a title that upset their record company, the band began to consolidate a style that would secure them a devout cult following for nearly the next 30 years. The lead track, "One Hundred Years," is a brooding, doom-laden canvas of expressionist angst; metallic, mechanical drum sounds; raging, moaning guitars; crying vocals; and a muffled, cloudy mix. The lyrics present an epic depiction of futility. Smith starts by singing, "It doesn't matter if we all die, Ambition in the back of a black car." The lyric and mood presume nightmares to follow. Smith sings of world endings, mournful lives, and apocalyptic frenzies, but despite the rigors of a long and hardy tour schedule, Smith's life has seemed regular and stable.

The 1987 double album *Kiss Me, Kiss Me, Kiss Me* is an appalling epic of anger and bile. Smith had threatened to quit the business, and the album seemed like a cry for help for someone tired of the anxiety of trying to please fans, record companies, and critics. Considering that Smith was only 28, carrying the weight of writing, and producing the band, touring regularly, spending long hours in rehearsal, promotion, and video and live performance, it was easy to see the roots of his exhaustion. The album had clever single tracks like "Hot, Hot, Hot" and the worldwide pop smash, "Why Can't I Be You?" Smith and the band danced about in gorilla suits and cavorted across the stage. The joking video suggested that the band was becoming a group of performing monkeys and that the group wanted to be an audience again, people who could afford to be normal. Smith's angst-ridden vocals explored his troubled psyche. For all the adulation, for all the money, and for all the copy generated, Smith was saying he wanted out. "Why Can't I Be You" is an aggressive track, with horns pounding against the beat, a frantic and jazzy arrangement, a delirious vocal that spirals out of control, and an ending that stops the madness abruptly. Smith's questioning identity seems best served when he is trying to lose himself in his work. Most disturbing is the thunderous title track "The Kiss," which beckons like a descent into hell. As crunch chords collide, Smith cries, "love me, love me, love me, your tongue's like poison, I wish you were dead, I wish you were dead." Ironically, that same year, Smith married longtime girlfriend Mary Poole. Despite the cacophony of his music, the violent emotions expressed in such songs, Smith seemed to have found a strong balance between the negativity expressed in his lyrics and his work life. One can only imagine that with Poole, Smith has established a stable and cleansing life environment that grounds the fiction of his lyrics and surreal soundscapes. Smith is like Picasso, who could paint fiercely surreal works all day and return home to discuss the mundane with friends and family.

The Cure rode a crest of fame in the late eighties and the early nineties. The album *Wish* was especially euphoric, with the single "High" describing a seemingly happier Robert Smith arguing, "I can't get that high," and the over-the-top "Friday I'm in Love." One would have thought, Smith's troubles were over with commercial success, a strong cult following, and critical respect to his credit. But in the next 15 years, the Cure continued to proliferate an astonishing number of tracks. *Wild Mood Swings* from 1996 accentuated the positive aspects of the band and moved to a more pop position. Singles like "Gone," "Mint Car," and "Strange Attraction" pointed to a poppy Robert Smith relinquishing his dark moods. But 2004's *The Cure* album and 2008's *4:13 Dream* rebooted the darker, gloomier side of Smith. Yet even these doomy tomes have lighter moments. In the 2004 *The Cure* album's "End of the World" video, Smith was crying, "go if you want to," while an entire house fell down about him and the band in stop motion animation. But by the song's end, the entire house was restored. Smith's character seemed confused but relieved. Later, in the band's *4:13 Dream* album, Smith and the Cure returned to dread with songs like "Sleep When I'm Dead."

GWAR AND COMEDY GLAM

At the bottom rung of the goth/glam contingent sits GWAR, a happy collective of vaudeville, camp, and metal clichés. More than anything, GWAR is indebted to Cooper for their popular and kinky show, and they take their cue as much from Cooper's humor as from his horror movie origins. Started in Richmond, Virginia, in 1985, GWAR's members wear complex costumes of foam, latex, rubber, and multiple padding that makes the band resemble bad TV aliens from *Star Trek*. They wage alien battles on stage, spew juices and concoctions on the audience, slash off alien limbs in mock wars, satirize newsworthy figures (O. J. Simpson, Michael Jackson, Paris Hilton) and politicians (Kerry, Bush, Gore, Reagan) while writing and performing demented songs based on H. P. Lovecraft and other horror fiction authors. Band members have alien aliases. Singer David Brockie is Oderus Urungus, and side performers appear with names like the Sexecutioner. GWAR welcomed humor into their act, and their debut album was entitled *Hell-O*. In 1999 they released *We Kill Everything*, and the next year produced the live album *You're All Worthless and Weak*. They still perform with an ever-changing cast of psychotic alien personas marketing their brand of heavy-metal vaudeville. While perhaps occupying only a small niche in the glam universe, GWAR had continually proved that there is a strong audience for effective theatrical rock using imaginative fantasy themes, topical references, and wild performance antics.

ELECTRONICA: SPARKS AND THE PET SHOP BOYS

> Their memorialization of the recent past emerges not through traditional historical research but through identification and acquisition of objects from the recent past, as well as the replication of its images and styles.
>
> —Elizabeth Guffey (2006)

Some groups use glam to conjure the past, and some use the theatrical to render a future world of dystopian anxieties. Bowie looked to a frightening goth future in *Diamond Dogs* and back to the Weimar Republic in his stage depiction of Brecht's *Baal* and his dance-hall tunes influenced by German cabaret. Alice Cooper explored crude road-warrior planets in the future and creepy gothic fantasies from the Victorian era for his performances. Some bands are more schizophrenic. They want to embrace various ideas from the past and simultaneously explore them with the latest technology. They sit in an uncomfortable position between technological electronica and rampant nostalgia, and they occupy a strange fissure in the glam landscape. Often comedic and often lush and romantic, groups like Sparks and the Pet Shop Boys offer a wild sense of exhibitionism and experimentation. Both have survived as duos, and both practice a heavily electrified sound that dabbles in theatrical motifs, classical music, and cutting-edge digital production.

Sparks

> He has sung from the point of view of a sperm, Mickey Mouse, suicidal supermodels, a Liberace sympathizer, and the suitor of a faded opera star.
>
> —Skylaire Alfvegren (1998)

The Mael brothers, Russell and Ron, married goofball humor, camp, twee pop, and a penchant for overheated performance nearly 40 years ago. Their band Halfnelson (management suggested the name change to Sparks) was snatched up by Todd Rundgren's Bearsville label, and he produced their first album. The Maels were from Los Angeles—Ron, a graphic design student, and Russell, a theatre/film major, merged their respective interests with the emerging glam pop style of T. Rex and David Bowie to form a band. Los Angeles was uninterested in Britpop, and the Maels protested, saying, "we detested folk music because it was cerebral and sedate and we had no time for that" (Hodgkinson 2002). They visited England, gigged at the seminal Marquee club, and were heckled as gay freaks for their artsy show, but drew attention from the venerable television program *The Old Grey Whistle Test*. Despite snide rebukes from the program's host, the Maels won a strong fan base in the UK, owing to a designer show, hyperbolic pop music, and an experimental sound that constantly evolved. With producer Muff Winwood, they produced the breakthrough *Kimono My House* and the hit singles "This Town Ain't Big Enough for the Both of Us" and "Amateur Hour." Russell related that Liam Gallagher of Oasis approached him at an awards show. "Yeah, he was charming and he told me that 'This Town . . .' was important to him while growing up" (McNair 2006). They were wedded to glam through their energetic/sugary pop, the bizarre contrast between Ron Mael, a psycho Chaplin on keyboards, and Russell Mael, who danced like Pinocchio on LSD. Their whimsical/absurdist performance was high in theatre/camp, wild videos, and musical experiments. The Maels flayed pop culture icons, explored the incompetency of technology, and skewered high art (design, opera, and film).

Their stage performance of 2008's *Exotic Creatures of the Deep* began with synth orchestral flourishes, Russell's extroverted vocals, and a squad of women in dresses with shopping carts perambulating the stage. The band was packed into framed apertures as the opening chords of "Good Morning" resonated and Ron Mael burst from a bed placed at center stage. Russell bounced in, dressed a "sailor-on-holiday" elegant stripped ensemble. Strutting, posturing, and singing like a demented manikin, handsome Russell Mael plays the impeccable, excitable front man, arms thrust akimbo, marching, strutting through hyper-speed pop like 1995's "When I Kiss You (I Hear Charlie Parker Playing)." Each song makes coded or overt references to pop culture. Brother Ron plays the psychotic twin, often appearing growling, glowering, or sneering at the audience like a demented Arkham Asylum escapee. Russell began (1970s) in long, girlish tresses, more like a Raggedy Ann doll than a live presence, while Ron favored the appearance of an anorexic Adolf Hitler on smack.

Alongside deeply theatrical albums and sets, the duo courted musical innovation, including a stint with disco producer Giorgio Moroder, making the innovative, Euro-disco "No. 1 in Heaven" (1978) that merged manic pop with electronica and helped to introduce the euro/disco/trance music that defined eighties nascent electro pop. They ditched "a group" for electronic production. Russell Mael told a reporter, "we thought the combination of the vocal with really cold electronic sound was amazing" (Alfvegren 1998).

MTV's arrival fitted the band's bizarro impulses, Brechtian sophistry, and surreal imagery. Jane Weidlin of the Go-Gos, a fan and supporter, lent her voice to their track "Cool Places," with Russell and Jane bouncing from cool date locales to weird places including a scene of Ron cutting up poor Jane. In "Dick Around" (2006), the duo take the sentiments of "messing around" to new heights, blending a performance in front of an audience of cats/people (go figure), to performing chamber pop with a band of orchestral cat musicians, to an emo-pop that straddles Green Day/Smashing Pumpkins bathos ("why the hell did she desert you when you told her she was so essential"), to a Wagnerian/Orwellian doom pop finale of prog/rock pretentions. "When Do I Get to Sing 'My Way,'" (1994) offers a tongue-in-cheek commentary on the ability to quote one's own sound as opposed to aping another artist. The video portrays the Maels as songwriting crooners from a forties noir thriller. Detailing the dilemmas of the cover band, Sparks plays in a Pet Shop Boys/Erasure/Electronic style that suggests bands can only succeed when they imitate, not innovate.

Lil' Beethoven (2002) mixed electronica with a few spare lines to create a concoction heavy on operatic flourishes, gags, and atmosphere with inserted musical philosophy. Russell Mael told the *Guardian*, "we spent a year in the studio, figuring out a way of making pop songs without using any of the usual pop conventions" (Hodgkinson 2002). The album is an electronic, classical thesis on pop, using "pop music" as a pretext not substance. The MusicOMH Web site called it "the best kind of concept album" (Hubbard 2004). In "How Do I Get to Carnegie Hall?" the Maels take the old Vaudeville one-line joke ("practice, buddy, practice") and turn it into a melodrama about the music business. In a 2008 live performance, Ron played the opening rubato piano passage with six-foot extensions to his arms (the passage was sequenced). When there was a treble clef left-hand solo, he raised the giant right arm into the air, an act of fake bravura. The audience burst into laughter and thunderous applause. Throughout, snatches of dialogue are merged with thunderous electro-symphonic beats and textures. The result is a mesmerizing blend of melody, challenging music, and surreal images. The album literally merges a "little Beethoven" and other classical styles with intoxicating flashes of electronica and poetic streams of dadaesque words. *Exotic Creatures from the Deep* features humorous songs such as "Let the Monkey Drive," "Lighten Up, Morrissey" (a plea to sob sister/angst singer Morrissey to tone down the overwrought histrionics), and "Photoshop" (me out of your life). On the earlier *Lil' Beethoven* release, they offered the robotic comedy of "Your Call Is Very Important to Us. Please Hold." in which a disconnected phone recording reassures the impatient listener that their phone call is important to the company receiving, but not answering. Skylaire Alfvegren referred to Ron Mael's songwriting as, "lyrically from the 'school of Cole Porter,' favoring caustic wit over trivial personal problems, his achingly clever lyrics seesaw between superficial gloss, profound sentiment, and the incomprehensibly bizarre" (Alfvegren 1998).

In 2008, the Maels toured England with typical eccentric zeal, replaying a whole album each night in sequence for a series of gigs that showcased their 35 years/21 albums of material. For a rendition of "Perfume," (2006), Ron gets up from the piano in mid-song to give a PowerPoint description of the olfactory sense, and why it is so powerful in human interaction. The performance was part performance art, part electronica, and a good measure of Warner Bros. cartoon schtick.

Pet Shop Boys

We have never really lost our fascination with pop, in all of its forms—the arts, clothes, music, fashion. We still go clubbing even though we're old.
—Jim Sullivan (2009)

The Pet Shop Boys have had a productive and nonstop career, with over 20 charting singles, over 50 million records sold, and a continuing 25-year career of performing, collaborating, and recording with many of the music business's

Combining disco, prog rock, and synth washes, the Pet Shop Boys are smart, caustic, and funny purveyors of an electronic form of glam storytelling. They make up for their deadpan expressions with extravagant videos and live shows. (Courtesy of EMI/ Photofest.)

most respected producers. Their patented electronica/disco sound is constantly evolving and changing, and yet their core components, the nasal voice of Neil Tennant and the rubbery synth programming of Chris Lowe, has remained largely unchanged through today.

Neil Tennant was a writer for *Smash Hits*, the magazine of the nascent new romantic movement of the eighties. After writing about Duran Duran, Talk Talk, Psychedelic Furs, Spandau Ballet, Culture Club, Soft Cell, Simple Minds, Eurthymics, and a host of synth pop duos and groups, Tennant quickly decided that he could parlay his modest voice and strong, satirical writing ability into a similar musical career. He found another ambitious and astute writer, synthesist, and partner in Chris Lowe. They met in a synthesizer shop in London, and together they ventured into the world of pop music, writing several demo tracks including "Opportunities," "West End Girls," and others. They thought of calling themselves "West End" because they were attracted to the fashionable shopping district in London, but they settled on the whimsical Pet Shop Boys because they had friends in Ealing who worked at a pet shop.

Their first album *Please* dealt with a range of classic glam and Warholian pop psychedelic issues: fame, money, suburban life, and love. Delivered in a deadpan flat monotone, Tennant seemed to be aping Warhol's own approach to publicity by appearing bored with everything. Like Warhol, the duo was oblique and distanced from the material, and they seemed to avoid direct emotionalism. The lead track, "Two Divided by Zero," used a spy/mystery tale format. Tennant sings, "Let's not go home, we'll catch the late train." We don't know who is running from whom, but it appears that two people are escaping to someplace far away. The video for the song makes the escape more concrete, Tennant, in evening wear, and Lowe, in bomber jacket and wool cap, are speeding away in an old car, while an announcer at an airplane tower is repeating "two divided by zero." Inside a hanger, a pilot is taking off in an old bi-plane in hot pursuit. The two stop to look at a map, and the pilot shoots them full of holes in a strafing run along an old, isolated stretch of road. The pilot seems deliriously happy that he has murdered them. The track has Tennant's tough sing-speak delivery, a multilayered percussion track, multiple synths, tight bass, and ambient vocal sound effects.

The clever "Opportunities (Let's Make Lots of Money)" could be read as a cynical ode to the Reagan years or as a game plan for the Pet Shop Boys. Tennant sings bluntly, "You can see I'm single-minded, I know what I could be." Tennant's delivery has the urgency of a car salesman and a lush atmospheric opening is quickly replaced by a tough beat, percussion, sampled orchestra sounds, keyboards, and backup vocals. The song established a long Pet Shop Boys tradition of contemporary satirical songs that jab at social issues. In 1986, the target was greedy yuppies of the eighties, and in the video,

Tennant's character, sitting in front of a grand car, simply turns to bones and dust in the end. The suggestion is that all the money in the world won't save us. "Love Comes Quickly" featured an early romantic side to the Pet Shop Boys with the lyrics "sooner or later, this happens to everyone." The video portrays Lowe and Tennant in a drifting and dreamy series of montage shots intercut with pretty young men and women. Again, the notion of being in love is so universal that the carefully contrived video can appeal to gay or straight audiences, and the lush romantic sound filled with Lowe's rubbery bass lines and throbbing rhythm track is equally popular with male and female listeners. The album cover was a pure white, with one tiny two-inch portrait of the duo off to one side. The duo rarely saw themselves as attractive and continually either evaded the limelight or situated themselves as comic or absurd figures in their own performances.

Clearly, Lowe and Tennant understood their limitations as performers and have always sought to surround themselves with opulent set pieces. The band performed lavish spectacles in costume and highly staged theatrics with backup singers, dancers, and visual screen displays to reinforce their act. Their 1989 performance, *Pet Shop Boys on Tour*, was staged by British stage and film director Derek Jarman. It began with the PSB instrumental "The Sound of the Atom Splitting." A group of actors wander around the stage in fantastic costuming, until Neil Tennant appears dressed as a bishop wearing a mask. He pops off his disguise and breaks into "It's a Sin." They follow this with a change of costume and a troop of dancers bouncing and snapping dressed as British public school children. They surround Tennant and start to tailor him in the tune "Shopping." The tightly choreographed dancers do a hip-hop routine while musicians appear, and we see a complete backup band supporting the duo.

In 1991, the two toured with the *Performance* show directed by David Alden. Here the show begins with an orchestral and dance interlude involving a little boy in school gear, a bizarrely costumed moth figure with a mysterious book of ancient wisdom, and an old blind man making abstract hand signs on a couch. The moth figure gives the book to the boy while the blind man frantically signs. Another figure stabs a man with a light saber. In the background, romantic classical music blares. A man falls dead. Then, while "This Must Be the Place I Waited Years to Leave" erupts in all of its synthesized toughness, Tennant and Lowe emerge as British schoolchildren, complete in short pants, school ties, and crested caps. A chorus of dancers also dressed in public school garb dance and mime behind them. They write cryptic phrases on chalk boards, like "Jesus Saves." In "It's a Sin," the schoolboys are now in beds. A vampish woman goes bed hopping to seduce the children. Then, a lecherous old, masked man comes out and touches the children all over their bodies. The vamp woman writhes in the bed. For "What Have I Done to Deserve

This?" Lowe and Tennant enter in yellow-and-pink suits, fake mustaches, and bowler hats. They stand on mini-stationary surfboards and appear to surf on the stage. On the left, a group of male dancers with clubs and mugger ski masks emerge. On the other end of the stage, a group of girl dancers carrying purses and wearing pumpkin head masks flirt with them. The show approaches animated surrealism with dazzling costume effects and expressionistic images that seem to come and go like waves of dreams.

In 2000, the Pet Shop Boys produced *Closer to Heaven* with writer Jonathan Harvey. Similar to *Rent* in that it talks about bohemians in the big city working in the music business, *Closer* discussed the London club scene culture. It was their final movement from pop band to actual stage musical. Tennant described it by saying, "we thought it would be great to see if you could put pop music back into musical theatre" (Pope 2001, 46–49). Though it closed quickly, the play had a strong following in the gay community, and the Pet Shop Boys argued that the play's message was "about taking control of your life . . . not being a victim" (Ibid.).

In 2009, while obtaining a lifetime achievement prize from the BRIT awards, the two appeared as 30-foot video projections. After brief thank yous, their faces swept open to reveal the two performers in costume. Tennant wore a long black jacket, sunglasses, and a bowler hat. Lowe was dressed in a Warhol-style pink wig and a frumpy fur with jeans. As the two performed a medley of their hits, Tennant would occasionally duet with his 30-foot video face image. Then, a chorus of 20 Asians came out and danced in a line to the tune, "Go West." The show was silly, over-the-top, theatrical fun peppered with commentary about world politics and messages of identity and individualism.

ART ROCK AND KATE BUSH

Not all the adherents to the glam style were male, and a fascination with make-believe, fantasy worlds, disguise, and narrative styles was equally appealing to many women artists. The trouble was, there was little encouragement for women to step into the limelight. There were few female artists being encouraged as composers, dancers, and performers, and few were being trained to transform the boundaries of gender and identity roles. Kate Bush was part of a generation of young performers bent on changing that. Born in 1958, Bush was a generation younger than many glam artists, and she was rasied in a family that encouraged music and theatrics. She grew up in an affluent family (her father was a doctor) living in the English countryside with a surplus of books, musical instruments and the benefit of a liberal Catholic convent school to support her ambitions. Kate and her brothers John and Paddy were artistically ambitious, singing and playing a variety of instruments. Kate's mother encouraged their ambitions; she took the children to plays and children's theatre, and enrolled them in mime, dance, and creative dramatics classes. She wanted them to be well-rounded, young people. But it was Kate's father, an amateur songwriter and pianist, that inspired her love of composing. Once he introduced her to the piano, she would sit for six hours a day exploring melodies and singing to herself. Her subject matter wasn't the typical romantic love ballads of the day, and Phil Sutcliffe reports that, "lyrics followed, influenced by kitchen table talk and a little heavy reading (*The Bible*, Gurdjieff, Kahlil Gibran)" (Sutcliffe 2003, 74). Even at an early age, Kate's compositions were mature. Bush and brother Paddy started an unsuccessful rock band, but along the way they made friends that reported the news about an extraordinary girl singer who wrote atmospheric songs, danced rapturously, and sang in a wide range of five octaves. Family friend Ricky Hopper recorded the child singer and passed the tapes to his friend, Pink Floyd guitarist David Gilmour. He put her in touch with executives at EMI records, who were looking for a female singing sensation to replace aging sixties popster Cilla Black. A guiding light was David Bowie, whose career and songwriting had greatly influenced her theatrical approach to rock. Like Bowie, she studied mime with avant-garde dancer Lindsey Kemp. Kemp encouraged the wild, outrageous, uninhibited style of performance that Bush sought. For Kemp, dance was a mad, frenzied pursuit of liberation, and Bush learned from him to be totally committed to the moment and the expression of the body. While many girls learned polite, withdrawn dance routines, Bush's style was vigorous, aggressive, playful, thrusting, jazzy, masculine, and forceful.

She valued her independence, and once compared herself to "a brain and a big pair of ears on legs, stuck in front of a mixing desk" (Sutcliffe 2003, 80). Eventually, in the late seventies when she began performing, she found engineers willing to make her an early prototypical headset microphone so her hands could be free and she could dance across the stage. She appeared in wild costumes playing witches, women in disguise, vixens, and child-like waifs. Mostly she was an expressionistic, interpretive dancer 10 years prior to Madonna, who performed an exotically choreographed show that left audiences breathless. Unlike Madonna, whose dance was tightly choreographed and dependent upon suggestion and sex over plot, Bush favored dance motifs that connected to stories. Her dances seek to reenact or produce a visual counterpart to the song's tale. In England, "Wuthering Heights" was a smashing success in 1978 establishing her overnight as a massive star. Her performances on stage and on television captivated the nation. She became more in charge of her own work and by her second album, *Lionheart*, also released in 1978, she was demanding copious retakes to perfect her vocals. She worked out for months in 1979 preparing a large concert tour, complete with complex choreography. She said,

"I saw our show as a complete experience, like a play . . . I can hide behind a role on stage, and really enjoy performing, but I think to an extent, I would become lost without costume and make-up" (Sutcliffe 2003, 77). In America, she appeared on *Saturday Night Live*. The comedy audience didn't know whether to take her seriously or as a parody of dance. Bush fizzled with an American audience who either wanted seductive dances or rough rock. The American crowd, raised on Springsteen, didn't know how to take a theatrical dance artist. Bush succeeded more clearly in the video for "Them, Heavy People" which offered Kate as a mobster moll roughhousing with two male dancers. Her use of hats, lots of expressive hip thrusts and overtly sexual grasps placed her work near Bob Fosse's rough-and-tumble, hip-gyrating, sexually charged work (*Cabaret, Chicago*) of the era. American audiences didn't know how to interpret a singing, writing, exhibitionistic, woman performer. Bush wanted to act her character, and she acted them loud and hard, in a manner too extreme and too vibrant for an American audience who liked attractive but mousey icons like Farrah Fawcett, Meryl Streep, and Olivia Newton-John. Bush's artistry would keep her a cult artist in America. This was acceptable for Bush, who craved independence and aesthetic artistry over adulation. As a feminist figure, she was a full-blown, sexualized, liberated, and empowered performer, keenly aware of how to project herself and lacking any sense of false modesty.

Bush's first album, *The Kick Inside*, showed mature songwriting (she was 19 when it was released) bright and varied singing, and a wide range of tones and qualities. Her second album, 1978's *Lionheart*, showed a mastery of the studio and Alan Parsons's orchestral arranger Andrew Powell produced a sophisticated orchestral sheen that packaged the singer beautifully. Her tribute to England, "Oh England, My Lionheart," is a winsome evocation of all things English: poetry, Shakespeare, and the beauty of the people/country. She mentions being dropped from "her black Spitfire," and in a video of the track she wears a bomber jacket and pilot's goggles circa the World War II era. During her 1978 "Tour of Life" concert performance, she sings the tune movingly, honoring her parents who grew up in that era. Her atmospheric "In Search of Peter Pan" invoked the classic tale of a boy who didn't grow up. Her singing is crystalline and she captures the mood of lost innocence and ultimately inserts a small snippet of "When You Wish upon a Star," for a captivating coda. It is a transforming and mystical melody. Bush's "Symphony in Blue" is a melancholy love song. We can think of Bush alone in her room when she sings, "I spend a lot of my time looking at blue, The colour of my room and my mood." The song chronicles her moods and feelings, but also reflects on her metaphysical quests. She codes her feelings and moods to colors, and in the end, she comes to no sure determination. The song has a strong, colorful pop arrangement, but liltingly turns jazzy in key changes and moves in a serpentine manner. It is an artful song, and one in Bush's distinctively eclectic style. "Wow!" is Bush's meditation on fame. She muses, "wow, wow, wow, unbelievable." The song mocks people who see her as a prodigious talent. The firmly grounded Bush perceives herself as a hardworking musician, and the song tends to suggest she disdains the massive adulation she had acquired.

"Don't Push Your Foot on the Heartbrake" is a rocking call to engage in love and not to place the brakes on love's desires. "Fullhouse" is another jazzy number, with strong melody lines, sophisticated accompaniment and a vibrant chorus. Bush chants, "remember yourself, you've got a fulhouse in your head tonight." "In the Warm Room" is another quiet love song with Bush's distinctive voice and solo piano accompaniment. "Kashka from Baghdad," is another story song about a woman and her love. It is an evocation of Bush's search for exotic tones and textures. Bush relates the story like a voyeur looking into the life of someone who exists down the road. It also showcases her interest in exotic countries and cultures. "Coffee Homeground," is a campy satirical song sung in the style of German music hall. Like many of Bush's songs, it tends to derive its mystery suspense plot from film noir and Hitchcock films. Bush sings, "Down in the cellar, You're getting into making poison." There is an oompah beat, a repeating motif, and Bush's wildly acrobatic voice, crawling up and down the scale. There is a similarity to Bowie's "Time," another tune derived from Weimar Cabaret style, but Bush plays the stylistic departure for humor.

Many consider her 1986 album *Hounds of Love* her masterpiece, and it does provide a marvelous top to some of Bush's themes. In *Hounds of Love*, Bush uses video in a story-centered manner, turning each tune into an operatic exercise. "Hounds of Love" is confessional and dramatic. Bush admits, "I don't know what's good for me," and "I've always been a coward." In "Running Up That Hill," Bush performs the video in a dance ensemble and again there is the contrasting moving forward and the struggle to break free as she sings, "If I only could, I'd make a deal with God, and I'd get him to swap our places." Originally, Bush entitled the song "A Deal with God," but her record company EMI felt uncomfortable with the implications of such a title and feared it would provoke controversy. "Cloudbusting" has a strong story video featuring Donald Sutherland as a half-mad inventor who has a rain machine. Bush, who played the inventor's daughter, and Sutherland drag the machine to the top of hill for experiments. Government agents accuse Sutherland of fraud and arrest the inventor, and Bush is left to operate the machine, start a cloudburst, and provide the definitive proof that her father is not a crank. The song is a metaphor. Bush had read Peter Reich's book *Book of Dreams*, about his father, famous psychologist Wilhelm Reich, who also was a controversial figure. In interviews, Bush referred to the performance as her first acting video in which she felt she acted more than performed.

"The Big Sky" has militaristic overtones and is a strong rave-up, with Bush and her band in military gear and marching/dancing through the song,

The year 1990 brought Bush's *The Sensual World*. Bush explores more earthy themes and dances in Elizabethan garb in the exquisite and elegant title track. The song pays homage to the joys of the flesh, and here Bush is at her most serene and focused. "This Woman's Work" was featured in the John Hughes film *She's Having a Baby*. The song deals with Bush seeking to avoid adult life issues—"Just make it go away." In the video, Bush is shown in a relationship with a man played by actor Tim McInnerny. She collapses and enters a hospital. A nurse comes out to reassure the grieving McInnerny, and at the end Bush closes the piano. "Love and Anger" features a strong performance by David Gilmour on guitar. The video features her band in performance.

In 1993's *The Red Shoes*, Bush reached out to other audiences, performing a less esoteric, straight-ahead rock. The crux of the album was a suite of six songs Bush composed for a long-form, 45-minute video she made to accompany the album. It is an introduction to her thinking about the music. "The Red Shoes" reflected her love of music and dance and her affection for the 1948 film *The Red Shoes* by Michael Powell. The film was a meta-theatrical exploration of the world of dance and ballet. The original tale, "The Red Shoes," was a fairy tale by Hans Christian Andersen concerning a little girl who wished to dance and obtained a pair of red ballet slippers that won't allow her to stop dancing. In the film version, a beautiful young dancer is invited to join a dance company, which is producing a stage version of the Anderson story. The film shows the struggles of a dancer to live the ballet life and the joys and sorrows that accompany such a sacrifice and fidelity to art. Bush had collaborated with Powell, who had made the original film, but he died while Bush was at work on the project. Still, his ideas inspired her own work. Guest stars in Bush's *The Red Shoes* included British actress Miranda Richardson, who plays an enchantress and Bush doppelganger, and Lindsey Kemp, who worked with both Bush and Bowie early in their careers. Bush is enticed by a mysterious woman who comes running out of a set of mirrors in a dance studio. She complains that she cannot return through the mirrors unless Bush draws a line, a cross, and a curve, magical symbols that will return her to the magical kingdom. In return for this, she gifts Bush with her red ballet slippers that lead her to a world of enchantment and chaos. Bush is thrust into the mirror world of Richardson, and like the character in the Anderson tale, she cannot control her dancing.

Wishing to devote more time to her family, Bush took a long-deserved hiatus from art for 12 years. She returned with the quiet and strong album, *Ariel*. In *Ariel*, there is a return to imagery of dancing and flying and Bush uses a trance-like technique in building songs for the album. There is a strong sense of flow as Bush sings, "I want to be up on the roof, I've gotta be up on the roof." The lead track, "King of the Mountain," is another meditation on fame and the famous life. Bush sings of paragons of fame, Elvis and Orson Welles's *Citizen Kane*, in the same breath. "Elvis are you out there somewhere, Looking like a happy man? In the snow with Rosebud, And king of the mountain." In *Citizen Kane*, Kane seeks an elusive and simpler past symbolized by Rosebud, his childhood sled from Colorado, buried in the snow, never to be seen again, always lost, and always pursued. It is a fitting symbol for Bush, who pursues the elusive balance between fame and happiness.

CONCLUSION

The continuing musicians of glam have found that to keep the style alive, they have had to hybridize their sound with other pop genres, such as prog, metal, goth, and pop. But each performer has returned to glam forms and ideas about media, theatre, fantasy, and pop art to keep their work vital and to inspire a new generation of glam performers.

Many of the glam artists realized early on that the style of theatre wedded to rock music would likely have limited appeal and might be popular to a mass audience for only a brief time. Many of these bands and performers not only accepted marginalization in the music business, they courted it. There are many glam performers who have existed comfortably in the margins of pop rock, and they still produce a lively blend of pop rock and theatrical excitement.

Chapter 7

POSTMILLENNIAL GLAM TENSION

This is a love story between a girl and her television set.
—David Bowie, introducing "TVC 15"

Glam evolved with the century, and new artists added their interpretation of glam aesthetics as the decades passed. Initial concerns with technology, identity, mixed genres, and the theatrical largely remained, but younger generations added new concerns and new insights. First, technology allowed bands to become virtual entities, thus birthing experiments like Gorillaz, a band made up of animations and studio musicians. Matters of identity made performers into synthetic creatures that changed faces and styles with ease. Pop performers like Madonna became chameleons, shedding identities multiple times. Styles of music expanded, allowing art pop bands like of Montreal, My Chemical Romance, and Bird and the Bee to flirt with French films, mod London, and Orwellian future worlds. Finally, overt theatricality gained societal prominence as postmodern aesthetics flourished. Everyone wanted to be reality stars, and the proliferation of YouTube videos gave more people a chance to proclaim their musical stylistics. An awareness of multiple theatrical eras allowed a concurrent flowering of different genres of theatre. Madonna plundered movie icons, Prince borrowed from soul divas, and of Montreal pulled from Surrealism. Glam survived the millennium to reemerge reenergized as Glam 2.0.

As the century waned, interest in issues of authenticity became less important as the matter of reality and originality was contested. Mary Harron expressed the problem with supposedly authentic rock in her analysis of Bruce Springsteen. "For a performer like Springsteen, the more he tries to detach his image from that sales process, the more artificial his image becomes—if only because the maintenance of his integrity requires a continual watchfulness and involvement in overseeing his own marketing process" (Harron 1993, 88). Harron argues that someone who is actively manipulating perceptions of image (like Madonna), is simply more authentic.

Ironically, in a society suffused with images, ghosts, and simulacra, the glams may be the last real artists. The pressures that intensified issues of identity and disguise, passing and playacting, gender and ethnic association, only grew with the end of the century. Media invaded every sector of life. The postmodern sense of lost-ness and the consequent quest for fame and some limited form of stardom (a television appearance, a Web page, a local cable talk show) magnified the public desperation for a life beyond life, one's own 15 minutes of fame for 15 people. Warhol explained back in the sixties that this modern process of identities was porous and not reliable or particularly stable. He said, "I'd prefer to remain a mystery. I never like to give my background, and anyway, I make it all up different every time I'm asked. It's not just that it's part of my image not to tell everything, it's just that I forget what I said the day before and I have to make it up all over again" (Berg 2004, 87).

Glam changed. Core interests in pop culture, media, identity, and theatre remained, but glam's mixture of acid rock, psychedelia, and dynamic pop production (Trevor Horn, Tony Visconti, Bob Ezrin) now enlarged to include twee pop, hip-hop/dub, and electronica. Certainly, the hybridizing of metal, pop, goth, disco, and eccentricity became only more frenzied as millennial forces sought to summarize the century.

Further, contemporary artists weren't just creating and recreating glam identities, but established artists also were involved in the process of self-reimagining. Theatre became an act of survival, as artists reinvented obtuse identities on the fly. Michael Dunne's *Metapop*, or pop that insists on referring to itself, commented that, "even if this singer does not see himself as the sort of 'star' epitomized by Frank Sinatra—or Neil Diamond, or Chubby Checker—he still finds his personal experience as a performer riveting enough to merit extended presentation to a crowd of strangers. He is at least a 'star' in his own mind and consequently, he assumes, of intrinsic interest to others" (Dunne 1992, 123). The availability of Facebook pages and other social media allowed a band to reinvent themselves overnight. Many bands were no longer bands, but canny individuals or sometimes cybernetic entities with little human agency.

Millennium artists were keenly aware of playacting as the substance of a musical/video career, and therefore saw glam as a natural strategy/precursor to their work. Video presentation of artists had become almost ubiquitous thanks to technologies like YouTube and Google video. Videos from 30 years prior coexisted with new product, providing a postmodern absence of history. Young artists could effortlessly research obscure artists like Gary Glitter or

Sweet through their widely disseminated Web fan bases and ubiquitous video performances. The endurance of glam as a style and the renewed popularity and continuance of artists such as Roxy Music, Bowie, Eno, Bolan, Bush, and Cooper placed those names and musical styles firmly in the consciousness of young musicians who wanted to rifle past styles for inspiration.

The tensions that promoted glam promoted a new digitalized glam. Factors contributing to this threshold state included (1) an increasing interest in identity politics; (2) the saturation of media as a connecting aspect of life; (3) the spiraling increase in technology; (4) the variety and acceptance of costuming and body decoration in every aspect of daily presentation; and (5) the conflation of human and cybernetic entities merged to a point where cyber/human hybrids often existed simultaneously on stage.

MADONNA

Three to four years ago dancing was the most important thing—now it's music. That will lead on to something else . . . acting. Above all I want to be an all-round entertainer.

—Madonna (*Smash Hits*)

In this early *Smash Hits* interview quoted above, Madonna indicated that dancing and music were simply steps towards acting and that acting was central to her performance work, despite superior gifts as a singer, composer, and producer. Madonna's career used theatrical role-playing in a deliberate manner, convincing the public in the eighties that she was a wanton sexual predator. Though some would consider Madonna an eighties persona and not a part of the millennial vanguard of new glam, it is only in the past decade that people have begun to see Madonna as a talent wedded to the theatrical. Finally, people are now able to discern that Madonna's various guises were a series of masks. She always thought of herself as a self-conceived entity. Despite adulation as a teen idol and later as a diva, Madonna has said of herself, "I'm too left of center, I'll never have mainstream acceptance, never" (Madonna 1998).

Susan McClary wrote that "she invokes a whole range of conventional signifiers and then causes them to rub up against one another in ways that are open to a variety of divergent readings" (McClary 1993, 108). Indeed, Madonna has taken pleasure in confusing critics with her abrupt changes in style. Her ideas and work are a perfect synthesis of what Jean Baudrillard called the hyperreal, something that is more than real and less than real at the same time. Baudrillard used the example of Disneyland (but Madonna works just as well) when he said, "to begin with it's a play of illusions and phantasms: pirates, the frontier, future world, etc." (Baudrillard 1992, 153). Madonna is able to spontaneously reconstruct herself (her 2004 tour was

Madonna successfully merged music, dance, stories, and spectacle into a cleverly packaged show that used sex to draw large crowds—and kept them coming back with her unique ability to mine a wide range of musical styles. Madonna represents one of the great synthetic minds in pop music, constantly sifting styles and finding appropriations she can use in the studio and in concert. Sadly, she's rarely respected for her intellect and too often derided for her dance skills. (Courtesy of Photofest.)

called the "Reinvention tour"), assuming a new look, sound, and context. In this she is inspired by Warhol and Bowie's notion of disposable self-images. Madonna is equally at home playing a pop act, a sex vamp, a camp crooner, a disco diva, a Euro-inspired electronica artist, or a hip-hop hussy. After an initial rush of fame with dance hits like "Holiday," "Borderline," and "Lucky Star," Madonna emulated a *Diamonds Are a Girl's Best Friend*–era Marilyn Monroe for the video "Material Girl." Madonna deftly merged her bad-girl image, pastiches of the curvaceous Monroe, and MTV's intercutting spectacle style into a video that mixed nostalgia, simulation, and sex. She courted associations with Marilyn, Veronica Lake, Bette Davis, and other movie sirens as touchstones to her work.

Mostly, early Madonna videos played with sexual references because the canny performer understood that sexual imagery was pungent and taboo. Strikingly, in 1986's "Open Your Heart," she appears as a peep show performer in a sultry backroom of a porn parlor. While couples, debauched losers, and weirdos drool over her frantic dance, a lone child watches out of innocent curiosity. Madonna's vigorous and athletic routine insinuates art into the maelstrom of seediness. Her dancing proclaims that artistry can prevail in the least likely environments, and at last, she and the boy dance from club to freedom, wholesomeness, and some undervalued sense of aesthetic integrity. Though, the video played in steady rotation on MTV, few saw Madonna's aesthetic manifesto about dance, video, and music as a means of empowerment through disguise and performance.

The video for "Vogue" (1990) extended her grasp of potent performing symbols. She mixed classic and contemporary images of women, creating a crazy salad of iconography for a new generation of artists. The video masterfully manipulated images from *Vogue* magazine as a touchstone. Blending iconic portrayals of women's fashion, Madonna infused the film with a cornucopia of performance meta-references. First, a series of model/dancers strike poses, becoming living gallery objects. Madonna couples an infectious club beat with her best Jean Harlow impersonation. Her costume is diamond-studded and sheer. As men and women regard their image in mirrors, Madonna calls out, "strike a pose."

The video had its genesis in history, current events, and practicality. Madonna and producer Shep Pettibone cobbled together a series of beats for a fast disco track. But Madonna's practical search for material was matched with a keen eye for local talent. Gay drag performer Willie Ninja had been doing a "Vogue" dance on the New York gay club circuit, patterned on a sequence of looks/gestures based on impressions of famous actresses/*Vogue* covers. Madonna grabbed the subcultural performance idea and melded it with her own film-icons infatuation. Madonna's lyrics explained that role-playing was universal for all people. Just as she impersonated past stars, people were at home fantasizing about her. The film's self-referential discussion of being an "other" summarizes Madonna's impact, her first decade of influence on pop culture, and the video culture of the eighties.

Stylistically, the video, in black and white, shines and shimmers like a Busby Berkeley musical number or a Cecil Beaton, thirties-star glamour photograph. The setups are presentational. Madonna directly addresses the audience in Brechtian style. Madonna's politics of identity are unmistakable. Some shots look like audition images for *Evita*. In other takes, Madonna is on display in a see-through top, her breasts an example of female power. Here her body becomes an object for her own glorification. Madonna's athletic dance workout uses drop-shouldered, hatted, Bob Fosse–school bump-and-grind pushed to a disco pace. The lyrics are: an invocation to "vogue" on the dance floor; instructions for taking control of a love life; a manipulation of the media; and a reinvention of one's self-image. Madonna sings, "It makes no difference if you're black or white; If you're a boy or a girl." Racial, gender, and social differences are erased by the resculpting power of the dance floor. Re-invoking disco's mantra that everyone can be a superstar through music, Madonna argues for the autoerotic. You don't need others; you can do it to yourself. Narcissism is no longer perceived as a malady, it is the situation du jour. In Madonna's aesthetic, it is a norm.

Over the decades, Madonna's carefully choreographed and performed shows became a gold standard of pop theatre, inspiring others to re-embrace the stage. Madonna told *Rolling Stone* that "acting is fun for me . . . for most people music is a very personal statement, but I've always liked to have different characters that I project" (Madonna 1987). In the nineties she formed the Maverick label with Warner Bros. and began to sign artists, exerting control over film, music, and publishing projects. Her recordings became more experimental/conceptual. She told *Spin*, "I like to work with people who take chances. Usually they're undiscovered, because once people are successful they don't like taking risks" (*Spin*). As the millennium approached, she crossed over from disco/pop to a darker, more adult cabaret music.

The year 1992 brought the complex *Erotica* experiment, first with a text: the *Sex* book, filled with graphic pictures and controversial dialogue. Simultaneously, she released *Erotica*, which focused separate tracks on different issues of sexual politics. The first song, "Erotica," dealt with sex hang-ups, and Madonna sang, "Will you let yourself go wild; Let my mouth go where it wants to." The pungent lines promoted sexual fantasy or perhaps images of rape. Her film work expanded with the sour documentary *Truth or Dare*, a box-office lemon; and a performance in a sexy mystery thriller, *Body of Evidence*, that critics dubbed neither sexy nor thrilling. But though controversial, *Erotica* did fascinate audiences with its candid portrayals of sexual relationships. "Deeper and Deeper" dealt with sexual obsession, and the fifties classic "Fever," was reborn as a drum machine techno-grinder. Madonna was playing a rakish character in her films, through the *Erotica* album and the *Sex* book, but unlike Bowie's portrayal of an alien, Madonna's taboo performances alienated audiences. Madonna dismissed the criticism, saying that "art and music can never be too permissive" (Rooksby 1998, 38). Madonna used her art to respond (like Warhol) to her conservative Catholic origins.

Stage performance seemed essential to developing her ever-changing personas. Working with dance companies, choreographers, and massive set designs allowed her to create strange exotic places, a world of environments she could control. Madonna retooled her act through successive shows. *The Girlie Show* (1992), grossing over $70 million, was such a reinvention. Reeling from critiques that the *Erotica* album had gone too far, Madonna turned bad press into a popular tour, working feverishly, handpicking her dance company, and producing an extravaganza that was part cabaret, part burlesque show, and part musical circus. Biographer Andrew Morton described her arduous preparations, including "putting in seventeen-hour days, arriving at her Los Angeles home just before midnight for a massage and sleep" (Morton 2001, 199).

The evening was carefully structured. International talents were used as opening acts. The opening orchestral parade mimicked circus show music. Things heated up as a half-naked pole dancer slithered down a metal pipe dangling high above the stage. Madonna decided not to run from *Erotica*'s controversial images, but to embrace their spicy suggestions. Madonna feminized Bowie's glam, exchanging future dystopian worlds for overtly political messages, confronting the conventions of the puritanical Reagan years, and responding to America's psychological fear of overt female sexuality. During her show, Madonna emerged from the stage behind pole dancers, dressed as a black-masked dominatrix. Against a lush, clubby orchestration, Madonna rubbed a riding crop between her legs while dancers posed and danced suggestively around her. This melded into "Fever," with Madonna aping sexually suggestive poses with two male dancers. "Vogue" was reimagined in Asian contexts with a Hindu-inspired headdress and gestural dances. Later, for "Deeper and Deeper," Madonna donned a Donna Summer–style disco ensemble and tackled the track in a retro-seventies mode. A drunken male jumped from the audience and tried to dance with Madonna as she called for security. Eventually, he ripped off a pair of breakaway pants, and the audience discovered he was simply another dancer in the pack. While toying with different guises for sexually empowered women—first as sex warriors, then as sex club vixens, and finally, as crazed autoerotic dancers—Madonna continually reminded us that her show is just an act. As disco balls flew across the stage from one furious dance after another, audience revelers saw that Madonna's ringmaster act revealed a professional performer, dressing, dancing wildly, and directing a fast-tempo stage review.

For her "Drowned" world tour in 2001, Madonna came out in post-punk kilt miniskirt and black top, singing the electronica piece "Substitute for Love." Against a startling grid stage, Madonna and her band thundered music mostly from the *Ray of Light* and *Music* albums. Madonna merged choreography with narrative for "Impressive Instant" when she and her dancers, dressed in robot headlamps, crossed the stage like machines. Madonna sang, "I'm in a trance, cosmic systems intertwine." As the company performed sinister,

1984-style, fascistic, robotic movements, the dancers tried to grope Madonna. She pushed them back, but one helmeted robot grabbed a huge hose and thrust it between Madonna's legs where it belched out fog onto the audience. Was Madonna suggesting an orgasm or urination on the crowd? "Frozen" was performed with a rear-screen Madonna video. The singer appeared in a red-and-white kimono, but onstage, the real Madonna appeared in a black kimono with 20-foot arm extensions. Other dancers made the wide cloth into waves as they carefully moved the draped material in time to Madonna's singing.

In 2008, Madonna returned with the *Hard Candy* album and "Sticky and Sweet" tour, promoting an image of rap/hip-hop culture, American dance music, and integrating her previous techno-electronica sound with an earthy, rough urban vibe. The "Sticky and Sweet" tour started with the pumping, distorted, compressed sounds of "Give It to Me," featuring an Asian beat and winding rhythms similar to the *Ray of Light* album; but here the sound was more frenzied, like an Indian raga. With rear projections flashing massive lighting displays, Madonna entered surrounded by dancers. Their dance routine was more spontaneous and choral, and Madonna simulated sex with a dancer, handed microphones to audience revelers, and bounced enthusiastically with her dance team. The spectacle resembled the funky, joyful community dance of the actors at the end of *Slumdog Millionaires*. Here, Madonna was inviting a world community vibe. But, Madonna never forgets to act a character, and during the show, she licks a plastic instrument, and taunts the audience singing, "my sugar is raw."

SUEDE

Brett Anderson formed Suede in the early nineties with girlfriend Justine Frischmann and childhood friend Matt Ossman. The name suggested the duality of a soft material that was simultaneously, incredibly durable and tough. It was a good description of their sound. They thought that they could develop a voice that was distinctly different from the prevailing Madchester disco sound of England and the emerging grunge style in America. All the group members were influenced by the strong lineage of glam. They played songs by the Beatles, Bowie, and the Smiths. They looked cool, and their early gigs led to a massive hype. According to Simon Fernand of the BBC, the influential British music newspaper *Melody Maker* called them the most important new English band of 1992, even before any recordings were released.

Lead guitarist Bernard Butler and singer Brett Anderson were convinced their future lay in creating great songs, and Anderson had a breakthrough with the song "The Drowners." "It was kind of like suddenly finding a key

Suede's mixture of pop, punk, and glam highlighted the decadent nineties London crowd and reminded people of the acidic, caustic, eruptive spirit of early glam. (Courtesy of Photofest.)

to a door that had been locked. It was really quite a spiritual experience" (Barnett 2003, 56). But "The Drowners," with its crunchy, *Ziggy Stardust*–era bright, distorted guitars and its lyrics suffused with sex and sleaze, sounded anything but spiritual. Anderson sings, "Won't someone give me some fun? We kiss in his room to a popular tune." The lyrics by themselves are less important than the sound of Anderson's insinuating voice, an invigorating melody and chorus, and an acidy, energized attack. Alexis Petridis, writing for the *Guardian*, called it "a snottily confident marriage of heavy-duty glam rock guitar riffs, and sexually ambiguous lyrics" (Petridis 2005). The video showed a girl and a well-dressed man kissing on a rooftop intercut with images of the girl becoming a dummy. The tune charted on the low end of the British pop charts, but Suede's unique sound was a signal of a new spirit in British music that was quickly defined as Britpop. Chris Jones, writing for the BBC, explained that the band was rooted in glitter, and that in their first album, "their bleak chronicles of urban dysfunction, modern love and sexual confusion were never a million miles away from Morrissey's home ground" (Jones 2007).

Like the glams of 20 years earlier, Suede profited from an image of outrage and excess, and their visual display caused puzzlement. They wore girlish outfits, and lead singer Anderson flounced on stage like a cross between Bowie and Morrissey. But mostly, their angry exterior was all press pose. Former manager Jon Eydmann commented that, "they tried to have a rock 'n roll party. And the extent of it was crushing crisps into my carpet" (Barnett 2003, 106). What they did represent was an unabashed return to British music. They played disastrously at the Brit Awards in 1992, but Brett Anderson lionized the band, saying, "We felt like snotty little kids that had gatecrashed this really glitzy party, and I felt great about it. I didn't feel intimidated. I thought all these people were a bunch of prats" (Barnett 2003, 107). More than anything, Anderson outraged audiences by wearing second-hand girls' lacey blouses and girlish haircuts. It wasn't that the hair was that long, but it was cut in a wedge or page-boy style, making audiences assume the band was focused merely on look and image. Anderson said, "I dunno where all the femininity came from . . . I think it sort of distorted . . . And even now people . . . often think, 'oh, they're that camp band'" (Barnett, 108).

A feminine identity, sources in earlier glam music, and a shrill, sour, and venomous style marked them as leaders of the Britpop movement. Though it was a minor event in America, Britpop in England was a huge musical and patriotic form. It was an attempt to reclaim music for British bands after a 10-year period of the ascendency of American music through artists such as Springsteen, Petty, Metallica, and Michael Jackson.

More than any other band since the seventies, Suede placed identity, look, and gaze front and center. This band intended to be a visceral punk/glam amalgam. Schaffner's description of Roxy Music as "arty decadence . . . the group's obsession with visual style, and Ferry's own brand of deadpan crooning . . . as key ingredients in the 'new' New Wave" (Schaffner 1983, 185) fits Suede, too. Suede mirrored punk's playful quality and its rage. Suede was a party band, but it was a sour party. Anderson saw his music as sorrowful. "For me, our initial vision of what became called Britpop was like a Mike Leigh film. [Other] Bands . . . turned it into a *Carry On* film" (Barnett 2003, 68). Leigh produced a series of downbeat British social dramas, and the *Carry On* films were a group of British satiric comedies.

Suede was interested in provoking audiences, and their show confused viewers. They wedded punk's fury with glam's visuals, suggesting a more psychotic brand of Roxy Music. The lyrics spoke of dissipated hipsters, and their music was powerful but often melancholy. Simon Fernand of the BBC wrote that, "lyrically, there's not a lot to get excited about; mainly sex, fashion, and suburbia, but this does create a cohesion" (Fernand 2002). Their debut album featured two androgynous figures kissing, and the insinuation of a gay subtext shocked audiences. David Barnett in his biography of the band, *Suede: Love and Poison*, explains that actually the photo was of two girls kissing in wheelchairs. Anderson's fey, self-stroking performances elicited media attention. He responded to suggestions that he was an autoerotic performer. "There was something I quite liked about it, the ridiculousness. I didn't feel it was a feminine in a soft way, it was quite aggressive, it was almost sexual" (Barnett 2003, 108). But on the whole, Suede's show retrofitted Warhol's notions of pop culture and McLuhan's view of media.

Their debut galvanized the British press behind their indigenous, aggressive, and retrospective sound. In the nineties, their heroic pop recalled the glory days of glam, one of the last times British music dominated the local culture. Like the sixties British pop bands that many nineties Britpoppers emulated (Oasis, Blur), the first album was filled with striking singles. "Animal Nitrate" is a thinly veiled reference to the drug amil nitrate, an inhalant that, like cocaine, causes paranoia, violence, and sexuality. Brett Anderson sings, "Well he said he'd show you his bed, and the delights of his chemical smile." Sexual excesses, and then rash outbreaks of violence, seem a common theme in Suede's tunes, and reflects the band's love affair with hard drugs: cocaine, Ecstasy, and heroin. The video featured men kissing and was banned on British television. It seemed to be a response to the political situation of people living in depressing government-financed high-rises. The camera zoomed in through a cold apartment structure, and we find a man and woman wearing face paint or masks as they perform ritualized sex acts with images of dogs and snakes intruding into the scene. Anderson sits in a chair caressing a pig mask. The video cuts to the band playing against a red curtain, with Anderson swinging his hips to the music. A dog attacks a pig-faced dummy. The images are squalid and disturbing. Anderson sings that it (animal nitrate) "turns you on."

The band offered the idea of updated glam with acid punk. Suede's sour, self-obsessed, narcissistic sound was a strong part of Britpop's identity. Compared with Oasis and Blur, Suede was demanding, bitter, and acidic. The other bands sought a brighter, Beatle-ish formula to win fans back to the British pop scene. Suede clung to a more theatrical sound. "Metal Mickey," also from their first album, described the overt sexuality of a young girl. "Well she's show showing it off then . . . and all the people shake their money in time." Suede's songs court images of raw sexuality, of people that are overt and straightforward exhibitionists. The subjects of their songs, mirror their own theatricality; there is little hidden about their rampant desire to be viewed. The video for "Metal Mickey" shows a young girl in drag dressed as a pimp, all in purple. She takes a frumpy girl from a meatpacking plant and dresses her. Glammed up and now quite attractive, she is placed as an attendant at the door of a peep show to lure men. A woman in drag pimps another woman to men. Deviant and commercialized mournful sex is part of the Suede package. The sexuality is confused, the purpose of sex is reduced to commerce, and the outcome is doubtful.

Suede doesn't dwell on straightforward messages or songs that try to teach a simple moral. That would be too didactic or meaningless. Instead, they serve as reporters on a hedonistic scene that dwells on its own narcissistic pleasure. Their songs are snapshots of Western decadence. Iain Chambers describes Suede's insular, inward music well when he writes, "the Nietzschean vision of the world, that is, a world of our making. Dependent on our activity and language for its existence, it here laid out as the human adventure in which the movements of peoples, and the rigors and rhythms of bodies, limbs, and voice, set the patterns, the design, the nomination, of the land, the country, our home" (Chambers 1985, 101). Surprisingly, this band that seems to care for nothing outside their own pleasure and visual scopophilia sensibility, a band that wallows in sensual sensation, is in the end strangely political, predicting a world in which the sense of the polis has fallen apart and what remains is merely individual gratification.

But despite criticism (like earlier glams) that they were apolitical, their fourth single, "So Young," expressed a personal philosophy. "Because we're young, because we're gone; we'll take the tide's electric mind, oh yeah? Oh yeah." Merging a touch of science fiction futurism and a sense of their next-generation destiny, Suede explains that they are the legitimate heirs to a youth culture. The song contains a languid guitar interlude and a piano break inspired by Mike Garson's work in "Aladdin Sane," a style that connects rock ballad and lounge lushness. They extend this mantra of the next era in the song, "New Generation," from 1995's *Dog Man Star* album. Anderson wrote, "While the styles turn and the books still burn, Yes it's there in the platinum spires." In a few lines, the band explains their outlook. They are avatars of style, postliterate denizens of the city, users of advanced technology, and adopters of the electronic techno soundscape.

Guitarist Bernard Butler left the band while it was producing its second album, and he was replaced by teen guitar phenom Richard Oakes. The band produced a wide range of massively successful singles in England, but never penetrated the American charts. The States preferred a conventional form of rock, rooted in rhythm and blues, punkish attitudes, and images of pseudo authenticity. "Trash" is perhaps their most self-descriptive single in which they respond to their critics who describe them as misanthropic losers. The band performs in a high-tech cabaret or model runway. The room is suffused in Day-Glo colors, while burned-out models sit around wearing cat-eye contacts, languid expressions, and designer clothing. Futuristic luminaries circulate around the room. The song's great hooks and upbeat energy contrast with the sense of model ennui. "Maybe, maybe it's the clothes we wear, The tasteless bracelets and the dye in our hair." Throughout the song, they make references to their sound, calling it "cellophane." This description accurately describes the band's brittle, thin, high, and wispy approach. Throughout, there is a sense of a future disco where people are at once stoned, enervated, and engaged. The look of the models is the central feature. Critic Simon Fernand referred to their sound as having "always oozed a kind of sexy suburban charm" (Fernand 2002).

Anderson and Butler, who had a falling out and stopped writing together, have mended fences and worked together in a post-Suede band called the Tears. Lately, Butler has produced Duffy, and Anderson has embarked on a solo career as a crooner. Anderson weaned himself off of various drug addictions, and his music has calmed considerably. But Suede's impression on the British scene was electrifying, using the glam imagery of the seventies to brilliant effect on a host of tunes ranging from science-fiction-inspired stories to media-drenched cautionary tales of people who live in a world of five-minute fame.

GORILLAZ

Millennial cyber identities began to birth bands that weren't really bands but instead acted as virtual corporate entities. Taking a cue from the manufacture of pop groups in the sixties (the Monkees), Damon Albarn of Blur decided to create a studio entity he entitled Gorillaz in 1998. The band didn't exist in real space or real people besides himself and artist Jamie Hewlett (creator of the *Tank Girl* comic books). The two decided to produce music using fictional cartoon characters (2D, Murdoc, Russel, and Noodle). The "band" members were drawn as anime/hip-hop characters by Hewlett and featured in a series of animated videos. What we see is a cartoon band. The players were an ever-changing cast of studio musicians recruited by Albarn to produce a variety of pop styles.

Their video for the popular track "Clint Eastwood" indicates the strategy. (Eastwood is never mentioned in the song, and his name is used to ground the song more in the pop culture than for any specific reference to the actor/director.) The band appears as their animated selves, tooling around a creepy nighttime graveyard setting as gorillas begin to erupt from the ground and threaten the characters. It is happy music with long rap interludes, but it has a spooky video that is more "Thriller" than Nicktoons. Writer Neil Gaiman explained their invented origins in an interview for *Wired*, saying that "the group inhabits Kong Studios, high on a mountain in Essex, northeast of London. There are no mountains in Essex. The band exists enough to make music, to produce videos, to remix, and to be remixed" (Gaiman 2009).

The band's style incorporates inner-city hip-hop, pop, old horror movie scores, sonic sound effects, sci-fi images, and anime graphics. Their first album, *Gorillaz* (2001), sold over six million copies and was released with animation, video games, and rock videos.

Their second album, *Demon Days* (2005), was coproduced by American electronica/hip-hop producer Danger Mouse. Danger Mouse (Brian Joseph Burton), himself no stranger to odd combinations of musical styles, had previously merged vocals from Jay-Z's *The Black Album* with instrumentals from the Beatles' *The White Album*, creating an amalgamation known appropriately as *The Grey Album*. Songs like that album's "Dare" are catchy trip-hop melodies with liberal doses of animation, surreal images, and vibrant psychedelic odes and effects. The 2005 single "Feels Good" offers a more upbeat tempo, with aspects of Japanese steam-punk technology intruding into graphics and animation. There are mixtures of trance and hip-hop styles, and often the funky Gorillaz band seems to be a campy parody of the hip-hop scene. If hip-hop is another genre (like Springsteen's rock) that thrives on an image of authenticity and "street cred," then Gorillaz seems to play with the sound, working *street crud* into poppy, child-friendly lullabies, sort of hip-hop for kids who watch Sesame Street.

Gaiman asked Albarn how Gorillaz links so many divergent styles together, and the singer answered that "more and more, cultural groups are cross-pollinating, and we're getting much more interesting art as a result" (Gaiman 2009). Following the glam creed that a complexity and mixture of musical styles is more colorful than straight-ahead rock, Gorillaz produced the slow-boiling rocker, "Kids with Guns," with Neneh Cherry on vocals. The tune discussed the dangerous dynamic of kids carrying guns in their social life. Gorillaz found a method to perform live and even shared the stage with Madonna for the 2006 Grammy Awards. The band was situated behind the stage, but holographic images of the band were projected on transparent screens giving the impression that the animated characters were alive and dancing with Madonna. If the band cleverly addressed the issue of cyber agency and even matters of cyber sexuality with the band's bass guitarist Murdoc, dressed in a G-string, cape, and police cap with a V-shaped guitar across his genitals. Gorillaz through its videos, music, and live appearances has explored new territory for glam, bringing in divergent musical styles while focusing on issues of representation and identity that has concerned glammers from the start.

Neo-glam artists arising in the nineties were deeply committed to the pop art creed promulgated by Andy Warhol and other pop artists. Warhol said, "I can't tell you what pop art is: it's too involved; it's just taking the outside and putting it on the inside" (Berg 2004, 90). This was an art that loved artifice, superficiality, and immodesty. It was diametrically opposed to the sort of sincere angst that propelled grunge to national prominence. Neo-glam emerged in the shadow of a renewed interest in British music, after a period of political and musical ennui encouraged a more strident sound. After the rough fiscal conservatism of eighties British politicians (Margaret Thatcher and John Major), the generation of the nineties wanted some fun and outrage. They plundered the highly superficial painting of British artists such as Richard Hamilton, Eduardo Paolozzi, and Peter Blake, whose "painting also prefigured and licensed mod fashion of the mid-sixties, particularly the attention to stylish clothing and the prominent display of badges" (McCarthy 2000, 11). British audiences bathed in a nostalgia for popism and absorbed the mantra of consumerist sixties culture. Glam's return paralleled new pop art from the Young British Artists (YBA), a group of controversial art students, mostly from Goldsmith's College who modeled their varied and eccentric works on Warhol's assaultive sixties work. Their principal attack was the Sensation show of 1997. Marcus Harvey's huge portrait of Myra Hindley (a child killer) compared to Warhol's *Death and Destruction* series. Another YBA, Damien Hirst, created a creepy dead shark in a tank of formaldehyde that was entitled *The Physical Impossibility of Death in the Mind of Someone Living*.

MY CHEMICAL ROMANCE

My Chemical Romance (MCR) is a band from New Jersey who pioneered a furious metal glam sound. Formed as punk rock, but quickly morphing into something grander under the leadership of singer/writer/performer Gerald Way, MCR gained a cult following. Way was depressed after seeing the 9/11 attacks. He felt that music, powerful, theatrical, and pop, could provide an antidote to the tragedy. Way began to experiment with elaborate costumes, Beatle-like band uniforms, dyed hair, and makeup. The stage show began to emulate the circus, with Way leading audiences in highly theatrical, over-the-top performances. In their third album, *The Black Parade*, the band created a misanthropic teen angst concept album. Borrowing from other glam groups, Way and company performed, "Mama" with its deliriously sick lyrics, "Mama, we all go to hell." In "Welcome to the Black Parade," Way sang of a young person who is empowered to free society through music. For a Halloween show, the band dressed as punk zombies to play their tunes.

Way saw each concert as providing a communal way to tell the stories in his songs. He acted out the characters and portrayed the emotions of a teen suffering the angst of coping with adulthood and responsibility, just like the overwhelming number of postadolescent boys in his audiences. Way's pop theatre aped Alice Cooper's horror/pop/metal. Teens investigated their own young adult anxieties. Pop rock theatre in this sense acted as a large scale form of cathartic generational therapy. For the tune "Dead!" the live band plunged through the tune with manic energy, blue lighting, Beatle-like band uniform outfits, and a flippant attitude. Way laughingly cries out, "and if your heart stops beating, I'll be here wondering." Though the lyrics are savage and cynical, the approach is joyful and poppy. Aside from the dark subject matter, MCR's performance resembles an early Beatles concert with a dash of macabre humor.

Despite the strong theatrical performance and powerful rock accompaniment, the band remained near their fan base. Way was a new media entrepreneur. He also wrote a highly successful comic book, entitled *The Umbrella Academy*, that chronicled the adventures of a French troupe of superheroes. The band has had enormous popularity, something rare in glam subculture. Their show merged pop rock with a subtext about a society struggling and often falling apart. Way's message is more optimistic and suggests that despite struggle, people can prevail. It is a positive message in an era when Americans have felt internal doubt about their country, their leadership, and their direction. Way commented that the band shares common roots with other struggling pop bands. "We both come from the same kind of place . . . basements, vans. . . . That's our world. We were both thrust into a position of importance" (Anderson 2006, 84).

OF MONTREAL

Of Montreal is more of an experimental collage created from elements of the recording label Elephant 6 Records than an actual band. The group or group concept is created by writer/singer/performer Kevin Barnes, who performs with a motley assortment of side performers that seem to be in constant flux. Rarely does the same set of performers appear on two albums, and most of the composition and recording is accomplished by Barnes himself. Performing first on the Elephant 6 label out of Athens, Georgia, Barnes carved a niche singing quirky personal songs and performing in a college alternative style. Over time, his music and performance have seemed steadily more bizarre and theatrical, expressing interests in subject matter as diverse as media, personal demons, the politics of fame, and the vicissitudes of love. The name of the band refers to a failed love affair Barnes had with a woman from Montreal.

Of Montreal's performances are colorful and wild. Barnes even performed a part of a set in Las Vegas in the nude. The 2007 album *Suffer for Fashion* is strongly glam-influenced, with a clever video of someone making an image of the band for the single. "For Our Elegant Caste" (2009) featured the members dressed in face and body paint, Indian headdresses, dark glasses, scarves, and partial nudity. They look like a dissipated version of the Village People on a particularly rough day. Barnes's lyrics are twisted little personal ditties with a humorous hint of perverse sexuality. He sings, "We can take it softcore if you want, but you know I take it both ways." The soft, upbeat poppy sound is nearly twee in its lightness, and Barnes uses brilliant and varied vocal arrangements to keep the music progressing. When asked what he thought of album reviews, he mused that he would only listen to reviews from "someone who's produced albums I really respect. Someone like David Bowie, or David Byrne, Brian Eno, Prince. The kind of people who are my idols" (Barnes 2009). Judging from his influences, Barnes sees himself in that frame and tradition of performers who theatricalize their work.

A good example is Barnes's surreal video for the single, "Heimdalsgate Like a Promethean Curse," from the *Hissing Fauna, Are You the Destroyer?* album (2007). Barnes wears a white bunny suit that covers his head and body like an industrial protective outfit. He is on a stage, and the curtains open and people flit about him wearing spaceship costumes like they are playacting a space attack. Then Barnes lays lengthwise on a table, and people run toy tanks up and down the outline of his body. Barnes morphs into a group of dancers performing a dance reminiscent of a Maurice Sendak story or a Picasso painting. The dancers wear black tights and oversized masks. There is a dancing bear in a red suit, Barnes is chased by a character in a shark suit, and performers wearing photo reflective gear dance and then explode behind him. Out front, people applaud politely while a character wearing a ghost sheet costume leaves the audience. In the end, Barnes and his troupe (presumably, members of the band) step out for a curtain call, with Barnes now wearing a prosthetic lobster arm. The crowd applauds, and a man bends over only to arise as Barnes in a Robin Hood outfit, The overall effect creates a gentle, pleasant, dreamy, surrealistic miasma. The music mimics progressive trance rock somewhere between Eno/Roxy and the band Stereolab.

Barnes's comprehensive studio technique (he had produced and played many of Montreal albums as a soloist, and only recently has had the involvement of a steady group of confederates) suggests a mind involved in all aspects of the production process. This makes Barnes seem similar to Todd Rundgren or Prince, as a consummate studio musician who also enjoys the variety and excitement of a live or video stage presentation. The event is eccentric, odd, charming, individual, eclectic, and highly danceable. The lyrics sound like the effects of a drug reaction. Barnes sings, "Chemicals, don't flatten my mind, Chemicals, don't mess me up this time." There doesn't seem to be anything recreational in what Barnes is describing. Drugs seem to be using him. In fact, there is a strong, clear, hallucinatory feel about the project, as if we are inside one of Breton's automatic writing projects during the surrealist evenings of the twenties. Barnes argues that his wacky and playful stage persona is a natural evolution of his performing music and that outside the performances he lives a relatively conventional life for a musician. He commented that, "I think that, in general, everybody is eccentric. Aside from a small minority of people that are as one-dimensional as they appear" (Barnes 2009). Barnes believes that most people have some other life underneath, and for him it is natural to want to express that hidden life on stage. He explained that, "Someone like Salvador Dali, who was just performing all the time, I mean, his whole life was a performance" (Ibid.).

While Barnes has been making music for over 20 years, his 10 years of experimental glam laboratory performance with of Montreal suggests that there is more to come from the imaginative mind of the Athens, Georgia, studio wizard.

SCISSOR SISTERS

Who said disco is dead? Scissor Sisters has led a one-group revival of seventies pop culture, becoming a sensation in Europe where their releases are megahits, but they remain relatively unknown in their own country. Formed in New York in 2001, the band champions the disco, glam, club scene of their youth and seeks to restore the fun and excitement that made that scene explode in the seventies. At times sounding like Elton John (who has actually cowritten some songs with the band) and alternately miming Abba, Village People, or Grace Jones, the five-piece ensemble writes a host of songs that cross categories while performing a flamboyant blend of pop disco tunes in shiny disco outfits, wild makeup, and lurid costumes. Jake Shears and Ana Matronic handle the outfront vocal duties, and the band contributes to the wide ranging repertory of songs that they produce. In 2005, the *Washington Post*'s Richard Harrington called them "dressed by Bob Mackie on acid."

The band scandalized the musical world in 2003 by tackling Pink Floyd's progressive rock masterpiece, *The Wall*. The Sisters chose to redo the ultimate downbeat bummer song, "Comfortably Numb," as a disco number. Worse, the band chose to shoot the video in a large pool setting it to complex choreography like a Busby Berkeley musical production, totally transforming the material from serious, reverent rock to silly, beat-oriented dance music. Oddly, the transplantation works quite effectively, elevating the song from a dull plod to a breathtaking and vigorous romp.

The band is openly sexual and political. After the exit of drummer Paddy Boom, the band's members are now officially all gay. But their mission is to make wide-ranging pop music, and though their gay identity helps to shape their performance style, the band wishes to refrain from becoming a gay-only group. Their first album sold only 150,000 copies in the United States—not bad, but not a big hit. In England, the album sold 10 times as many copies, and the band became a staple with their massive European hit

"I Don't Feel Like Dancin' " (cowritten by Sir Elton John). The tune took its cue from Leo Sayer's disco tune "I Feel Like Dancin" but went in strategically different directions, with a rocking beat, emphatic percussion, and great keyboard solos. The clever video featured the band in shiny silver disco gear and even had them transformed into robot automatons. Harrington for the *Post* described them as " '70s singer-songwriter craftsmanship mixing with disco camp and stadium rock, punk attitude melding with new romantic couture, transatlantic influences revisited with sincerity and authority rather than kitsch coyness" (Harrington 2005, WE 06).

The band returned to the studio to blend another mix of pop, disco, and performance rock. They hope they can break their glam mix on American soil, but the resistance to openly gay musicians and music that tends to promote quirkiness for its own sake often fails in the American market. Still, if Katie Perry's "I Kissed a Girl" can be a hit, anything is possible for the winsome Sisters.

THE BIRD AND THE BEE

While there are many different formats that have embraced glam, there is a brand of glam that borders on synth pop. Such a group is Inara George and Greg Kurstin, collectively known as the Bird and the Bee (Inara is the Bird, and Greg is the Bee). The group formed when Kurstin was working on George's solo album. Kurstin had done substantial production work on a variety of rock albums. The concept behind the Bird and the Bee was to form an art duo that produced sophisticated pop. George was the daughter of Little Feat founder Lowell George. She had a strong musical background and was versatile in a variety of musical formats. George and Kurstin found they had a common love of jazz standards, and they played that music to each other. Determined to record an album together, they found a willing record company in the jazz label Blue Note. They adopted a persona that was strongly influenced by the mod look of the sixties. George wore minis and Twiggy-length hair. Kurstin dressed in dapper conservative suits. They made a capable cabaret act, with George on bass and vocals, and Kurstin running drum machines and keyboards.

The group also had a penchant for catchy titles, videos, and performances. "Fucking Boyfriend" was a complaint to a boy that a girl wants to come closer, but he is reluctant. The title dissuaded stations from airplay, but underground buzz made the group a strong alternative draw. Their self-titled first album, *The Bird and the Bee*, also featured the light and charming "My Love," with the clever video featuring George in a sixties polka-dot plastic dress and a chorus of girls in minis hiding behind balloons. The video for "Again and Again" features the duo in a retro-sixties Mercedes driving about. They stop off and see a little girl wearing black and holding a bunch of helium-filled black balloons. A little boy dressed in black flashes them an okay sign. They open a box that has black creatures that fly away. They walk down the street holding hands. The video has the quality of a spacey, New Wave, sixties French film. There is a surreal series of events, and the group bathes in a retro vibe. In particular, The Bird in the Bee ponders an odd past that envisioned a different future. For all the electronic sheen of their music, George and Kurstin are obsessed with a vision of the past. Elizabeth Guffey referred to this as "the oxymoron, retro-futurism, the discrepancy between what the future once represented and what it no longer means" (Guffey 2006, 152). The Bird and the Bee explore the disparity between what was thought to be future images (their dress and jazzy setting) and a music that is deeply intellectual, cerebral, and electronic.

The band has caught a sense of the future that argues that the past is a part of our conception of the future. The theatricality, the costumes, and the playfulness of the group define the Bird and the Bee as a new generation of twee retro futurists bent on defining glam for students of pop and jazz, not just rock. Their MySpace music site describes their sound as, "A futuristic 1960's American film set in Brazil." The band blazes a nostalgic lounge jazz path to a Disneyesque, whimsical future world.

LADY GAGA

Techno glam. Lady Gaga is a recent addition to the resurgent glam culture. Although signed to Def Jam Records in mid-decade, she was soon dropped but began songwriting for Interscope records. The label quickly signed her as a performer, and she performed an electronic pastiche of Bowie- and Queen-style theatrics while transforming herself into a disco diva under hard techno influenced beats on songs like "Pokerface" and "Paparazzi." To date, she has released one album, sold millions of Internet singles, and performed in long-form videos wearing skimpy costumes and dancing manically with ensembles of male dancers. Her music is a blend of disco and hard techno with pungent crunch guitars, drum machines, and distorted electronica.

Gaga, despite her highly upbeat techno dance music, returns to principal qualities of glam: fun, outrage, and fashionista costuming. She never looks the same way in two different appearances and has assured reporters she'll never be seen working in jeans and a T-shirt. Often, her outfits mimic early Roxy Music space suits filtered through fifties sci-fi films. She can change from beguiling songstress, to platinum blonde, to raven tresses, to pink or blue hair in a heartbeat. She wears bizarre combinations of fringed, tight, see-through ensembles, wild glasses and masks, massive shoulder pads and art-deco futuristic designs borrowing from Erté drawings. Sometimes she will appear in Daisy Mae sex-kitten shorts, 12-inch silver platform shoes, and

The wild and exaggerated dress and music of Lady Gaga stands as an expressionistic departure from techno, disco, and glam. Gaga utilizes shocking visuals, narrative performance, and dense technology in her complex matrix of sound and vision. (Courtesy of NBC/Photofest.)

dresses inspired by flowers in full bloom. The *Sunday Times*'s Ruby Warrington described her as wearing "trademark panties vintage shades, shoulder pads, and bullet-proof blonde bangs" (Warrington 2009). On occasion she has adopted face paint, paying homage to Bowie's seventies Aladdin Sane lighting strike makeup design.

She is strictly a commercial artist with an impressive Web site hosting a wide range of Gaga images from her 2009 "Monster's Ball" tour, and news of her 2009 release *The Fame Monster*—which is actually a reissue of her

2008 release *The Fame*, with eight new tracks appended to it. The album has already birthed six hit dance singles, and the site extends Gaga's offerings with a collectable art book for over one hundred dollars. The gift book includes "a lock of Lady Gaga's hair, a behind the scenes look at her creative process, and 3-D glasses to view forthcoming Gaga visuals" (Lady Gaga Web site).

As an artist, Gaga's lyrics reflect themes about fame and love and how the two either intertwine or poison each other. In "Poker Face," she explains, "I wanna hold em like they do in Texas plays." Presumably she is discussing keeping her cool in front of her lover. Actor Christopher Walken did a clever send-up of "Poker Face," reducing her lyrics to a series of shouts of "ohs." In "Paparazzi," she talks about being followed. "I'm your biggest fan, I'll follow you until you love me, Papa-paparazzi." The song "Starstruck," rather than discussing fame and stars, discussed the mechanics of building dance techno tracks. Gaga sings, "put your hand around my waist, pull the fader, run it back." The lyrics sound like a prescription for creating a disco track.

Gaga's videos are modeled on extravagant musical productions. The seven-minute promotional video for "Paparazzi" featured popular *True Blood* HBO actor Alexander Skarsgård and offered a Hollywood Noir look with titles and forties style scene transtions. The video opens with Skarsgård and Gaga romping in bed together. He drags her playfully outside and kisses her affectionately as she sits on a ledge. When the singer realizes he has done this to expose her to paparazzi, she bashes him over the head with a wine bottle. He throws her off a high balcony, and she plunges to almost certain death. News headlines flash across the screen: "Gaga Hits Rock Bottom." She returns as a singer in wheelchair and chrome crutches wearing metal under garments inspired by Fritz Lang's 1925 art-deco science fiction, *Metropolis*. Eventually she returns to Skarsgård and poisons and kills him, and in the end, the paparazzi get their pictures. The video indicates that media attention can be both valuable and dangerous.

Gaga's music is intense percussive techno, beat music with a nod to Madonna and hop-hop culture. A *Times* (London) profile from 2008 commented on her origins in the Convent of the Sacred Hearts School in Manhattan, where she was the "artsy, musical-theatre, nerdy girl who got good grades, and who learnt the tricks of self-reinvention" (Collins 2008). In the article she claimed her favorite record was David Bowie's *Let's Dance*, a dance record that has influenced many artists, and she uses the techniques of Bowie, changing character, and Warhol, being oblique and controversial, with ease. She claimed that "her influences range from Warhol to Bowie to Versace" (Ibid.). Indeed Gaga does meld a sense of art, glam music, and over-the-top fashion statements in her performances.

In Hattie Collins's discussion for the *Times*, she described the singer as "a perplexing somewhat camp combination of brash, bright, and slightly strange" (Ibid.). Gaga's complex matrix includes video screens, ornate choreography, backup dancers, computerized and story-centered videos, costumes, and a wild art style that favors expressionistic or Dadaesque excess. She has said, "my art is my whole life" (Ibid.). She works continually, even posting self-made documentaries on her work on her social networking sites. Like many glam artists, she takes the music and the show equally serious.

Gaga's costuming for the 2009 MTV Video Music Awards drew attention to her innate theatricality. She walked the red carpet in a steampunk neo-Victorian outfit that was floor length, with a large gold necklace, a deflated top hat, and a phantom of the opera half mask. During the show, she wore a white bunny mask, white leggings, and white underwear for "Paparazzi." After a cathartic dance, she played piano in the style of Elton John bouncing and using her feet. She emerged with blood gushing from her chest. She fell to the floor, and the backup dancers suspended her from a pole, a totem to the pursuit of fame. As she dangled lifeless and bleeding, photographers snapped images of her dead body. Then when she won the award for new artist, she appeared in a red see-through lace outfit with a red crown and face mask. She looked like Sissy Spacek's Carrie, drenched in blood after winning the school prom. Finally, she appeared in a bizarre white wedding dress with blackened eye makeup, almost like a corpse bride. While many commented that she made her appearance too theatrical, her acceptance speech was charming and brief as she accepted the award for "God and the gays." Gaga's uncompromising portrayal of media in our lives, her self-theatricalization, and her willingness to assault conventional ideas of pop music with thrilling set pieces makes her a good example of glam's continuing importance as a musical style.

Appendix

TOP GLAM SONGS BY DECADE

PRE-GLAM ERA: 1960–70

1. Gene McDaniel, "Tower of Strength"
2. James Brown, "Please, Please, Please"
3. *Jesus Christ Superstar*, "Gesemmene"
4. The Monkees, "Daddy's Song"
5. The Monkees, "Tapioca Tundra"
6. The Beatles, "Rain"
7. The Turtles, "Sound Asleep"
8. Paul Revere and the Raiders, "Him or Me (What's It Gonna Be?)"
9. The Who, "Go to the Mirror, Boy" (*Tommy*)
10. The Rolling Stones, "She's a Rainbow"

FIRST GLAM ERA: 1970–80

1. T. Rex, "Ride a White Swan"
2. David Bowie, "Changes"
3. Roxy Music, "Virginia Plain"
4. Sparks, "This Town Ain't Big Enough for the Both of Us"
5. David Bowie, "Starman"
6. 10cc, "Wall Street Shuffle"
7. Roxy Music, "Street Life"
8. David Bowie, "Boys Keep Swinging"/"DJ"
9. Bryan Ferry, "Heart on My Sleeve"

10. Kate Bush, "Symphony in Blue"
11. Brian Eno, "Cindy Tells Me"

POST-GLAM RESURGENCE: 1980–90

1. Pet Shop Boys, "West End Girls"
2. Frankie Goes to Hollywood, "Welcome to the Pleasuredome"
3. Duran Duran, "Girls on Film"
4. Bryan Ferry, "Slave to Love"
5. David Bowie, "Scary Monsters"
6. David Bowie, "Blue Jean"
7. The Cure, "One Hundred Years"
8. Siouxsie and the Banshees, "Hong Kong Garden"
9. Pet Shop Boys, "Two Divided by Zero"
10. Grace Jones, "I'm Not Perfect (but I'm Perfect for You)"

GLAM REVIVED: 1990–2000

1. Suede, "Trash"
2. Prince, "7" (seven)
3. Suede, "Film Star"
4. Pet Shop Boys, "Closer to Heaven"
5. Bryan Ferry, "Mamounma"
6. David Bowie, "Jump They Say"
7. The Cure, "Strange Attraction"
8. Kate Bush, "Sensual World"
9. Peter Gabriel, "Digging in the Dirt"
10. Kate Bush, "Rubber Band Girl"

MILLENNIAL GLAM: 2000–2009

1. Madonna, "Music"
2. Madonna, "Beautiful Stranger"
3. My Chemical Romance, "The Black Parade"
4. Of Montreal, "Heimdalsgate Like a Promethean Curse"
5. The Bird and the Bee, "Again and Again"
6. David Bowie, "New Killer Star"
7. Grace Jones, "Williams Blood"
8. Lady Gaga, "Paparazzi"
9. Scissor Sisters, "Don't Feel Like Dancin'"
10. Gorillaz, "Clint Eastwood"

WORKS CITED

Adorno, Theodor. "The Musical Material." In *Cultural Theory and Popular Culture*, ed. John Storey. Athens: University of Georgia Press, 1998.

Alfvegren, Skylaire. "Shooting Off Sparks." LAWeekly.com, November 12, 1998. http://www.laweekly.com/1998-11-12/music/shooting-off-sparks/ (accessed May 3, 2009).

"Alice Cooper Interview 1973" (Finnish television), Helsinki, Finland, 1973. YouTube. http://www.youtube.com/watch?v=LrPN6dkM7fw&feature=related and http://www.youtube.com/watch?v=PH5CcWGf16s&feature=related (accessed February 15, 2010).

Anderson, Kyle. "Dungeon." (An interview with Geald Way of My Chemical Romance.) *Spin*, March 2006, 82–85.

Anthony, Jason. "Kraftwerk." In *The All Music Guide to Rock*. Ann Arbor, MI: All Media Guide, 2002.

Appignanesi, Richard, and David Garratt. *Introducing Postmodernism*. Cambridge: Icon Books, 2003.

Archer, Michael. *Art since 1960*. London: Thames and Hudson, 1997.

Auslander, Philip. *Performing Glam Rock*. Ann Arbor: University of Michigan Press, 2006.

Bangs, Lester. "Alice Cooper: Punch and Judy Play the Toilets." *Creem*, July 1975, 48–52.

Barker, Hugh, and Yuval Taylor. *Faking It: The Quest for Authenticity in Popular Music*. New York: Norton, 2007.

Barnes, Kevin. "Of Montreal's Kevin Barnes." Interview by Jay Hathaway. Suicide Girls Web site, August 18, 2009. http://suicidegirls.com/interviews/of+Montreal%27s+Kevin+Barnes/ (accessed February 17, 2010).

Barnett, David. *Suede: Love and Poison*. London: Andre Deutsch, 2003.

Baudrillard, Jean. "Simulacra and Simulations." In *Modernism/Postmodernism*, ed. Peter Brooker. Harlow, Essex: Longman, 1992.

BBC Four. "The Roxy Music Story" (television documentary). Martin R. Smith, producer, Bob Smeaton, director. 2008.

Benton, Janetta, and Robert DiYanni. *Arts and Culture*. Upper Saddle River, NJ: Pearson, 2008.

Berg, Gretchen. "Andy Warhol: My True Story" in *I'll Be Your Mirror: The Selected Andy Warhol Interviews*, ed. Kenneth Goldstein. New York: Carroll & Graf Publishers, 2004, 85–95.

Best, Steven, and Douglas Kellner. *Postmodern Theory*. New York: Guilford Press, 1991.

"Bolan People." http://www.tilldawn.net/trexpeople.html (accessed February 15, 2010).

Booker, M. Keith. *Alternate Americas: Science Fiction Film and American Culture*. Westport, CT: Praeger, 2006.

———. *Postmodern Hollywood: What's New in Film and Why It Makes Us Feel So Strange*. Westport, CT: Praeger, 2007.

Bracewell, Michael. "Her Dark Materials." *Guardian* (UK), September 24, 2005.

Brecht, Bertolt. *Brecht on Theatre: The Development of an Aesthetice*, ed. John Willett. New York: Hill and Wang, 1992.

Buckley, David. *The Thrill of It All: The Story of Bryan Ferry and Roxy Music*. Chicago: A Cappella Books, 2004.

Burns, Bree. *America in the 1970s*. New York: Facts on File, 2006.

Bush, Kate. "Biography." Kate Bush official Web site. http://www.katebush.co.uk/katebush_html/ (accessed August 5, 2009).

Cagle, Van. *Reconstructing Pop/Subculture*. Thousand Oaks, CA: Sage, 1995.

Cameron, Keith. "Siouxsie Sioux: Interview." *MOJO*, October 2007, 44–50.

Cann, Kevin. *David Bowie: A Chronology*. New York: Simon and Schuster, 1983.

Caramanica, Jon. "Warm Leatherette with Beats and Plumage." *New York Times*, August 1, 2009, C5. http://www.nytimes.com/2009/08/01/arts/music/01grace.html.

Carr, Roy, and Charles Shaar Murray. *David Bowie: An Illustrated Record*. New York: Avon, 1994.

Castiglia, Christopher. "The Way We Were, Remembering the Gay Seventies." In *The Seventies: The Age of Glitter in Popular Culture*, ed. Shelton Waldrep. New York: Routledge, 2000.

Chambers, Iain. *Urban Rhythms*. New York: St. Martin's Press, 1985.

Charlton, Katherine. *Rock Music Styles: A History*. Boston: McGraw Hill, 1994.

Christgau, Robert. "Diamond Dogs" (review). In *Christgau's Record Guide*. New York: Knopf Doubleday Publishing, 1981.

Christie, Ian. *Sound of the Beast*. New York: HarperEntertainment, 2004.

Collins, Hattie. "Lady Gaga: The Future of Pop?" *Sunday Times* (London), December 14, 2008. Times Online, http://entertainment.timesonline.co.uk/tol/arts_and _entertainment/music/article5325327.ece (accessed October 31, 2009).

Cox, Cristoph, and Daniel Warner, eds. *Audio Culture: Readings in Modern Music*. New York: Continuum, 2004.

Crimlis, Roger, and Alwyn W. Turner. *Cult Rock Posters*. New York: Billboard Books, 2006.

Crone, Rainer. *Andy Warhol, A Picture Show by the Artist*. New York: Rizoli, 1987.

Debord, Guy. *The Society of Spectacle*. Translated by Ken Knabb. London: Aldgate Press, 1983.

Dellio, Phil, and Scott Woods. *I Wanna Be Sedated: Pop Music in the Seventies*. Toronto: Sound and Vision, 1993.

DeRogatis, Jim. *Turn on Your Mind*. Milwaukee, WI: Hal Leonard, 2003.

Dick. Philip K. *The Philip K. Dick Reader*. New York: Citadel, 2001.

Doran, John. "Siouxsie Sioux Interviewed: The Banshees and the BBC." *The Quietus*, July 20, 2009. http://thequietus.com/articles/02219-siouxsie-sioux-interviewed -the-banshees-and-their-assault-on-the-bbc (accessed August 15, 2009).

Downie, Alec. *Glam Rock.* Video documentary. Glasgow: TV Dir. Eve Nicol, GMCTV, 2007.

Duncan, Robert, and David Surkamp. "Sparks: From Taco Bell to Fish and Chips." *CREEM*, July 1975, 38–39.

Dunne, Michael. *Metapop: Self-Referentiality in Contemporary American Popular Culture.* Oxford: University Press of Mississippi, 1992.

Du Noyer, Paul. "Contact: David Bowie." *MOJO*, July 2002, 74–90.

Eco, Umberto. "A City of Robots." In *Postmodernism: A Reader*, ed. Thomas Docherty, 200–206. New York: Columbia University Press, 1993.

———. "Postmodernism, Irony, and the Enjoyable." In *Modernism/Postmodernism*, ed. Peter Brooker. Harlow, England: Longman, 1992.

Eno, Brian. *Oblique Strategies Cards.* Random card generator at http://music.hyperreal.org/artists/brian_eno/oblique/oblique.html (accessed February 15, 2010).

Erlewine, Stephen Thomas. "Queen." All Music Guide. http://www.allmusic.com/cg/amg.dll?p=amg&sql=11:jifpxqr5ldje~T1.

Fernand, Simon. "Singles" (Review of Suede's Singles album) November 20, 2002. http://www.bbc.co.uk/music/reviews/qdn8 (accessed September 15, 2009).

Frith, Simon, and Howard Horne. *Art into Pop.* New York: Methuen, 1989.

Fussman, Cal. "Alice Cooper: What I've Learned." *Esquire*, January 2, 2009. http://www.esquire.com/features/what-ive-learned/alice-cooper-quotes-0109 (accessed July 25, 2009).

Gaiman, Neil. "Keeping it (Un)real." *Wired*, issue 13.07, July 2005. http://www.wired.com/wired/archive/13.07/gorillaz.html (accessed April 15, 2009).

Goddard, Simon. "The Scream: Liner notes." *The Scream* (reissue). Polydor Records, 2005.

Goodall, Nigel. *Elton John: A Visual Documentary.* London: Omnibus Press, 1993.

Goodlad, Lauren M., and Michael Bibby, eds. *Goth/Undead Subculture.* Durham, NC: Duke University Press, 2007.

"Grace Jones." In *Notable Black American Women*, vol. 2, ed. Jessie Carney Smith. Detroit, MI: Gale Research, 1996. Reproduced in Biography Resource Center. Farmington Hills, MI: Gale, 2009. http://library.columbiastate.edu:2057/servlet/BioRC (accessed August 2009).

Grace Jones fan site. http://www.gracejones.org (accessed July 2009).

Greenberg, Jan, and Sandra Jordan. *Andy Warhol: Prince of Pop.* New York: Delacorte Press, 2004.

Grossman, Loyd. *A Social History of Rock Music.* New York: David McKay, 1976.

Grunenberg, Christoph, ed. *Gothic: Tranmutations of Horror in Late Twentieth Century Art.* Cambridge, MA: MIT Press, 1997.

Guffey, Elizabeth E. *Retro: The Culture of Revival.* London: Reakton Books, 2006.

"Hamilton, Richard." In *Twentieth-Century Artists on Art*, ed. Dore Ashton. New York: Pantheon Books, 1985.

Harrington, Richard. "Scissor Sisters: On the Cutting Edge." *Washington Post*, January 7, 2005, WE 06. http://www.washingtonpost.com/wp-dyn/articles/A53256-2005 Jan6.html (accessed August 24, 2009).

Harron, Mary. "On Madonna vs. Bruce." In *Desperately Seeking Madonna*, ed. Adam Sexton. New York: Dell (Delta), 1993.

Hebdige, Dick. *Subculture.* London: Routledge, 1979.

Hodgkinson, Will. "Home Entertainment: Sparks." *Guardian* (UK), November 1, 2002. http://www.guardian.co.uk/culture/2002/nov/01/artsfeatures6 (accessed May 2009).

Hoskyns, Barney. *Glam!* New York: Pocket Books, 1998.

Hubbard, Michael. "Sparks: Melting Down Beethoven." MusicOMH.com Interviews, April 2004. http://web.archive.org/web/20071222025303/http://www.musicomh .com/interviews/sparks.htm/ (accessed May 2009).

"In Memoriam: June Feld." http://www.tilldawn.net/images/junemem.jpg (accessed February 15, 2010).

Jones, Chris. "Suede" (review of first Suede album). BBC Music, April 19, 2007. http:// www.bbc.co.uk/music/artists/a55c2f1b-3f3f-4d6a-aa30-5e186dbadce6 (accessed September 11, 2009).

Kilpatrick, Nancy. *The Goth Bible: A Compendium for the Darkly Inclined*. New York: St. Martin's Griffin, 2004.

Koskoff, Ellen, ed. *Music Cultures in the United States*. New York: Routledge, 2005.

Kuznets, Lois Rostow. *When Toys Come Alive*. New Haven, CT: Yale University Press, 1994.

"Livewire's One on One: The Vincent Price of Rock 'n' Roll." Livewire, October 20, 2001. http://www.concertlivewire.com/interviews/alice.htm (accessed July 2009).

Loss, Archie. *Pop Dreams, Music, Movies and Media in the 1960s*. Fort Worth, TX: Harcourt Brace, 1999.

Lucie-Smith, Edward. *Art in the Seventies*. New York: Phaidon Press, 1980.

Madonna. "Interview: On Being a Star." *Rolling Stone*, September, 1987.

———. "Interview." *Spin*, April 1998.

———. "Madonna Interview." *Smash Hits*, February 1984. http://allaboutmadonna.com/ madonna-interviews-articles/smash-hits-february-1984 (accessed August 9, 2009).

May, Brian. *Guitar Greats* (radio program). BBC One, 1983. http://www.queenpedia.com/ index.php?title=Father_To_Son (accessed February 17, 2010).

McCarthy, David. *Pop Art*. Movements in Modern Art series. Cambridge: Cambridge University Press, 2000.

McClary, Susan. "Living to Tell: Madonna's Resurrection of the Fleshly." In *Desperately Seeking Madonna*, ed. Adam Sexton, 101–27. New York: Delta Books, 1993.

McLaren, Malcolm. "Punk and History." In *Literary Theory: An Anthology*, ed. Julie Rivkin and Michael Ryan, 1076–81. London: Blackwell, 1998.

McLenehan, Cliff. *Marc Bolan, 1947–1977: A Chronology*. London: Helter Skelter Publishing, 2002.

McLuhan, Marshall. *Understanding Media*. New York: McGraw Hill, 1964.

McNair, James. "Sparks: Creating Mischief Again with Their Latest Album." *Independent* (UK), February 22, 2006. http://web.archive.org/web/20070124130940/ http:// enjoyment.independent.co.uk/music/features/article347014.ece/ (accessed May 2009).

Melly, George. *Revolt into Style*. Oxford: Oxford University Press, 1989.

Mendelsohn, John. "David Bowie? Pantomime Rock?" In *The Bowie Companion*, ed. Elizabeth Thomson and David Gutman. New York: Da Capo Press, 1996.

Mercer, Mick. *The Gothic Rock Black Book*. London: Omnibus Press, 1988.

The Monkees. *Pisces, Aquarius, Capricorn, and Jones*, liner notes. Rhino/WEA, 1995.

Moriarty, Frank. *Seventies Rock: The Decade of Creative Chaos*. London: Taylor Trade, 2003.

Morton, Andrew. *Madonna*. New York: Bedford Books, 2001.

Murray, Charles Shaar. *Shots from the Hip*. London: Penguin, 1991.

"The New Rock: Bittersweet and Low." *Time*, March 1, 1971, 45.

Parkinson, Judy. *Elton: Made in England*. London: Michael O'Mara Books, 2003.

Pattie, David. *Rock Music in Performance*. Basingstoke: Palgrave Macmillan, 2007.

Pattison, Robert. *The Triumph of Vulgarity*. London: Oxford University Press, 1987.

Paytress, Mark. *Bolan: Rise and Fall of a 20th Century Superstar*. London: Omnibus Press, 2002.

Perone, James E. *The Words and Music of David Bowie*. Westport, CT: Praeger, 2006.

Petridis, Alexis. "Frankly, I Hated Suede." *Guardian* (UK), April 22, 2005. http://www.guardian.co.uk/music/2005/apr/22/popandrock (accessed October 9, 2009).

Pioneers: Brian Eno. Directed by Phoebe Collins. Produced by BBC Channel 4, UK, 1999.

Pope, Carole. "West End" (interview with The Pet Shop Boys). *Advocate*. July 17, 2001, 46–49.

Queen: The Days of Our Lives. Directed by Rudi Dolezal and Hannes Rossacher. Buena Vista, 1991.

Queen. "Death on Two Legs." *A Night at the Opera* (record). Electra, 1975.

Ratcliff, Carter. *Andy Warhol*. New York: Abbeville Press, 1983.

Redfern, Mark. "Of Montreal: In the Studio" (interview with Kevin Barnes). *Under the Radar* (online edition), August 21, 2009. http://www.undertheradarmag.com/interviews/of_montreal_in_the_studio (accessed September 5, 2009).

Rensin, David. "George Lucas, Skywalker." In *Very Seventies*, ed. Peter Knobler and Greg Michell, 233–36. New York: Fireside, 1995.

Reynolds, Simon. *Rip It Up and Start Again: Post Punk, 1978–1984*. New York: Penguin, 2006.

Rider, Stephen. *Queen: These Are the Days of Our Lives*. London: Castle Communications, 1994.

Rigby, Jonathan. *Roxy Music: Both Ends Burning*. London: Reynolds and Hearn Ltd., 2005.

Robins, Wayne. *A Brief History of Rock, Off the Record*. New York: Routledge, 2008.

Rock, Mick. *Classic Queen*. New York: Sterling, 2007.

———. *Glam! An Eyewitness Account*. London: Vision on Publishing, 2006.

Romanowski, Patricia, and Holly George-Warren. *The Rolling Stone Encyclopedia of Rock and Roll*. New York: Fireside, 1995.

Rooksby, Rikky. *The Complete Guide to the Music of Madonna*. London: Omnibus Press, 1998.

Rose, Judd. "Encore: A Look at the Many Faces of David Bowie." *Newstand* (CNN/Entertainment Weekly), September 29, 1998. http://www.cnn.com/SHOWBIZ/Music/9809/29/david.bowie/index.html (accessed September 14, 2009).

Sagert, Kelly Boyer. *The 1970s*. Westport, CT: Greenwood Press, 2007.

Scaruffi, Piero. *A History of Rock*. New York: IUniverse, 2003.

Schaffner, Nicholas. *The British Invasion*. New York: McGraw-Hill, 1983.

Schinder, Scott. "Heart of Darkness" (Robert Smith interview). *Pulse!* March, 2000.

Sexton, Adam, ed. *Desperately Seeking Madonna*. New York: Dell (Delta), 1993.

Siegel, Carol. *Goth's Dark Empire*. Bloomington: Indiana University Press, 2005.

Sinclair, Paul. *Electric Warrior: The Marc Bolan Story*. London: Omnibus Press, 1982.

Siouxsie/Dreamshow. Performed by Siouxsie Sioux and Budgie. Produced by Sophie Coolbaugh and Paul M. Green. Rhino/Warner, 2005.

Sontag, Susan. *A Susan Sontag Reader*. New York: Vintage Books, 1983.

Spitz, Bob. *The Beatles: The Biography*. New York: Little Brown, 2005.

Starr, Larry, and Christopher Waterman. *American Popular Music: The Rock Years*. New York: Oxford University Press, 2008.

Stratton, Joe. "Why Doesn't Anybody Write Anything About Glam Rock?" *Australian Journal of Cultural Studies* 4, no. 1 (1986): 14–38.

Stump, Paul. *Unknown Pleasures: A Cultural History of Roxy Music*. New York: Thunder's Mouth Press, 1998.

Stussey, Joe, and Scott Lipscomb. *Rock and Roll: Its History and Stylistic Development.* Upper Saddle River, NJ: Prentice Hall, 2008.

Sullivan, Jim. "OK Computers: Pet Shop Boys Dazzle with Electro-pop Extravaganza." *Boston Herald,* September 5, 2009.

The Supremes. "Love Child." *Love Child.* Motown, 1969.

Sutcliffe, Phil. "Kate Bush: Season of the Witch." *MOJO,* February 2003, 72–82.

Szatmary, David P. *Rockin' in Time.* Upper Saddle River, NJ: Prentice Hall, 2006.

Tamm, Eric. *Brian Eno: His Music and the Vertical Color of Sound.* New York: DeCapo, 1995.

Thompson, Dave. *Glam Rock.* Burlington, ON: Collector's Guide Publishing, 2000.

Thompson, Dave, and Jo-Anne Greene. *The Cure: A Visual Documentary.* London: Omnibus Press, 1993.

Tomas, David. "Art, Psychasthenic Assimilation, and Cybernetic Automaton." In *The Cyborg Handbook,* ed. Chris Hables Gray. New York: Routledge, 1995.

Toth, Csaba. "Like Cancer in the System." In *Gothic,* ed. Christoph Grunenberg. Cambridge, MA: MIT Press, 1997.

Valdez, Stephen. *A History of Rock Music.* Iowa: Kendall-Hunt, 2006.

Waldrep, Shelton. *The Seventies: The Age of Glitter in Popular Culture.* New York: Routledge, 2000.

Walker, John A. *Cross-Overs: Art into Pop/Pop into Art.* London: Methuen, 1987.

Warhol, Andy, and Pat Hackett. *Popism: The Warhol Sixties.* San Diego, CA: Havest/HBJ, 1989.

Warrington, Ruby. "Lady Gaga: Ready for Her Close-Up." *Sunday Times* (London), February 22, 2009.

Williams, Richard. "Roxy Music: The Sound of Surprise." *Melody Maker,* July 1, 1972. http://rocksbackpages.com/article.html?ArticleID=6163 (accessed June 4, 2009).

Wood, Mikael. "Parents' Night Out." *Spin,* February 2007, 96.

INDEX

Adorno, Theodor, 24, 33, 34, 70, 77
American Bandstand (American pop
   music television program), 26
American Popular Music (Starr and
   Waterman's history of pop music), 2
Art into Pop (Frith and Horne), 44,
   74, 167
art rock (and glam), 126–37
art schools, 37, 44, 69–70
Avalon (Roxy Music album), 84, 86,
   87, 88

Baudrillard, Jean, 24, 71, 141
Beatles, the, 29–32; confluence of video
   and television broadcasts, 26; decline in
   quality during *Let It Be* sessions, 11;
   image making and video, 31; indirect
   influence on Bowie, 44; indirect
   influence on Roxy Music, 75; influence
   of their films on pop musicals, 40; as
   leaders in the psychedelic movement,
   38; media interest in, 29; as musicians,
   30; and psychedelia, 13; and "Rain"
   31–32; and television, 25; television
   and their film career, 29; use of media
   20; *Yellow Submarine* and their cartoon
   show as elements of psychedelic
   culture, 38

Benjamin, Walter (media theorist), 24
Billion Dollar Babies (Alice Cooper
   album), 117, 118
Bird and the Bee, the, 157–58
"Black Parade (The)" (My Chemical
   Romance), 13, 153, 164
"Bohemian Rhapsody" (Queen), 90,
   103, 105
Bolan, Marc, 91–99; early career, 92; early
   childhood, 91; and founding of
   Tyrannosaurus Rex (later T. Rex), 92
Bowie, Angela (wife of David Bowie),
   45–46
Bowie, David, 10, 43–65; *Aladdin Sane*
   (album), 57–59; "Andy Warhol," 53;
   career of, 12, 36, 45, 64, 94, 97, 100,
   110; compared to Roxy Music, 84; and
   criticism of his work, 17; *Diamond Dogs*
   (album), 60–61, 83, 126; education of,
   44; *Hunky Dory* (album), 8, 49–53;
   image of, 4, 119, 121; influence on
   Madonna, 142; influence on rock, 90,
   99–101, 106–7, 123, 127, 133, 139, 141,
   145–46, 148, 155, 158–60; *The Man
   Who Sold the World* (album), 47–48;
   music styles of, 6, 8–9, 88; personal life
   of, 29, 46, 95; *Pin-ups* (album), 59;
   relationship to Brian Eno, 75;

"West End Girls" (Pet Shop Boys),
130, 164

Yellow Submarine (Beatles' cartoon
film), 38

Young British Artists
(YBA), 153

Ziggy Stardust (David Bowie album) 53,
54, 55, 56, 64; influence of, 1–2